raising your hearing-impaired child:

a guideline for parents

shirley hanawalt mcarthur

ALEXANDER GRAHAM BELL
ASSOCIATION FOR THE DEAF
3417 VOLTA PLACE, N.W.
WASHINGTON, D.C. 20007

Permissions for quotations:

p. 55   From <u>Edison</u> by Josephson. Copyright 1959. Used with the permission of McGraw-Hill Book Company.

p. 130   <u>Encyclopedia Americana</u>. Copyright 1979. Reprinted by permission of Americana Corp. and Grolier Inc.

pp. 173–74 Copyright 1975 by <u>Newsweek Inc.</u> All rights reserved. Reprinted by permission.

p. 199   Editorial, <u>Indianapolis News</u>, 1974. All rights reserved. Reprinted by permission.

p. 210   Copyright 1978, <u>Los Angeles Times</u>. Reprinted by permission.

Library of Congress Cataloging in Publication Data

McArthur, Shirley Hanawalt   Raising your hearing-impaired child: a guideline for parents

Card Catalog Number 82–70282
ISBN 0–88200–150–7

© 1982 Alexander Graham Bell Association for the Deaf
3417 Volta Place, N.W.
Washington, D.C. 20007

10 9 8 7 6 5 4 3 2 1

Printed in the United States of America

214679

With God's grace,

I dedicate this book

to my husband, Pete,

and our children,

Linda, Peter, Laurie, and Leslie

sources of opening quotations

Introduction:
>   *The Holy Bible,* Mark 5:36.

Part I, In the Beginning:
>   Paraphrase from speech given by Dr. James C. Marsters to the Parents of John Tracy Clinic, Fall of 1973.

Part II, The Preschool Years:
>   Mary E. Numbers, *My Words Fell on Deaf Ears; A History of Clarke School for the Deaf,* Alexander Graham Bell Association for the Deaf, Washington, D.C., 1974.

Part III, The Elementary School Years:
>   Charles McCarry, "Kyoto and Nara: Keepers of Japan's Past," *National Geographic,* 1976, 149(*6*), 849.

Part IV, The Junior and Senior High School Years:
>   Editorial in *Indianapolis News,* June 27, 1974, Part Four, p. 309 reported by Dr. H. Latham Breunig in his article, "The Right to Independence," *Volta Review,* 1978, 80(*4*), 203.

Epilogue:
>   Old Saying, Anonymous.

contents

about the author

In a variety of ways, Shirley Hanawalt McArthur has been a teacher of the hearing impaired since 1950. On one level, she has served as a student, substitute, itinerant, and full-time teacher in California oral day programs, working with students of every age description, preschool to senior high school. In addition, she has been a parent in the full sense of the term—raising two hearing children and two hearing-impaired daughters, conveying classroom experiences to her home program and vice versa.

Born July 1, 1916 in Los Angeles, Mrs. McArthur received her B.A. in English from Stanford University in 1938 and was certified as a teacher of the deaf in the state of California in 1965. Her husband of 41 years, Peter R. McArthur, 64, is a 1939 petroleum engineering graduate of Stanford now retired from engineering and construction sales. Two of their children have normal hearing: Peter R. McArthur, Jr., 32 (M.A. Chem. Engr., Stanford Univ. '72), is a project manager at Cetus Corporation, a genetic engineering company in Berkeley, CA, and Laurie McArthur Kincheloe, 30 (B.A. Math., Cal. State Univ., Chico '76), is a high school math teacher in Chico, CA.

Linda Gray McArthur, 34, has been profoundly deaf from birth (97 dB hearing loss). After earning her B.A. in physical education from California Polytechnic State Univ., San Luis Obispo, and M.A. from Western Washington State University in 1973, she joined the faculty of Cal Poly as an instructor of physical education, also serving as the coach for the women's track team. Currently, she is working on a doctorate in biomechanics at the University of New Mexico. And Leslie Marie McArthur, the youngest at 26 (and with an 82 dB hearing loss), received her B.A. in English in 1977 from the University of California, Irvine, and is now a caption editor with the National Captioning Institute in Hollywood.

introduction

One day in 1950 we discovered, with all the accompanying heartache, that our first child had a severe hearing loss. Details of this revelation probably vary but slightly from your own experience, for this discovery is remarkably similar from parent to parent, dissolving into:

"Why didn't someone tell me sooner?"
"Why me?"
"WHY?"

So often there is no convincing explanation for a child having been born with this birth defect. The bewildered parents, totally ignorant of the problems involved in educating a child who is lacking the major avenue for building communication skills, must begin at the beginning to understand the problems themselves. They soon find the problems to be so complex, albeit unapparent physically, that even the educators who specialize in this field cannot agree among themselves upon the best method for overcoming this handicap.

To complicate the matter further, the parents must apply what they do learn to their particular child and to his immediate family. This is no easy task since children differ one from the other and families differ in background, makeup, and values. Moreover, no hearing-impaired child is quite like any other, for the differences in his hearing, plus all the other variables in his personality, add up to the special individual that he is.

I approach this book, then, on the premise that each child is unique in his needs. If only there were a "method" for each individual child, how wonderful it would be! In spite of helpful legislation, education remains largely, for practical and economic reasons, a grouping situation that is amenable to an area's school system rather than to the needs of an individual child. Thus, it remains for parents to decide on raising their hearing-impaired child in the best way they possibly can, utilizing the facilities that are available and practical. Slowly, the right of the parents to decide how their child will be educated is emerging, and rightly so.

Actually, the one place that a child can receive help tailored to his individual needs is in the home. As his parents, you know best what he requires to get along in his family circle and in his ever-widening horizons.

Being parents of this special child is difficult—we must face this fact—but it is surmountable. We have proof of this from the many active, independent, hearing-impaired adults with fine character that we meet. The handicap can be overcome given the positive attitude, courage, and patience of the parents who will it to be so and who determine that their child shall realize his full potential as a member of his family, community, and country.

In order to make intelligent decisions through the growing years, parents should set realistic goals for their child, but these goals should not be absolute. As situations change, the child should be evaluated by both parents, with an assist from professionals in the field, and the goals adjusted when necessary. For example, adjust your sights after a change in environment, for newly developed personality traits, and occasionally because of a change in hearing level.

There is one prime, overall goal that every parent should reach for: to raise a hearing-impaired child to become a responsible, independent, and happy adult. It is toward this goal that this book is addressed. It won't solve all your problems, but it will perhaps point the way, warn of pitfalls before they arise, and set forth some helpful ideas that in many cases you would have to learn by trial and error— ideas that I wish, how I wish, someone had told me thirty years ago!

I believe that the raising of a child should come to a reasonable end. A child must be allowed, indeed encouraged, to grow and develop independence, leading to a time when he is able to think out, decide, and act on matters for himself. I arbitrarily place this time at the completion of high school, or soon thereafter, as your child should for all practical purposes be raised by then. To prolong his taking responsibilities leads to a further handicap.

This book is limited to the problems of children with hearing losses, realizing at the same time that a sizeable percentage of these have other handicaps as well. The goals for such children must often be limited further by the multiplicity of their problems. However, the evaluation method I suggest can be expanded to include categories that apply to the multihandicapped child.

In this book, references are to an average, middle-income family consisting of a mother, a father, one hearing-impaired child (who will be termed in the masculine gender for literary usage), and possibly additional children. I used the Thorndike diacritical markings because they are widely used in the schools and thus familiar to many (Thorndike & Barnhart, 1965). If your child's school uses other markings, follow the school's method. I have chosen to use the term *hearing impaired* instead of *deaf* because it best describes a child with a hearing loss of whatever degree—in this day of excellent hearing aids, to label a child with a mild loss *deaf* is a debilitating misnomer. I have also chosen to use the word *speechreading* rather than *lipreading* because it more accurately describes the art—understanding speech through reading the whole face, expressions of the eyes and eyebrows, gestures of the head and body, and movements of the muscles of the neck, face, and jaw as well as the all-important lips and mouth.

I prefer in most instances to bring you "what you can do" about raising your hearing-impaired child and leave "how to do it" to your own planning, since individual differences prevail, and parts of what I suggest may fit some cases but not others. There is a further, more important reason for not strictly following another person's pro-grammed learning schedule at home. It can be an exercise in futility if it does not relate to your particular child and the communication needs and living pattern of your family. Undoubtedly, in planning your own schedule, you will invent, discover by necessity, and end up proudly practicing many of your own ideas.

The amount to be done for a hearing-impaired child may seem overwhelming. It is hoped that you will come to terms with just how much you can do, and not fret over what is left undone. Guard against tenseness in yourself or your child in trying to do too much too fast or too soon—stop before you are dead tired. Plan your campaign carefully. If you falter, try again another way, but follow through. Avoid comparisons—what other parents accomplish may be miles away from what you accomplish with greater effort.

My background includes teaching hearing-impaired children in an oral day school program for four years, substitute teaching, and tutoring, but I write primarily as a parent to parents and anyone involved in raising a hearing-impaired child. There are educators devoting their lives to the education of the hearing impaired for whom I have great respect; I do not pretend to speak for them or experts in related fields. I also acknowledge the many parents who could testify to the ingenious, successful ideas that they used in raising their hearing-impaired children. Finally, I am less familiar with the total communication method of teaching than the oral method, and with residential schools than day schools. But for the benefit of other parents of hearing-impaired children, I have felt for some time a deep, overriding desire to put on paper the practical ideas I have accumulated through the years.

My underlying theme is that the need to develop good communication in the framework of the home is common to all parents, regardless of the placement or method of education they choose for their child. And my sincere hope is that this book will give you, as parents, some guidelines and the resolve, confidence, and courage to raise your hearing-impaired child successfully.

You rightfully ask in the beginning, and also sometimes when frustrated in midstream, "What can I do to help my hearing-impaired child adjust to his family, his school, and the hearing world? What can I do to raise him to be a happy, independent adult?"

And my answer is, "So very much!"

Have faith in yourself and in your child.

SHM

part I

in the beginning

"We should never treat deafness as a great big balloon in front of our child—so huge we cannot see the person."

Dr. James C. Marsters,
Deaf Orthodontist

chapter *1*

seeking help and other family concerns

In the beginning there is the family doctor or pediatrician, then the ear doctor, the audiometrist, and the hearing aid dealer—and after that, education and mostly you. Through all this the baby smiles, happy and lovable, but, for you, a maddening question mark.

It was probably you, the parents, who noted that your baby did not begin to talk when he should, and it was you who first questioned your doctor. All too often valuable time is lost by the doctor or pediatrician who has had no training or professional experience with a child with a hearing loss and does not recognize the symptoms. "Your child is young, wait awhile," he says.

There may be further delay when you finally see an eye-ear-nose-and-throat doctor whose only testing equipment is a tuning fork. "Come back to see me again in a month," he is likely to say.

Such experiences have left many parents bitter about the need-less loss of time when they later learn how valuable the early years are to a hearing-impaired child's development of communication skills. A wise doctor will take the time to explain the communication problem and make suggestions.

Learning facts about your child's hearing loss, what can be done about it, and how, is crucial at this stage and is the greatest known balm for shock and grief. The period of recovery for parents can be shortened in direct relation to effective information given them plus assurances they receive as to the possibilities open for their child's future.

For those who have not already gone through this painful process, I would only pause to say: Don't wait! Go to the experts and spend the time and money to do whatever is necessary to get as fine and thorough diagnostic services as you can.

If you live in a small town or an isolated area, travel to where you can obtain expert advice from highly qualified doctors and audiometrists who can test your small child properly. If other handicaps are suspected, such as often occur with babies whose mothers contracted rubella (German measles) during pregnancy, you will need additional consultation with experts in other fields. A metropolitan city clinic, connected with a hospital or university, usually furnishes all these services in one location and is the most desirable arrangement. Be prepared to stay as long as necessary to learn all you can about your child's problems.

The incidence of a child with a hearing loss in the total population is small enough that your child may be the only one in your immediate vicinity with this problem. To cope with his needs in your home environment and community, you must have answers. You must know, to the extent of the best abilities of the experts who study your child, just what his problem really is and what can be done about it. On this basis, parents can function with purpose and go forward in a positive manner—this knowledge and direction are doubly important when you live in a remote area.

You will never regret the effort and money you spend if what you receive is truly the best professional help available.

IN THE INTEREST OF THE WHOLE FAMILY

Parents new to the problems of a hearing loss are hungry for knowledge and advice. Help is available.

For example, the Alexander Graham Bell Association for the Deaf, Washington, DC, will send upon request booklists, advice, and information on clinics and schools in your area. The John Tracy Clinic in Los Angeles will send material and its excellent correspondence course on early education in the home free upon request. (Addresses and other sources of material are listed in Chapter 2.)

Above all else, parents should arrange to visit an educational facility and watch the teaching of hearing-impaired children, not once, but as often as possible. In several large cities, there are clinics that offer short summer sessions for parents who live a considerable distance away.

Think carefully and decide for yourself if you should move the whole family to a new area for the sake of the education of this one child. Advice, even though excellent and well intentioned, should be weighed within the context of your particular family situation. Investigate carefully all possibilities for help and education within your reach. Many factors are involved, and whether or not to move is the first and one of the most important decisions that a young family will make.

I have known moves made for the benefit of one child that have been a disaster for the father who was unhappy with a forced change of jobs. Also, if other children in the family are well placed in school, they must be considered in the uprooting of the whole family for the sake of the schooling of this one child. And I have known mothers who have gone alone to the area of a clinic or educational center with her child for a year or more. This long a period with the mother away from the home can be traumatic. If this separation is indicated, be sure it is the best possible solution; some families have divided for a time successfully and feel the sacrifice was worth it, while others have been most unhappy. You must judge for yourself in the light of the many circumstances involved: your spouse's work, your family home, and the other children in the family. The "whole" of the family should have priority.

If you decide to move closer to educational facilities, or happen to live where they are available, then you will have an opportunity to learn and observe for yourself the early educational needs of your child. If you decide to stay where you are, and are in an isolated area, then you must find the answers yourself. But do not despair if the latter is your decision and situation—your family will have the security and happiness that come from being together in the area where you really want to live, and there are so many constructive things that you can do on your own. In fact, during the preschool years, work in the home to start a hearing-impaired child on his way is by far the most valuable single source of help he can receive.

Seek out information with determination. Learn what you need to know to help your child, and at the same time spread this information to others around him.

WHO WILL HELP?

Everybody!

Help will come from people whom you least expect to offer it; from the druggist, who sells your child a piece of candy and speaks to him kindly with a bit of language and a new face to speechread, to the understanding neighbor who supplies needed companionship by arranging that her child play with yours. The help other children will give is invaluable, and often unrealized. While you are busy with other matters and the children play together, the child's need to communicate with someone approximately the same age is so strong that learning can be at its peak. Never underestimate such play periods, even if it seems to you that they play often in silence. In later years, your child will tell you how much he learned from friends.

In your relations with people, enthusiasm and attitudes of absolute acceptance and pride of accomplishment emanating from you will frequently transfer to others and will pay off tenfold. However, do your best to take other people's attitudes philosophically—some will understand your child's special needs, some won't, and the some who won't may be your closest friends.

Within the family, everyone must make a concerted effort to help in developing communication, and will gladly do so if feelings of love, understanding, and closeness prevail.

Expose your hearing-impaired child to as many people, circumstances, and unusual happenings as humanly possible. Encourage all—the butcher, the baker, and the candlestick maker, as well as your family and close friends—to talk to your child. Talk, talk, and more talk!

Mothers

It is understandable that Mother will carry the greatest burden of teaching in the early years. This is true for a hearing child as well as a hearing-impaired child. Because this child needs a little more help in communication than her other children does not mean that the others do not need their share. A delicate balance must be maintained to keep the harmony, and a harmonious family will do more to bring this small hearing-impaired child a sense of security and confidence than anything else. When I was teaching a hearing-impaired class, I recall a young, handsome boy from a large, well-adjusted Mexican-American family. He had other problems besides his hearing loss: his eyes needed correction, and, as time passed, we found some learning problems as well. But he was the most secure, lovable, well-behaved little boy in the classroom. He knew how to get along with people, how to play properly on the playground, and he tried hard to learn. It was a joy to work with him, even though progress was slow; I felt, in spite of his considerable handicap, he would lead a happy life thanks to his warm, accepting family.

Mother usually sets the tone for the family. Her wholehearted acceptance of the hearing-impaired child and her joy in his accomplishments will lead the way for others in and out of the family to feel the same way. Aside from his communication problems, she must always remember: he is a person who happens to have a hearing loss.

He must be raised to take his position in the family as any of the other children. He must not have special favors, he must carry his burden of the family duties, and be treated like everyone else. There is no excuse for a hearing-impaired child's bad behavior. He will benefit from neither special treatment nor coddling. He can learn to care for himself as well as any other child. Future behavior problems can be avoided by stressing wholesome attitudes, firmness, continuity, and positive expectations in the early years. Try to anticipate problems before they arise, the better to cope with them. Set your sights high for proper behavior, and your hopes realistic, but high, for continuous improvement in his communication skills.

Working Mothers

If possible, a mother should try to stay home and give all the help she can to her hearing-impaired child during the early years between three and six years old. However, if this is economically unfeasible, I would urge her to guard against a feeling of guilt; face the facts squarely and make the necessary adjustments. Consider working part-time or irregular hours that allow you to be with your child longer.

I recall reading about a research project on the subject of hearing children of working mothers that concluded, to the surprise of most, that there was no significant difference between the progress of children with working mothers and those with nonworking mothers. Granted, for a hearing-impaired child there is an additional need to stimulate his communication skills, but the working mother by careful planning and efficient use of time can see her child progress satisfactorily.

Much depends on the arrangements the working mother makes for the care of her child during working hours. She can carefully choose the sitter her child is placed with and take the time to teach this person as much as possible about her child's hearing handicap, how to talk to him, and how to teach him. A substitute mother is a positive approach, and can be a good answer, if she is receptive, willing, and has the necessary understanding and love.

Some sitters are so challenged by a special child that they are eager to observe teaching sessions at a school for the hearing impaired or to read literature on the subject. Later, the child can enter nursery school, and the child interplay will benefit him greatly. But again, it is imperative that care be taken in choosing the right environment, and the time taken to instruct the nursery school teachers.

When you are at home with your child, realize that your energy level often becomes low after a long day's work. When it does, take this into account during home instruction. Thus, if your child is well placed in a nursery or daily care situation and you feel he is getting the best language-building experience possible while you are at work, continue your instruction at home as your strength allows in a relaxed, natural way. You don't have to teach a child a lesson when you are tired; just use the nearby objects, encouraging his interests, and surrounding him with a natural conversational environment. However, take the time to make a weekly language-building plan that you (and a sitter) can follow. Always take advantage of natural opportunities to stimulate his hearing and speech, and to continue to develop his vocabulary. Try to get away together on weekends, even for a little while, for an experience at the park or the store, and then be sure to talk about it.

Fathers

The role Father plays is different from a mother's, but no less important. He must establish a healthy attitude of acceptance of his child and support of his wife's efforts to raise him to be an independent, productive, well-adjusted young adult. It is important that he and his wife function as a unit, especially around the child, because a child can feel disunity with or without full hearing capacity. Some compromise must be made so that just one parent, whichever one, makes the final decisions in disciplinary matters, and the other upholds these decisions at all times. Settle any disagreements in private. The child must not be confused by a parent who lets him do what the other parent does not let him do, or be a witness to bitter arguments whether they involve him or not. Such a child can soon learn to defy discipline, and to play one parent against the other with disastrous results. Naturally, a deficiency in discipline will reflect most on the parents.

The first order of business for fathers, then, is acceptance of the child and harmony at home. Beyond this a father can do many things that will mold the all-around character of his child and add to his communication skills. Before listing several of the most important, consideration should be given to father's traditional role as the provider.

Usually, the time of greatest need in building a hearing-impaired child's communication skills coincides exactly with the greatest potential progress in a father's business career. In these years he is probably working the hardest toward success and family security. It is right that he place his greatest energies, at this time, on his ability to supply his family's needs. A wife should understand this. Too often, I've heard a wife exclaim bitterly, "I never have any help from my husband with our hearing-impaired child!"

Should she, in fact, expect all that much help from him at this time in their married life? Yes and no. She should expect him to read material and attend necessary meetings with her whenever he can. He should be knowledgeable enough about hearing losses to understand what should be done for his child and participate in periodic evaluations. He should be a strong, supportive arm and bring an objective outlook to family decisions.

A wife must face the fact that he is tired when he comes home from work, that his work week may involve traveling, and his energy is not unlimited. He should not be made to feel guilty if his work schedule sometimes leaves him unable to assist in a major way at home.

Looking out over the span of years while this child is growing up, there is valuable help you fathers can give your child informally, with a minimum of time and effort:

1. Talk to your child about anything and everything that interests the two of you. You are bringing him a new vocabulary, new subjects, a new voice to listen to, and a new face to speechread. Develop conversation through questions, answers, and directions; pose questions and lead him into the correct way to answer. The change from Mother is invaluable. And it both rests and benefits your wife for her to study your child from a distance for a few minutes in an environment other than her own.

2. Use idioms, colloquialisms, and exclamations with your child. Sometimes a man's speech is laced with more of a variety of these descriptive words and phrases than a woman's. *Oh boy!*, *Wow!*, and *That's great!* mark the type of small talk that is difficult for the hearing-impaired to pick up. Use and explain such common figures of speech as "raining cats and dogs," "fat as a pig," "hot as a poker," and "lazybones."

3. Try to develop in your child a sense of humor—he certainly needs one. Often a hearing-impaired child doesn't develop a

sense of humor because he doesn't always grasp the reasons for laughter around him. In light conversation, keep the hearing-impaired child aware of the subject matter.

Fathers can best introduce a little teasing in relaxed moments, helping the child to laugh at himself and see the humorous side of life. For example, help him to begin to understand what is funny in a cartoon; these frequently depend on colloquial language, and even if they don't, the meaning as often as not escapes him. He will understand with a little help, and the next time the meaning will strike home. A sense of humor is one of the most valuable assets your child can possess as he expands his relationships with other people and begins to cope with his impairment.

4. Help him to learn the rules of games. In most instances, hearing-impaired children don't learn game rules as easily as hearing children. Speech on a playing field is lost to them by distance and open spaces, so it is important that they learn the rules for athletic games by a means other than trial and error to avoid embarrassing mistakes and ridicule. There are many ways to teach game rules; athletic contests shown on your television screen offer an excellent opportunity and board games offer another. The best way to learn is to actually play the games. Teach him to play games for the fun of it, and play games of all kinds, indoors and out. Help him learn to lose gracefully, win humbly, take his turn, and follow the rules. If he learns these basics at home, he will transfer them to the schoolyard where he can become a coveted player on the field instead of a left-out on the sidelines. A child must succeed to be happy with himself and your hearing-impaired child needs a bigger boost in this direction than most.

5. Set up opportunities for all kinds of experiences for your child. Take him, or arrange for a member of the family to take him, places to see things, hear things, do things, feel things, collect things, and talk, talk, talk to him about them.

6. Suggest simple problems of arithmetic to him and help him with his reasoning and thinking processes.

If you can do all of the above, at least part-time, you will give your wife a much-needed lift and your child immeasurable help.

Once I visited a family with a small hearing-impaired boy. The father, anxious to help his young son, showed me a deck of playing cards he was using with his boy to teach him to match and to count.

He told me rather ruefully that a teacher had suggested that he could find better teaching materials than a deck of cards.

I wholly disagree with this opinion!

Not only was the teacher unnecessarily discouraging a willing father, but she underestimated the value of that deck of cards in the hands of that father. If Mother has the time and inclination to cut out pictures, that's fine, but if father feels comfortable with a handy deck of cards, the teaching possibilities in that deck are endless, from matching likenesses to seeing differences, from learning to count to putting things in sequence. They can be used as flash cards for arithmetic. Again, they can be used to play a simple game like Fish. There is a certain value to using abstracts, like the dots on a domino that is often pictured in first-grade arithmetic.

I equate that father's deck of cards with the Kendall Five-Flavor puppy biscuits that I used in the very beginning for matching colors, shapes, and for counting, because they were handy.

A man's approach is often a welcome change. My eldest hearing-impaired daughter, Linda, had her first male teacher when she was eight. In the two years that he taught her, she picked up many expressive, in-between phrases and colloquialisms. We have been forever grateful to him; he brought vigor, enthusiasm, and a new approach to the classroom.

Another man who influenced her in the early years was the taxi driver who drove Linda and others to and from hearing-impaired classes each day. Among other things, he taught her the names of the different cars on the road, and how to identify them.

Brothers and Sisters

A devoted mother of a highly successful hearing-impaired young man often said to me, "My greatest mistake was not having more children. They would have been a great help in building his communication skills."

Years later one realizes more fully the value of the companionship of children with each other. They help develop a child's language in many small ways, encourage him to talk, and expect him to participate.

If your family is large, consider it fortunate, even though you are too busy to give your hearing-impaired child as much time as you might if he were the only one. Your other children will fill in for you, and in some ways that you, as a parent, never can. Brothers and sisters quickly discover how to talk with him and will take an interest in plans for his improvement. So be enthusiastic, share your joy in his accomplishments with them, and assign them small teaching tasks. They can be particularly helpful in keeping him informed of what is going on. One family I know of assigns a different member each week to keep their hearing-impaired child abreast of the dinner table conversation. Also, hearing-impaired children appreciate being filled in on what is being said on television.

Children are amazingly willing, and like to be occupied. It cannot be expected that they will curtail their own activities, but there will be family hours before dinner and time in the evenings and on weekends when they have spare time.

One day I visited a small boy from my class with a severe hearing loss and a mother who was unable emotionally to teach him. She had had several mental breakdowns, and although she was able to feed and clothe her large family, she was unable to concentrate to the extent necessary to help the boy learn language. While I sat giving him a simple lesson, the other children came in from school, and their interest in what I was doing was intense. They begged to help. If only someone could have somehow tapped that energy more often, channeled that enthusiasm, the boy might have received the spark he needed. What a shame! They were like a group of enthusiastic volunteers with a cause but no leader.

Grandparents

Grandparents are very special people. Their grown children hold them very dear, and their grandchildren find them a source of wise council and a wide range of knowledge. Grandparents stand in the unique position of being able to dearly love, spoil, pamper, and thoroughly enjoy a grandchild for periods of time without being shouldered with the responsibility of parenthood. They usually have no desire to take on that responsibility twice over, and indeed they should not be expected to. For them, physical and mental energy may be on the wane. It is better not to burden them with the fine points of educating a hearing-impaired child if they seem unable or unwilling to absorb them. Grandparents will be effective as long as they hold a positive attitude and provide acceptance and more conversation-building opportunities. The time they spend taking their hearing-impaired grandchild to the zoo or the beach will be of great service, by adding more experience upon which language can be built and by giving tired parents a respite.

When a child comes home spoiled and difficult to handle from his grandparents' house, realize that he knows very well the difference between what he can do at his grandparents' house and his own house.

Remind him of this in short order and your routine will quickly be reestablished and maintained as "what is done at mother's and father's house" is not "what is done at grandmother's and grandfather's house." This appears to be a better method than trying to change the habits of grandparents.

ACCEPTING YOUR CHILD

If, after an honest personal appraisal, you feel that you have not really accepted your child's handicap, consider looking deeper into yourself. Perhaps you have not matured sufficiently to face this special problem. You need to see it as the God-given challenge that it is, for all its joys more than its sorrows. Know for a fact that as you watch and help this child of yours overcome his handicap, you will be rewarded many times over with pride and joy in accomplishment. You will greatly enrich your own life by discovering that, if you can solve the tough problems of raising a hearing-impaired child, you will have gained the self-confidence to handle other major problems that arise.

Not everyone is cut out to undertake this challenge, but most parents can stand up to the pressures of the situation, to the benefit of those near and dear to them.

Acceptance is the subject of deep concern to educators of the deaf. In setting up the John Tracy Clinic, Mrs. Tracy first employed a psychologist. She did not hire her for the children, but for the parents' individual and group therapy classes.

Acceptance is a necessary ingredient in the help that must be given a hearing-impaired child by his parents. Parents themselves are not always fully aware of their hidden, often guilt-ridden rejection of their child. Parents have admitted to me that they never really accepted the situation, only tolerated it; later, after a change of attitude, there was a marked improvement in the parent-child relationship. Free your mind of these distracting thoughts of nonacceptance. You can build a wall or you can open a gate. If your child is going to accept your corrections, your attempts to teach him to listen, to understand, and to speak, the gate must be open wide.

KEEPING A BALANCE

As the entire picture of the complexity of communication becomes clearer, many parents of a hearing-impaired child experience a feeling of urgency and try to accomplish too much for their child in too short a time.

Not only does this lead to undesirable tenseness, but one must be aware of not losing a sense of balance within the family structure. You must not pour excessive energy into helping your hearing-impaired child while neglecting others in the family. This child needs special attention, but your spouse and the other children do also. It is a wise parent who gives each child undivided attention for a portion of the day when he comes home from school (or another more convenient time) in order to assure each child that he has a listening ear. This will alleviate any jealousy toward the hearing-impaired child.

Results of an imbalance in attention are sometimes difficult to avoid. For example, my hearing-impaired daughter, Linda, grew up with a hearing brother, Peter. I well remember when I noticed one day that two-year-old Peter wasn't talking much, if at all, and he was, as a hearing child, certainly overdue. I realized that in my urgency to teach four-year-old Linda to speechread that my face and attention, when we were all three seated at the kitchen table, were directed only to her. Peter was listening well enough, but he was not receiving any direct contact with my face and eyes. I should have noted this sooner and made better seating arrangements so that they both faced me. This episode taught me that hearing as well as hearing-impaired children need a front view of your face and your complete attention when they are learning to talk.

Hearing children also will imitate the speech patterns they hear the most. Since Linda and Peter were inseparable and played together hours on end, they talked together in a wonderful, incomprehensible language all their own for several years. It consisted of all vowels, practically no consonants, and many gestures. Peter finally developed the last of his consonants in kindergarten.

And, if the husband-wife relationship is to remain happy, an occasional change in scenery is advisable. Get away together for short trips to enjoy new sights or old ones that bring back pleasant memories. Or, perhaps with congenial friends, take a trip long enough to give you a refreshed outlook. Your hearing-impaired child, placed with a trustworthy and understanding sitter, will not only survive, but have an opportunity to learn to understand another's speech. If you have other children at home, all the better—you will find that the learning process will continue.

Even in your relationship with friends, be conscious of maintaining a balance. Everyone may not want to hear at length about your work with your hearing-impaired child; therefore, use discretion in your conversations on this subject.

There will always be unexpected interruptions in any balanced household. If someone is ill, he must be cared for, and when a child has a problem, he must have your counsel.

A balanced family team attains the best results.

chapter 2

what you should know about a hearing loss

Learn all you can about a hearing loss so that you will be prepared to make intelligent decisions on behalf of your hearing-impaired child. Knowing your subject is the key to any successful endeavor.

Besides absorbing all the information and advice on hearing losses given by your doctor, specialist, audiometrist, and hearing aid dealer, you should reinforce and add to your knowledge of the fundamentals of hearing losses. Read books and articles on the subject, attend parent classes, and observe children in every teaching situation. You are building a solid base for evaluating your child's potential.

Among the first subjects to learn about are the ear and how one hears, hearing tests and their interpretation, hearing aid evaluations, and the workings of the hearing aid your child will wear. Also become aware of the special problems that may beset a hearing-impaired child in later school years. Often parents wait until a particular problem is upon them before realizing there are methods to use in the early years to solve or at least to ease the problem. Look forward to the later years and prepare for any stumbling blocks that might arise.

READING MATERIAL

One source of reading material for parents is the Alexander Graham Bell Association for the Deaf (3417 Volta Place, N.W., Washington, DC 20007). The material offered for sale includes books and inexpensive reprints of articles. The Association publishes a journal, *The Volta Review*, seven times a year with pertinent articles and information. It operates a lending library for members where a list of books is available by mail for a fee to cover postage. (Check less expensive postal rates for returning books.)

The John Tracy Clinic (806 West Adams Boulevard, Los Angeles, CA 90007) offers a free correspondence course to parents of preschool children, as well as a suggested reading list for parents.

The National Association for the Deaf (814 Thayer Avenue, Silver Spring, MD 20910) publishes useful books for parents and material on the language of signs.

American Annals of the Deaf (814 Thayer Avenue, Silver Spring, MD 20910) is a periodical published five times a year with various articles of interest to parents of children using either the oral or total communication method. Each year they publish a *Directory of Services for the Deaf in the United States* covering schools, classes, and clinics for the hearing impaired in the United States, Canada, and Mexico.

Recent articles and books on the subject of the hearing-impaired child written by educators, linguists, and other experts in the field often use a new vocabulary and style that are difficult reading for the average parent. When I puzzle over such words as: *associative selectivity, experiential, phenomenalistic, causality, and contiguity*, I ask, How can a parent without an advanced degree in education or equivalent possibly understand this?

For parents, a simpler reading source that I highly recommend is the early editions of *The Volta Review*, 1950 to 1960 and earlier. They contain gems of material for parents with timeless suggestions on teaching hearing-impaired children at home in clear, plain language. Letters from parents in "The Parents Talk It Over with Harriet Montague" and interesting first-hand observations from hearing-impaired adults in "Molly Mather's Mailbox" are featured columns in the older editions. You may have to hunt for a full set of bound *Volta*s. Try the large city libraries first (Los Angeles County's downtown library has a set). Other sources are libraries in colleges having programs for the education of teachers of the deaf and libraries in schools for the deaf.

One book I would like to bring to your attention, because it has been an inspiration to me and to others who have been fortunate enough to read it, is *My Life Transformed* by Helen Heckman (1928). It was written by a young deaf woman whose stepmother took her to her heart at age eleven. She transformed her from an awkward, shuffling, introverted, nearly illiterate child into a bright, attractive young woman with excellent speechreading and speech, who became a talented concert dancer. How she did it is a story as exciting and informative as the Helen Keller–Ann Sullivan saga. Unfortunately, this book is out of print, but you will find it worthwhile to search for in libraries and used book stores.

THE EAR

Set about learning about the human ear; study a diagram of the ear, its parts, and functions. Learn something of what can go wrong with the mechanisms of the ear. Be knowledgeable enough about the ear to understand what your doctor tells you about your child's hearing loss and the source of the trouble. Ask questions and insist upon explanations to better understand, develop, and care for your child's residual hearing. Your child's hearing is already low, which is reason enough that the utmost care be taken that no further loss occurs.

Note the relationship of the middle ear to the throat by way of the opening of the eustachian tube. Infections of the throat can easily pass into the ear from this avenue, particularly in children. Viruses, bacterial infections, allergies, and childhood diseases can seriously affect hearing. Infections carried in the bloodstream can affect the inner ear fluid through the arteries around the ear, which serve the ear with oxygen and other nutrients. Such an infection could result from an allergy problem.

If your child has other handicaps, seek consultation with experts and become knowledgeable in those fields as well. There should be a hard-and-fast rule that all children with a hearing loss should have an eye examination. With the hearing sense impaired, the eyes become doubly important for speechreading. They will carry much of the load for both senses, and parents should ensure they are as acute as is physically possible, providing their child with glasses if prescribed.

The Hearing Test

A careful and accurate test to determine the amount of your child's residual hearing forms the basis for selecting the proper hearing aid or aids he will wear. The expert who gives this test should be not only an experienced audiologist but also one who knows how to test a very small child with what is called "play audiometry." With the aid of a pure-tone audiometer, a test machine to measure a person's hearing, he can get a relatively accurate picture of your young child's hearing capability and chart it on an audiogram.

Be sure you learn how to read intelligently your child's audiogram and the accompanying report. Insist on receiving your own copy each time an audiogram is taken. In periodic tests as he grows older, these audiograms will help you understand what he actually hears as well as attest to whether his hearing is fluctuating or remaining fairly constant. My experience has been that a good audiogram is quite reliable as a visual image of a child's hearing "threshold," the point at which he first hears a sound loud enough to react to it.

Furthermore, the audiogram is a valuable comparative record. It tells you what potential your child has for hearing, his capacity to hear measured as hearing loss in decibel units for different frequencies, and indicates your child's frequency range.

This is, I know, a complicated subject for some parents, but I urge you to learn all you can about sound—the volume units of sound, called decibels (dB), and the high and low characteristics of sound, called frequencies, measured in Hertz (Hz). Figure 1 shows the frequency range most important for speech. This range contains most, but not all, of the speech sounds. Whereas your child's audiogram shows what he hears at one specific frequency by means of a pure tone emitted by the audiometer, speech sounds consist of a fundamental frequency plus a rich assortment of other tones on ever higher frequencies, similiar to octaves on the piano. The variety and peculiar makeup of these overtones give one speech sound the quality that enables you to recognize it from another. The vowels range from slightly below 125 Hz to 3000 Hz and are nearly all low frequency; vowels are perceived by most hearing-impaired persons with a hearing aid. The consonants have a higher and even wider range, from 200 Hz to as much as 6000 Hz. Table 1 shows the important frequencies of the consonants. Significantly, some of the consonants lie only in the higher frequencies and are not heard at all by many of the hearing impaired, since hearing losses tend to increase (dip on the audiogram) in the higher frequencies. Those consonants lying exclusively in the higher frequencies are (very high) *th, s, f,* and *t,* and (medium high) *sh, ch, p,* and *h.*

Even though the relevant frequency range for speech lies between 400 Hz and 3000 Hz, many components of our speech sounds lie well below and above that range. For this reason, hearing aids that amplify the low tones often are of added value to some hearing-impaired persons, while hearing aids with a good, wide range into the higher tones benefit nearly all those with hearing losses.

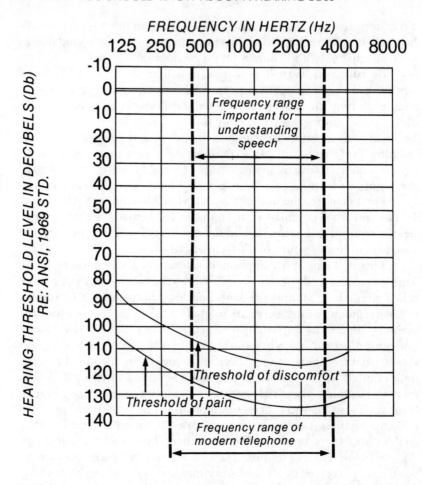

figure 1. Audiogram showing the frequency range important for understanding speech, the threshold of discomfort, and the threshold of pain. (Information obtained from Western Electric Company and Gloria Hoversten, audiologist of Los Angeles, CA.)

In addition, speech sounds vary in volume. The table of speech sounds in Table 2 is based on the loudest sound, the *ô* as in *ball*, spoken in a normal voice in a quiet atmosphere at 60 dB, with the other sounds relative in volume to the base sound, *ô*. You can see that there is a variation of 21.3 dB between the sounds. For normal hearing this is not enough to cause difficulty in understanding, but for someone who does not hear until the volume is raised to 80 dB, a difference of over 20 dB for the sound *th* can put this sound out of his hearing range.

TABLE 1. Frequencies of consonants

θ*				*About 6000*
o	*250–300*			*4500 – 6000*
s				*5000 – 6000*
z	*200–300*			*4000 – 5000*
f				*4500 – 5000*
v	*300 – 400*		*3500 – 4500*	
t			*2500 – 3500*	
d	*300 – 400*		*2500 – 3000*	
k	*300 – 400*		*2000 – 2500*	
g	*200 – 300*		*2000 – 3000*	
l	*250 – 400*		*2000 – 3000*	
p		*1500 – 2000*		
b	*300 – 400*		*2000 – 3000*	
h		*1500 – 2000*		
sh		*1500 – 2000*	*4500 – 5500*	
ch		*1500 – 2000*	*4000–5000*	
j	*200 – 300*		*2000 – 3000*	
m	*250 – 350*	*1000 – 1500*	*2500 – 3500*	
n	*250 – 350*	*1000 – 1500*	*2500 – 3000*	
ng	*250 – 400*	*1000 – 1500*	*2000 – 3000*	
r	*600 – 800*	*1000–1500*	*2000 – 2100*	

From D.M.C. Dale, Ph.D., Applied Audiology for Children, *1970; adapted from Harvey Fletcher,* Speech and Hearing, *van Nostrand, 1929. Courtesy of Charles C. Thomas, publisher, Springfield, Illinois.*

*Note: The sign θ is the same as th as in thin, and the sign o is the same as Th as in the.

Use these tables to determine what beginning words you will choose to teach your child to hear and to speechread. Be sure that those words have strong intensity vowels (those with tonal energy which produce the quality of loudness) and that their initial consonants are of low frequency and strong intensity.

Returning to Figure 1, note the "threshold of discomfort," the point at which sound becomes too loud for comfort, and the "threshold of pain," where sound entering the ear is so loud it becomes painful and possibly damaging. These levels are true for someone with impaired hearing as well as for someone with perfect hearing. These thresholds limit, at calculated points, the amount of sound that can be artificially put into the ear through a hearing aid. More volume

TABLE 2. The relative intensity level of 33 speech sounds*

			dB				dB
ô	as in	ball	60.0	n	as in	no	46.8
u	as in	sun	59.6	m	as in	me	45.4
ō	as in	home	59.6	Th	as in	the	44.2
ī	as in	mine	59.5	t	as in	tap	44.1
ou	as in	house	59.2	h	as in	hat	43.9
a	as in	cat	59.2	k	as in	key	43.8
e	as in	ten	58.4	j	as in	jump	43.7
o	as in	top	57.4	f	as in	four	43.6
u̇	as in	cook	57.1	g	as in	girl	42.9
ü	as in	school	55.9	s	as in	sit	42.4
l	as in	lamb	53.5	z	as in	zip	41.6
ā	as in	play	53.3	v	as in	van	41.4
i	as in	bit	52.6	p	as in	pet	40.6
ē	as in	team	49.4	d	as in	doll	38.9
ng	as in	ring	48.9	b	as in	bat	38.8
sh	as in	sheep	48.9	th	as in	thin	38.7
ch	as in	chair	47.2				

*Table presented by the late Dr. Janet Jeffers in her course, Aural Rehabilitation, given at the California State University in Los Angeles in 1962.

will not necessarily bring better hearing. Hearing aids are equipped to compensate for a very loud sound that would, when amplified, cause injury and pain to the ear, by cutting off the volume of sound above a certain point.

It is very difficult for those of us with good hearing to imagine what it would be like to hear with partial hearing. I doubt that we can ever really know exactly what our child "hears," aided or unaided. He may learn to enjoy music as much as we do, even though it has a different sound to him. No matter, he enjoys it. I've known many hearing-impaired people who relish their stereos as much as the normally hearing person.

Still, one way to partially experience the sound one would hear with a hearing loss is to listen to the sound of a voice on the radio turned very low. The volume of normal speech is considered to be 65 dB. If the radio voice is at a point where you can barely hear it, too low to distinguish what is being said, you are experiencing approximately a 60 dB loss. Also, I have heard a recording designed to show the effect of hearing loss ("How They Hear," by Gordon N. Stowe and Associates, Northbrook, Illinois). It allows you to hear the human voice speaking at normal volume, then cuts off to a 20 dB loss, then to a 40 dB loss, and finally to a 60 dB loss. It was truly revealing how difficult it was to understand the speech at 40 dB lower volume, and how impossible at 60 dB. Hearing this record for yourself will convince you of how rapidly the intensity of sound drops for every 20 dB. However, due to frequency variations, it will never duplicate, but only approximate, what a hearing-impaired child actually hears.

A recurring question asked of a parent with a hearing-impaired child is "How great is his loss?" The best and most accurate answer is to give his average loss in decibels through the speech range for the better ear. To arrive at this figure, read from his audiogram the decibel levels at 500, 1000, and 2000 Hz. These are the most important frequencies for speech. Add the three figures together, divide by three, and the result is his average decibel loss. For example, if a child's audiogram shows:

500 Hz	65 dB	loss
1000 Hz	85 dB	loss
2000 Hz	95 dB	loss
Total =	245 dB	

Therefore, average loss = 245 ÷ 3 = 81⅔ or 82 dB. This is by no means a complete picture of his hearing loss, but it does serve the purpose of giving you an answer to a question that is asked over and over, and it is approximate and meaningful enough to most people.

In this age of improved hearing aids, to describe a child's hearing loss as mild, severe, or profound is often misleading, as much depends on his ability to use the residual hearing he has when aided. Not infrequently, a child with a severe loss may function as hard of hearing after learning to listen with a properly fitted hearing aid. Nowadays a hearing loss is not considered profound unless it lies in the 95 to 100 dB range, and even then a child can learn to discriminate speech sounds enough to belie such a labeling. In fact, because of the complexity and the individuality of hearing losses, labeling should be avoided, except when referring to groups in a general, descriptive way.

The Speech Test

Providing your child's loss is not severe and he has developed some speech, the audiologist will conduct a test to determine his threshold for hearing of speech. This consists of giving him orally a list of words to see if he can repeat them from hearing alone, first unaided and then aided. Among the many speech tests, those used most frequently are the Spondee and the PB-50 Word Lists.

The easiest to understand are lists of ten spondaic words—two-syllable words in which both syllables are equally stressed (*cowboy* and *toothbrush*). The PB-50 lists are more extensive, consisting of fifty one-syllable words designed to represent all the speech sounds and point out those that are faulty or unintelligible, in terms of the child's discrimination. The results will show the percentage of words heard correctly and at what volume level of sound. The common mistakes are substituting one sound for another or missing a sound altogether. In using the PB lists, it is helpful if the tester will jot down the mistakes for you so that you can see what sounds your child hears imperfectly. Knowing his trouble spots, for example, substituting *b* for the *p* in *path*, you will be able to work at home or in conjunction with his teacher toward improving his discrimination and, ultimately, his articulation.

In both the hearing test and the speech test reports, audiologists use symbols, initials, and abbreviations that are highly confusing to parents. Nevertheless, they do contain valuable information for deciding what and where your child's problem is and what can be done about it, so be sure to ask for assistance in their interpretation.

THE HEARING AID EVALUATION

Arrange for a hearing aid evaluation, preferably through your audiologist or a comparable specialist, before you contact any hearing aid dealer. The audiologist is usually equipped to give you a hearing aid evaluation after your child's audiogram establishes the extent of his hearing loss and his need for a hearing aid. (Before this evaluation, it is best to have an earmold made—or even better, two ear-molds, one for each ear—so that hearing aids from different manufacturers can be accurately evaluated for use with your child.) An adequate supply of hearing aids in good working order should be available to examine and try on your child. From speech tests and an interpretation of the audiogram, the audiologist will make a recommendation as to which aid, or aids, are best suited to your child.

Audiograms and hearing aid tests can stretch over several months for a very small child, and are likely to try your patience. Weeks of conditioning your child to listening for sound may be necessary before a clear picture evolves of his hearing. At home, you can play listening games suggested by the audiologist to help him respond more readily to sound in a test situation.

The audiological recommendation on the basis of technical considerations is your prime concern. However, there are other factors to consider in deciding which of several acceptable aids to purchase, such as:

1. Extent of the frequency range. An aid that has a wide range of frequencies, particularly in the high frequencies, is more likely to maximize your child's hearing potential for the high-frequency speech sounds that he will hear as his auditory training progresses. The wider the range of amplified frequencies, the better the sound quality reproduced, as in a good high fidelity set of earphones.

2. Reliability and sturdiness. The aid, tested on a hearing aid analyzer machine, should show smooth amplification over its frequency range without sudden peaks and valleys which cause distortion. Inquire regarding the warranty given with the instrument.

3. Location of the microphone on the aid. For some children who are highly sensitive to distracting noise, a microphone on a body aid that is located at the top of the aid will be less susceptible to the annoying, rubbing sound of clothing.

4. The variety of settings available and the inner adjustments which allow for individualized amplification.

5. Availability of parts and reliability of repair service. Consider the distance from your home to the center where you can obtain hearing aid parts and prompt repair service. Receive positive assurance that an aid manufacturer, miles away or in Europe, has an outlet for parts and repairs within a reasonable distance from your home.

6. Cost. Other considerations being equal, selecting an aid that costs less does not necessarily mean its quality is less, and for a young family the savings can be important. Paraphrasing Dr. Hayes A. Newby of Stanford University, in the absence of evidence that a child would do better with a more expensive aid, it is advisable first to select an inexpensive one (Newby, 1958).

The Hearing Aid

When the decision is made on the exact hearing aid(s) to be purchased for your child, the audiologist will give you the manufacturer's name and model of the instrument and instructions for its proper settings. Consider this comparable to a prescription from a medical doctor. Go to a recommended hearing aid dealer, with luck, close by, and purchase the exact prescribed instrument. Remember, your audiologist is the authority on the hearing aid best suited to your child—do not let the hearing aid salesman persuade you to accept a substitute.

Expect to receive detailed instructions on how the aid functions and the possibilities of the different settings, such as the telephone control. Learn what cord model it takes, lengths and weights of cords available, and the batteries required. You need to know how to test it at home for power and performance. Since your small child will be unable to tell you how it sounds to him for a long time, you will want to know all you can about his aid to keep it in good working order. Also, check with the dealer regarding parts and repairs for your particular instrument—what parts does he have on hand, how long does the manufacturer take to make normal repairs, does he have an extra instrument that he will loan you during repairs? Your child should not be without a hearing aid at any time.

OVERCOMING THE SPECIAL PROBLEMS OF A HEARING LOSS

Because hearing impairment affects the communication skills, it directly affects related learning during the school years. Parents of a young hearing-impaired child should be aware of the learning problems that confront an older hearing-impaired child; nearly always there are things you can do in the early years to ease these later problems. How little parents know of the future of their small child, and how much they really want to know! As a telling example, I've seen parents come in droves to a panel presentation by hearing-impaired teenagers and adults, avidly watching and listening to the panel members in order to relate all they see and hear to their own child.

Several problems common to most older hearing-impaired children are:

1. Hearing-impaired children have great difficulty using proper grammar in their writing. Many can't write good letters, reports, or compositions by the time they finish school.
2. Too many hearing-impaired children are poor readers, which further handicaps their learning ability.
3. Hearing-impaired children often find it hard to learn to formulate ideas, to think creatively, to question, and to reason.
4. Vocabulary is an unending problem. Idioms and figures of speech are especially difficult.

5. Social conversation or "small talk" is often so poorly developed that the hearing-impaired person has trouble keeping a conversation running smoothly.

These are the most glaring problems that come to mind, and all can be diminished if you start working on them early. A hearing-impaired child can learn to write well, read well, and converse well, but it takes longer and more practice to become proficient in these skills. Specific ideas for such improvement are discussed in later chapters.

From a practical standpoint, in order to apply for and hold down a basic job, a person must at least be able to: complete forms or questionnaires intelligently; follow oral and written directions; explain himself and his particular work orally; and write simple memos, letters, and reports.

This is our goal, to raise our child to be self-sufficient. He must be able to get a job, hold it, and make a living for himself and his family. This is not easily attained by the hearing-impaired. Your young child will need all the assistance and guidance you can give him to be capable of finally making it on his own.

PROBLEMS IN ADJUSTING TO SOCIETY

Most hearing-impaired children must enter the mainstream of society to make their living, but society will not adjust to them—they must adjust to society.

In order to cope with society's demands and expectations, parents should encourage their child to:

1. Accept his hearing loss.
2. Give and take in everyday life without preferential treatment.
3. Develop a pleasing personality and a sense of humor.
4. Be comfortable and trusting with all people, the hearing impaired and the hearing alike.
5. Learn from and contribute to society.

One after another, writers and speakers on the subject of vocational training for the hearing impaired echo the words of Roger M. Falberg: "the attitudes of the deaf worker determine even more than his skills what degree of success the individual will meet in his chosen vocational area" (Falberg, 1963).

Two disagreeable habits peculiar to the hearing impaired should not be allowed to develop. One is the use of a hearing loss as a weapon in an argument with a hearing person. Be firm in not allowing your child to use his hearing loss as an excuse. Do not allow him, as a defense, to close his eyes, turn off his hearing aid, or turn and walk away from a conversation with a hearing person. Nothing leaves a person more frustrated and furious than to be treated to this kind of retaliation. It is unfair and rude.

The other habit to discourage is becoming suspicious of the unheard portion of other people's conversation. Hearing-impaired persons tend to believe that other people talking together are talking about them. This can mushroom, resulting in a suspicious, untrusting, and even psychotic person, thoroughly disagreeable to be around. If you see signs of this trait developing in your child, have a heart-to-heart talk with him—declare firmly that you know positively that people are not talking about him 99 percent of the time, and if they are at an odd time, they are just as likely to be saying something good.

Perhaps this is partly what my daughter Linda had in mind when she said, "I feel that the greatest mistake the deaf can make is not to trust the goodwill of people" (McArthur, 1967).

RELATING MATERIALS TO YOUR NEEDS

As you listen to teachers and experts in the field of hearing impairment, read, and observe children being taught, relate what you learn to your own child's abilities and interests within the family environment. Bear in mind that a valuable suggestion for one child may not carry the same value for another.

The best way to teach your child at home may not evolve by following to the letter all you learn from the spoken or written word, but rather from a combination of that knowledge and your own creative ideas.

Put another way, convert the best of what you learn and apply it to your own independent, unique style of raising your child. Then, through calm determination and patience, you will develop a suitable home learning program for your child with which you both will be comfortable. After all, you are with your child around the clock and you know his needs better than anyone else.

chapter 3

evaluating your own child

It is more important today than ever before that parents be capable of forming for themselves a knowledgeable estimate of the potential of their hearing-impaired child. Recent government legislation (such as the 1973 Education of All Handicapped Children Act—P.L. 94-142) has placed the parents squarely in a responsible position as part of the team evaluating and actively involved in the planning and implementation of their child's education. This opportunity can only be of value if parents are fully prepared to state their opinions with certainty and with a clear picture of their child's abilities to back them up.

In order to feel that you, as a parent, have made the wisest decisions possible, evaluate your child not only through the counsel of professionals, but also, more importantly, through your own observations as he grows to maturity. To evaluate your own child is not a simple task; it is difficult to be objective about one's own child. However, careful analysis of all factors is the best approach to solving the problem.

Decide on two sets of goals: those you want your child to attain in the near future, or short-term goals, and those you want him to attain by adulthood, or long-term goals. You also need to differentiate between what you want for him and what you think he is capable of achieving. "Reaching" is desirable, yet be wary of reaching while losing sight of reality. And then, on the other hand, it is disheartening to see a child who has never been allowed to reach for his ultimate potential.

In evaluating, try not to compare him with another child when you are observing hearing-impaired children. Nevertheless, based on such observations, you should come away with a general, realistic impression of what can be accomplished by hearing-impaired children near his age. Then look at your own child in all his aspects as the individual that he is and set your goals.

Evaluate your child as you see him now and reevaluate him again at least once a year, or more often if warranted by a substantial change.

Do not simply consider his age level but rather his overall ability, or maturity level. The hearing-impaired child, taking much longer to learn communication skills than a normally hearing child, may lag one or two years behind hearing children in school. This difference will seem significant in the early years but by adulthood it will seem minor.

The areas to consider in evaluating your child fall into four general categories:

1. Individual differences in all children,
2. Individual differences in hearing-impaired children of pre-school age,
3. Individual differences in hearing-impaired children of school age, and
4. Individual differences in environment.

PARENTS' HOMEWORK

Before beginning to evaluate your own child, you must have a broad basis for comparison. Be sure it is not based on only one or two other children.

Observe and listen to hearing-impaired adults, teenagers, and children of all ages as well as children the same age or maturity level as your own child. When observing hearing-impaired adults, particularly those 35 years and older, realize that many—when young and developing their communication skills—did not have the benefit of the improved hearing aids that children do today. But don't stop here; make it a point to watch normally hearing children of your own child's maturity level—seeing too much of a handicap warps a parent's clear perspective.

The very term "deafness" in itself is a defeating term. Mark Ross and Donald R. Calvert (1967) have pointed out that:

> The label of "deafness" or the response to a child with a significant amount of residual hearing as if he were "deaf" destroys the usual frame of reference one holds for expected standards of achievement. The frequent result is a greatly lowered standard, reduced motivation, with consequent limited achievement. Parents often have little understanding of their hearing handicapped child's potential. As they become aware of the limitations imposed by a hearing loss and as they broaden their experience with other hearing handicapped children, they tend to set their expectations too low. (p. 647)

But parents can expect too much of their child as well as too little. They can become so involved in their child's handicap that they expect him to perform a task that the average hearing child of the same maturity level is not yet performing. It is often recommended and sometimes insisted upon that teachers have experience in a hearing class before becoming teachers of the deaf. I have also known teachers of the deaf who have returned to teaching hearing children for a short period because they felt they were losing their perspective on programming for the hearing impaired. It is no less important for parents to regularly reinforce and broaden their views to keep their expectations in focus.

Mrs. Veneda Martin, parent of a son with a hearing loss, in *Parents in Action: A Handbook of Experiences With Their Hearing-Impaired Children* (Bitter, 1978), gives excellent advice:

> Parents of younger children have often asked me if I was always sure I was making the right decisions when I had to make them. The answer is no. Such saintly insight is not prevalent among the parents of hearing-impaired children I know, and I would venture to say it's not prevalent among any group of human beings. Now if you were to ask me if the decisions I made eventually led to the desired results . . . the answer would be yes. There are a couple of reasons why. The first is always following the 3 steps I'm going to give you. The biggest mistake we can make is focusing our time and energy on troubles. Instead, focus your attention and energy on finding the best solution to it. These are the 3 steps I have used:
>
> 1. Gather as much, and the *best* information you can find about the particular problem;

2. Study this information, and from what you learn, decide on the best course of action to take in this particular situation;

3. Take it!

Now there is a good chance that along the way, you might come across some new information. Study it, and if you decide it is important or it would help you reach the desired solution, revise your original decision accordingly. A good rule to follow is, never allow any problem to remain in your life for more than 24 hours without doing something to start solving it. (p. 16)

INDIVIDUAL DIFFERENCES IN ALL CHILDREN

On the assumption that one should begin with the child himself and not his handicap, the individual differences that affect all children affect your hearing-impaired child as well. The areas of importance to consider in evaluating your child are:

1. Maturity—learning and social,
2. Intelligence,
3. Personality,
4. Attention span, and
5. Motivation and curiosity.

Maturity—Learning and Social

A child's maturity level, or his readiness to learn, does not necessarily correspond to his age level. If a child is not ready to learn a specific task, the struggle for him to do so wastes time and is sometimes damaging to the child. For a hearing-impaired child, it is best that he have a safe measure of maturity above the average maturity of the class, particularly if he is in a regular classroom. A hearing-impaired child needs a head start. If, in your opinion, he is below average in readiness for kindergarten, it would be wise to wait one year to enroll him. The additional year of growth and learning development will give him the edge—the maturity—necessary to be a success, physically and mentally. And you do want to start on a good note, if possible.

Despite your hearing-impaired child's probable lag in communication skills, try to have him mature in all other respects prior to entering school. This brings to mind our daughter, Laurie, who entered kindergarten with perfectly good hearing and an October birthdate. By the opening of school in September she was eligible to enter even though not yet five, but so were those children with January birthdates of the same year, now over five and a half years old. Competition given this much difference in age would be difficult for many, and it was for Laurie. Thus, she entered school with several weak spots in her readiness to learn and in her attention span, but not in her social maturity—she was certainly advanced there!

As it happened, Laurie struggled with several learning abilities throughout elementary school, particularly reading and taking tests. By second grade, she hadn't learned to read in spite of help at home and her teacher's concentrated efforts. But by fourth grade she was reading at grade level, although I think her ego and desire to read were dampened for awhile. Also in fourth grade she came up against her first, simple test. She experienced nearly a total freeze, but by sixth grade this problem had leveled off. While her short attention span continued to slow her learning abilities in these elementary years, she showed, at the same time, an excellent ability to grasp the fundamentals of mathematics and continued to be well above average in social adjustment.

It is difficult enough to determine whether a child, who can do some things well and others almost not at all at a given level, should be held back, much less factoring in a child's hearing impairment. A hearing-impaired child with an uneven maturity (as described in Laurie's case) would undoubtedly improve his chances for success in school by waiting a year.

In an integrated situation your hearing-impaired child should either be socially ready or be placed in an understanding and carefully planned program. A happy child learns while a social outcast is rarely happy, and consequently his learning is impeded. Hearing-impaired children are often at least one year behind in social maturity, due in part to their slow development in language and their inability to hear the kind of backup conversation that hearing children naturally absorb.

Intelligence

Much has been written on the value of an intelligence quotient (IQ) rating. It is generally considered a valuable indicator, but not the overall, absolute intelligence guideline that it once was. In years past, children were commonly advanced a grade solely on the strength of their IQs, only to flounder in a more socially mature class. Not enough regard was given to the many features of their individual personalities.

Still, early intelligence tests should be taken into consideration by a parent as a starting point for evaluating his child's potential. For instance, when Laurie couldn't pass a test in fourth grade, I said in exasperation to the teacher, "No one has ever told me what she has to work with; her IQ test results have been held top-secret. Please tell me what we are dealing with." Her teacher consulted the files and reported her IQ indicated a very good intelligence. I was then able to consider her in the light of her intelligence potential, not just her present achievement. This was helpful for my peace of mind. Indeed, it turned out to be a true picture as the years passed; her abilities caught up with her maturity patterns and she began to learn at her potential.

I hope that a competent psychologist will give every parent some picture, however sketchy, of the intelligence of his or her hearing-impaired child in the early years by using nonverbal tests. Where language is retarded and thought patterns slow to form, and where there are other handicaps, children with low-scoring test results should be retested from time to time to see if maturity, learning, and other factors may have changed the initial result. If so, this can be cause for a new evaluation and fresh expectations.

Observation at home of your child's abilities, for example, solving simple puzzles and games, can add to an informed evaluation of his learning potential. Your personal opinion of his intelligence is an important addition to any test he may be given because you are able to watch him closely for longer periods of time.

A hearing-impaired child with average intelligence, not a high IQ, is capable of integrating successfully in a regular classroom if he rates high in your evaluation in such other respects as: personality, attention span, motivation, and differences connected with his hearing loss. Be sure to take everything into consideration—his other pluses may outweigh an average intelligence. A determined, hard worker can be as successful as a brilliant person, although he may take a longer, more arduous route.

Personality

Extreme shyness and satisfaction with things as they are, and, on the other hand, high degrees of confidence and drive can affect the learning patterns of children. Also, very intelligent children may become so spellbound with one subject that they neglect others. These children are not apt to learn with ease, or at the same pace, subjects outside their special interest, and their goals will differ from children with more diversified interests. Potential artists, musicians, and scientists are likely candidates for this classification; examples of men of science who had learning difficulties in some subjects and great insights in others are Albert Einstein and Thomas A. Edison.

A child goes through personality phases as he matures. Your child, who seemed outgoing a month ago, may suddenly reverse gears and become unbelievably shy. Possibly belligerence or contrariness or emotional upsets may suddenly develop, traits which will affect a child's ability to learn and to accept correction. Most children grow out of these phases, since they are linked to environmental problems, such as moving and having to make new friends, or temporary elements of unknown origin. For others, these traits could be inherent and more permanent. (People might say, "He acts like his grandfather.") In time, children can learn to control a disagreeable personality trait, such as a volatile temper. In judging your child's potential, carefully consider his personality as it is now, and how it might affect his learning and social adjustment. Review it again as he matures, gains better self-control, and experiences environmental changes.

Attention Span

The attention span of different children at a given age varies considerably. It is a crucial factor to the hearing-impaired child who relies on his undivided attention to speechread and to listen. The wriggly child in first grade isn't going to follow the lesson like the child who can sit still and watch. One glance away, and all is lost. He will forever be trying to play catch-up: "What happened? What did teacher say? What do we do next?" An exasperated teacher must then stop to fill him in or give up and go on to the next subject for the sake of the whole class.

Attention span is, to a large extent, a discipline. It comes easily to some motivated children, harder to others who are hyperactive by nature, physically disabled, or "dreamy" children, seemingly living in a world of their own.

As a rule of thumb, a young child's attention span is considered equal to one minute for each year of age. But, five minutes is not enough for your five-year-old hearing-impaired speechreader in kindergarten. He should be able to last at least through a story time, which at that age takes ten to fifteen minutes.

Consider your experiences with your children's birthday parties—it's a major feat to keep a party for five and six year olds running smoothly. It takes preparation and organization to prevent excessive delays that could lead to bedlam. Games, refreshments, and the opening of presents, in whatever order, have to be timed for their attention span and arranged to follow each other closely.

It is even the case with older children; I recall working with fourth-grade Cub Scouts who could not be depended upon to complete a ten- or fifteen-minute project without their attention drifting.

Suffice it to say, that a good attention span is a big plus in your evaluation of your hearing-impaired child, as it weighs heavily in the learning process.

Motivation and Curiosity

Everything can come together for your child if he has sufficient motivation for learning. He will listen, absorb, think, and react, if he is motivated. Your hearing-impaired child, who has the added burden of a communication handicap, will probably be a faster learner if he is not indifferent. Motivation can be encouraged by enthusiastic parents, family members, friends, and skilled teachers.

An evaluation should reflect motivation. If your previously listless child begins to react actively to learning, a new dimension can be given to the goals you set for him. If your child doesn't react positively to either motivation or the experience of learning something new, try not to be discouraged—a spark can light the way for him at any time. One bright, hearing-impaired young adult I know didn't begin to take an interest in school subjects until sixth grade. At that time she suddenly settled down at school and began to want to learn; a few years ago she graduated from Gallaudet College with high honors.

If your child has an innate curiosity you're fortunate. It's more than awareness; he wants to know the whys and the wherefores of everything around him, and you should encourage him. Heed his questions and give him answers that satisfy him. Other children need stimulation to pique their interest. Find the opportunities to take your child to the zoo, museum, rodeo, or any event or scene uncommon to his environment and daily routine. Such experiences can bubble over into related areas, and he will have the urge to learn new things.

INDIVIDUAL DIFFERENCES IN HEARING-IMPAIRED CHILDREN OF PRESCHOOL AGE

Evaluating your preschool age child in relation to his hearing loss centers around communication skills. Your personal evaluation checklist for your child should cover:

1. Extent of hearing loss,
2. Ability to use residual hearing,
3. Ability to speechread,
4. Extent of receptive vocabulary and language,

5. Progress and willingness to use expressive language, and

6. Ability to start to think independently and creatively, and to reason.

Extent of Hearing Loss

In evaluating and setting goals for your child, consider how much hearing he has unaided. Does he have the hearing potential to recognize sounds, particularly some speech sounds? Further, how much does a hearing aid add to his hearing ability? A severe hearing loss cannot be fully evaluated in the early years in the same way as a mild loss; a child with a severe loss, even with amplification, will usually take longer to perfect his communication skills, and the ultimate effect of hearing loss upon these skills cannot be foreseen with certainty.

Later, when your child is about to be placed in a learning situation, hearing loss should not be the only criterion for placement. A profoundly hearing-impaired child with the potential to develop other favorable factors can sometimes achieve at a higher level than a child with better hearing whose potential is depressed for whatever reasons.

Ability to Use Residual Hearing

An audiologist will tell you that two identical audiograms seldom assure that the two children tested "hear" alike. Children with a hearing loss do not respond similarly to sound, nor do they when it is amplified. There is a certain element of hearing discrimination which makes it more difficult for some to distinguish small differences between sounds. Moreover, there are complex problems in the transmission of sound to the brain and its decoding into meanings, the magnitude of which varies between children. So, in the use of residual hearing, evaluate your child individually and do not try to compare him to any other child.

Specifically, determine if he is beginning to listen and to identify sounds. For a small child with a severe loss, learning to listen with meaning is a slow process; give him time before reaching a decision on this point. If he is listening, is he listening only some of the time, or has listening become a constant habit, part of his sensual being? A child who listens for sound around him all the time as naturally as a hearing person, although the signal received may be small and imperfect, is a "hearing" child. If your child reaches this stage, however slight the residual hearing, you can raise the goals you set for him with justification.

If you are knowledgeable about the hearing he has and the amplification he is receiving, you can come to a realistic conclusion as to whether or not he is using his hearing to its best advantage.

Ability to Speechread

No one has been able yet to come up with a satisfactory solution to the problem of the child who is very slow learning to speechread. The ability of your child to speechread should be taken into consideration for your immediate goals, but give him plenty of time for practice as there may be impróvement later. From time to time, reassess his ability to speechread. One area to monitor is how well he speechreads people outside his own family.

There are gradations of reliance on speechreading depending on the capacity to use residual hearing; the child who is developing a good use of his residual hearing may learn early to combine his hearing through an aid and his speechreading. He is likely to prove more proficient when he can combine the two capabilities and less proficient when deprived of either one. Therefore, evaluate more critically the speechreading of a child whose loss is so great that he receives only slight supplementary help from his hearing; speechreading is both more difficult for and more important to this child.

Extent of Receptive Vocabulary and Language

Upon making a list of the words and phrases your child knows, you now have firm evidence of his progress. Is it a list made up of both nouns and verbs, descriptive adjectives, and words describing feelings? Does his vocabulary grow steadily and expand? Is he able to understand questions and follow directions? Each step is a step forward in building language.

Progress and Willingness to Use Expressive Language

How well is he expressing the vocabulary and language that he knows? Is his expression spontaneous? Is he using one-word, two-word, or longer sentences? Can he answer commands and questions? Can he carry on any kind of a simple conversation? Keep in mind that all children must understand a great deal of language before they begin to express themselves.

Further, is his voice quality pleasant and not strained? Does it flow on a breath? While intelligibility of speech at an early age is less important than his awareness of the possibilities of speech and his desire to speak, natural timing and rhythm of speech and the beginnings of inflection are the first indicators of future speech intelligibility.

Ability to Start to Think Independently and Creatively, and to Reason

Does he show an ability to think out a problem and express it in words? Is he asking questions? Is he able to absorb knowledge as it is presented? Does he surprise you occasionally with a new thought?

As your child learns language and speech, challenge his thinking processes and explore how well he is progressing in creative thinking and reasoning. There is now some evidence suggesting that the ability to reason begins to develop earlier than had been judged possible in the past, probably in the first year of life. If this is so, it also will be delayed, along with the hearing-impaired child's language and speech, past the point in nature's timetable of optimum development.

INDIVIDUAL DIFFERENCES IN HEARING-IMPAIRED CHILDREN OF SCHOOL AGE

When your child enters school, continue to question his communication skills as suggested in the above section, but now add evaluations of his school subjects and his adjustment to the class situation. These further evaluations should include:

1. Reading ability,
2. Writing ability,
3. Mathematical ability,
4. Clarity of speech,
5. Language and vocabulary pertaining to school subjects, and
6. Special talents.

Reading Ability

How well is he reading? This is an absolutely essential skill for his future education. By reading he can make up the vocabulary and knowledge he misses in and out of the classroom. Keep abreast of his grade level in reading so that he does not slip too far behind. When he is older, consider how well he is able to read a standard textbook written for his grade level. If he likes to read, he will read for pleasure, thereby substantially increasing his reading ability.

Writing Ability

How well is he writing? As he progresses, is he improving his ability to write letters, reports, and compositions without excessive errors and outside help? Writing is the most difficult skill for all children to master, and for the hearing-impaired child, it is a pronounced stumbling block.

Mathematical Ability

Is he keeping abreast of the class in math? He should become proficient in basic arithmetic and practical math problems involving percentages, interest, proportions, and money. This is a concrete subject that a hearing-impaired child finds easier to learn than a more abstract subject.

Clarity of Speech

As your child grows older, clarity of speech becomes increasingly important for his future. If he can achieve understandable speech, more doors will open to him in education and employment. Since the immediate family becomes accustomed to his speech, periodically ask others their impressions of the intelligibility of his speech.

Vocabulary and Language Pertaining to School Subjects

His vocabulary and language should continue to build steadily. He should be able to carry on a conversation in straightforward language and keep it moving. Is he participating in class discussions? Also, how well is he handling his homework? Does he need help frequently? If so, gradually reduce your assistance as he gets older; however, for an especially difficult subject, he may continue to need help for some time. Generally speaking, in the last two years of high school he should be able to do most of his homework by himself.

Special Talents

A special talent can be of great value in school, such as competence in sports and games, dancing, and art. This gives him a special status with other students and the teacher, and builds self-confidence.

INDIVIDUAL DIFFERENCES IN ENVIRONMENT

Finally, your evaluation of your child is not complete without taking into consideration his environment. Points to evaluate are:

1. Assistance by family
2. School placement
3. Economic problems
4. Learning environment

Assistance by Family

The prerequisite for learning is that a child be happy, loved, and feel secure. A family that has a solid and supportive structure offers a child more of a chance to learn. Sometimes family circumstances are not favorable for creating the conditions of support and understanding a hearing-impaired child needs. Divorce, illness, business travel, frequent moves, and other personal problems can become so overwhelming as to leave the parents unable to give the child adequate help. Bilingual families have the added difficulty of seeing that their child gets good grounding in English.

A child who receives sufficient help at home, particularly in the preschool years, will benefit greatly. Conversely, if family members don't give the hearing-impaired child encouragement, direction, and stimulation to communicate at home, there are not enough total hours at school to offset this shortcoming.

School Placement

It is a serious problem if your hearing-impaired child is poorly placed in school. If this is the case and no other options are open in the vicinity of your home, you will either have to acquire help from outside sources or do more yourself, or both. As a result, the goals you are setting for him should be adjusted accordingly.

Economic Problems

An economically disadvantaged family may be unable to give their hearing-impaired child adequate nutrition, proper sleeping facilities, or a quiet study area, any or all of which would affect his ability to learn. Also, they may not be able to afford or have the time to take him to places outside the home (for example, an amusement park, fair, or sports event) which would broaden his experiences. Because of his hearing loss and other variables, these circumstances may slow his otherwise anticipated progress.

Learning Environment

There is a very special relationship between learning and a child who is surrounded by people who are continually learning themselves. Reading books, playing games, having animated converstaions, and visiting new places are great motivation boosters that awaken a child's curiosity and drive to learn. Some homes supply these learning needs and some are starkly deprived of them; affluence has little to do with it. It's the people who live in the home who set the tone—people who are wide awake and curious, seeking knowledge, challenging a child to think more, and whetting his appetite for learning. A family like this living in a climate of learning, can bring out the most of a child's potential.

part II

the preschool years

"Parents and teachers who anticipate a child's every need without making him speak distinctly for what he wants, after speech teaching has begun, retard both speech and language and retard his development as an independent human being."

Miss Mary E. Numbers,
Author and Revered Teacher of the Deaf

chapter 4

points to ponder

Find encouragement in the knowledge that in the years ahead of you all is not forever struggle, fatigue, and time-consuming effort. These things are telescoped into a span of about four years, when your hearing-impaired child needs your help more than any other time in his life if he is to be self-sufficient and able to communicate successfully as an adult. True, you will need to continue to assist throughout his growing years by encouraging, motivating, correcting, and reminding him. For many years, you must be his ever-present dictionary against that two-headed monster that stalks him—vocabulary and straight language.

But the time when you should drop many of your personal activities, leaving the dishes in the sink, turning your back on the unmade beds, and giving him your attention and carefully planned thought, is the preschool years. These are roughly from the moment you first learn of his loss until he is about six years old, or whenever he is ready for full-time school. At this point you can relax somewhat and say to yourself, "I did my best to give him his start." Then, other people will become important to his learning and you can begin to pick up the pieces of your interrupted life; teachers will be educating him and he will spend more time with children his own age. Father will find it easier to step in and give him those particular elements that are Dad's forte.

By all odds these early years are Mother's years and the most formative of all for every child. It is in these years that a child is most ready for communication and establishes a sound basis for later learning. At this time:

1. He is learning to listen for specific sounds.
2. He is developing a mental vocabulary of meaningful words.
3. He is experimenting with speech sounds and speech.
4. Finally, he is beginning to lay the groundwork for his verbal thinking processes.

A child's verbal thinking processes develop after he has been parroting what he hears for some time, repeating the words you say. One day he will say something on his own in a particular situation. Perhaps it will be "more" as he holds up his empty cup. Or it may be "shoe" when one shoe is lost. Everyone present shows pleasure at this voluntary word. He tries other words, is encouraged, and thus his expressive ability begins to grow.

Your hearing-impaired child will follow the same pattern, but often children six years and older will be still stuck at the parroting stage, repeating, seemingly forever, like a broken record. They may have several hundred words of vocabulary at their disposal, but they don't try to use them even for their own needs without prompting. At this age, it seems to take months to unstick the needle. Time and again in the classroom a question such as "Who are you?" would echo right back at me, "Who are you?"

At an early age your child should be actively stimulated to use the words he knows. He should learn to think independently in words and to use them in conversing and answering questions. If you do all the thinking and speaking for your child, he will stay in one place or possibly regress in his development.

PLATEAUS

As an adult, past the growing stage, you are capable of controlling and activating your motivation. But your hearing-impaired child, who is experiencing a growing process that includes other motivating forces besides speech and language, is torn by priorities for his attention.

Your child must develop physically as well as mentally, and there are natural periods in his growth timetable for learning physical skills.

There are times when his desire to achieve new skills, such as skating, riding a bicycle, kicking, throwing and catching a ball, swinging, and climbing, overrides all other interests. With his attention centered on these skills you may sense that his interest and ability to learn speech and language are being put on the back burner.

Resign yourself to these flat periods of improvement in communication, these plateaus.

Communication skills don't always improve at a constant rate—typically, there will be rapid improvement to one level, followed by slow improvement to a new plateau. During the plateaus, curb your anxiety, plug along, taking advantage of the language that centers around any new physical skills, and wait. When he gains proficiency in some of the new skills, he will be willing once again to work on his speech and language, and progress.

Never underestimate the importance of learning physical skills. They help to bridge the gap in a hearing-impaired child's relations with other children. How important it is to his ego that he rides his bike with pride, and throws and catches with the best of them! Through elementary school, children are more apt to praise one skilled in physical abilities rather than perfect speech.

CORRECTING YOUR CHILD

Corrections are a form of criticism, and no one likes to be criticized. However, your hearing-impaired child desperately needs your good ears to monitor his speech and language, bring attention to his mistakes, and encourage him to use and improve his communication skills.

First of all, then, a warm relationship between you and your hearing-impaired child should be cultivated as carefully as you would a prized flower garden. It will be the soil in which you plant the seeds of new language and better speech. Your garden should be cared for with love, understanding, and respect and fed with patience. If love flows between you, then understanding will follow. You will understand his moments of discovery and achievement as well as times of fatigue and preoccupation, and, in turn, he will understand why you correct him and be willing to accept it in the spirit it is given.

After developing an atmosphere conducive to giving and accepting correction, the amount of correction and its timing should be given serious consideration.

To push too much and too often can backfire. If he expects to be corrected every time he comes to you with something to say, he may think to himself, "What's the use? She isn't interested in what I have to say, only how I say it." He may stop talking to you, or he may tacitly resent your correction and later reject what you have taught him. Many proud, overzealous parents have spoiled the potential careers of talented musicians and athletes by pressing too hard for what they want their child to achieve.

An example more closely associated with the subject of this book was brought to my attention a few years ago when I heard a panel discussion among hearing-impaired adults. An attractive, middle-aged woman with a severe hearing loss told how she had been taught orally by her parents and teachers with such concentration that she became resentful. As a teenager, she rebelled, turned to the language of signs, and refused to use her voice altogether. After marriage and raising her children, she began to refocus her life. She realized the benefits of her early teaching and longed to learn to speak again. Her speech was intelligible when I heard her because of her childhood training and, undoubtedly, has improved since then as she expressed a determination to start speech lessons. Her experience left a profound impression on me. It emphasized the risk of carrying the training of your hearing-impaired child to extremes.

So, in choosing the time for correcting your child, you should be sensitive to the atmosphere in which you correct—the parent and child should be interacting harmoniously.

Avoid dampening your child's enthusiasm by interrupting him in mid-thought. Listen to what he has to say to the very end before replying. Give him your full attention and show him that you are interested and that you understand him. After acknowledging his idea, then, and only then, go back and correct the faulty portion of his language and speech. Or wait until a better time to bring it up, when it will be a more acceptable correction, perhaps using a blackboard or pencil and paper.

Correct him when you are relaxed, and avoid correcting him when you are angry, tired, anxious, or hurried. You are your child's mirror—he will copy what he sees and hears. He will react with tenseness when he is surrounded by tenseness and relax when he is with someone who is relaxed.

And there will be times when his energy is spent or he's preoccupied (for example, after school when his eyes are tired) that it would be unwise to correct his language and speech for any reason. He may also be quite sensitive to correction in front of other people. Become attuned to his feelings and your corrections are more likely to accomplish their intended purpose.

HABITS

Throughout this book, there will be many references to "habits." By this I mean, generally, any functions that have been repeated in one way so often that they have become unconscious acts.

We all have many habits we have formed over the years, good and bad. Look at yourself as objectively as possible to see if any of your habits can be changed for the benefit of your hearing-impaired child. We know that a child first learns from his parents and others around him through imitation. In a television documentary recently, a scientific experiment illustrated this point in nature: a young song-bird raised without its mother and father in isolated surroundings didn't learn to sing its native song, demonstrating that some songbirds' identifying songs are not inherent but are learned from their parents.

Examining your own habits of communication as they may be imitated by your child may reveal some interesting findings. If your voice has a nasal quality, it is more than likely to be copied by your young child. Hearing-impaired children frequently develop a nasal voice, and hearing this at home will just compound the problem. Also, speechreading is made more difficult by habits that are tolerable to a hearing person but distressing to a hearing-impaired person, such as: having an inexpressive face, compressing your lips, mumbling, covering your mouth with your hand, and looking away while speaking.

Your hearing-impaired child must be encouraged to change any bad speech habits that you see developing. The longer your child hangs on to a bad speech habit, the harder it is to break; the earlier in a child's life you start changing the habit, the easier it will be to change.

Suppose your hearing-impaired child had never before been able to make a *k* sound, but now he can easily make a *k* when asked by you or his teacher. This is an accomplishment, but actually there's a big difference in making the sound and using *k* in the words he knows. That is, he may still happily tell you he wants to go for a ride in the "ar" and would like to have an "oo-ie" from the cooky jar. The trouble is that he has already formed a habit of incorrectly saying these words without the *k* for months. This habit must be changed. In Chapter 8, I suggest a corrective method to follow involving consciously and systematically repeating a new habit many times over until it becomes automatic. Progress in changing habits will evolve slowly, taking many hours of practice with marked retreats and advances.

GROWTH IN INDEPENDENCE

It has often been said about raising a hearing-impaired child, don't do for him what he can do for himself.

The primary task of parents is to teach their child during the growing years to take care of himself when he becomes an adult. Most creatures rear their young by gradually encouraging them toward more and more independence until they can cope with their environment. Although time varies for different species, parents abruptly leave their young when they feel the youngsters are ready to fend for themselves.

Growing up in the human race has become a sophisticated social process, in comparison to birds and animals, being largely dependent on a good communication system. However, the process of raising a child also has a time limit; generally, it is considered that a child should be independent by the time he is between eighteen and twenty years old. I submit that if a child is not acting independently by then, there is a better-than-average possibility that he will not have the ability to strike out for himself in our complicated civilization.

The desire to shelter a child with a handicap is strong—you must guard against it! While you are busily concerned with helping your hearing-impaired child understand and speak, by all means, remember your ultimate goal: to raise a self-reliant adult, able to care for himself and able to get along in a world of hearing people in the mainstream of society. The hearing impaired who tend to cling together may find happiness in each other's company, but at the same time, they must work to make a living, shop for their necessities, hire a plumber, engage a lawyer or doctor, travel, and encounter the mainstream at every turn in their lives.

It is imperative that parents vigorously attack the task of raising their child to face this world of hearing people, beginning at the earliest possible time. If independence is significantly delayed, it soon is beyond parents' control to transmit it, and later professional rehabilitation becomes a slow and painful process. The small seeds of independence should be sewn in the very small child and nourished as he grows. By young adulthood, your child should have not only the tools he needs, but also the many opportunities to practice independence along the way. As Mary E. Numbers says eloquently in her book, *My Words Fell on Deaf Ears* (1974), "Every time a youngster faces a real difficulty and masters it, his wings become stronger. Every time he makes a choice or a decision, he acquires more confidence and courage." p. 190.

chapter 5

materials

Time and again when I was teaching in a classroom, it would occur to me how lacking the conventional, sterile classroom is in props for teaching small hearing-impaired children vocabulary and language for "life situations," as Dr. Boris V. Morkovin (1960) was fond of calling them. The majority of the materials needed for teaching language to a small child are at home, right at a parent's fingertips, whereas a teacher must duplicate them with pictures, miniature furniture, play houses, empty cereal boxes, make-believe stores, and so forth. True, these makeshift classroom materials are interesting and different, a valuable new medium, but they are substitutes compared to the real thing.

Parents, look about your home and use in your conversation with your hearing-impaired child all the objects that you can see. Begin with the common objects used for family living and supplement with miniatures, toys, and pictures. While your child is home much of the time in the preschool years, you have a golden opportunity to give him a good start with language. There is no satisfactory way a teacher can duplicate this experience.

TOYS

The amount of money that can be spent on toys for a single child is appalling, especially if parents are intent on satisfying the child's every whim. Even those parents who try to resist are sometimes overwhelmed by the "spirit" of Christmas and television ads.

Whether or not your funds are limited, don't lose sight of the first rule for parents of a hearing-impaired child; he is first a child, who happens to have a hearing loss. He doesn't need, nor will he respond any better to, masses of toys that you purchase thinking they will be invaluable teaching aids. There are real things to see and examine, pictures in magazines, and small inexpensive items at the variety store that will serve as well or better. Homemade toys are usually sturdier, more durable, more popular, and infused with a parent's love.

Having watched my children play, and having succumbed to a parent's temptations to generosity and the desire to satisfy the handicapped child just because he is handicapped, I have formed some solid opinions on the value of toys, the ones that are worthwhile to learning opportunities and pleasure.

First on my list of "must" toys would be a set of blocks. This could be the most expensive item, unless homemade, but the most essential. Disturbed at the high price of blocks, I investigated the possibility of a cabinetmaker making blocks for me on special order. However, by the time he added his small-shop overhead and profit to his materials and labor, his price was higher than the toy store's comparable, mass-produced set.

Our children built such fascinating things with blocks that we kept adding blocks until we had accumulated a large bin full. Blocks: I am talking about some big ones (finished 2¾ inches wide by 11 inches long by 1¼ inches thick), many half that length with the same width and thickness, and smaller blocks in rectangular, square, triangular, and cylindrical shapes cut to the same scale. These building blocks took the place of many other toys, survived seventeen years, and were well worth the expense. For instance, when the girls acquired a much-desired metal dollhouse, their interest in it lasted barely a week. It was much more fun to create rooms having sizes and shapes of their own design with doors that swung open (blocks with a doorknob drawn in crayon), and to be able to reach in easily to move things about. All through the years, hundreds of houses with different floor plans were built, replete with stairs, second stories, split levels, and patios. No matter that their prized house had no roof, or that its occupants lived there no more than one day—next playtime a new fantasy would be built.

Our son, Peter, enjoyed building around his train almost as much as he did operating it. The blocks formed towers, buildings, bridges, tunnels, and elevated tracks. If your child likes to build as much as Peter did, go to a cabinetmaker and ask for some scrap wood. These pieces, usually smooth, thin, and irregular, can supplement or substitute for the more permanent blocks. Peter would nail and glue this free scrap wood into all sorts of miniature structures—houses, factories, Frosty stands, and firehouses—around his train. If you have adequate space and extra track, it is better not to secure the train track to a board. Making different track layouts develops ingenuity and keeps up a child's interest.

Next on my list would be miniature toys: furniture, a few small dolls (including a boy doll to play the father), and a collection of small cars and trucks. Some of the furniture can be made easily at home, like a bed with sheets made from a small box and cloth remnants, or tables and chairs made from scrap wood and doweling or popsicle sticks and toothpicks. Our girls often converted the blocks themselves into beds, chairs, stoves, and chests of drawers with the help of crayons. If the furniture is not homemade, the stores offer play furniture made of wood or plastic. The plastic is preferred because it is molded into a greater variety of shapes and is less expensive. It breaks easily, but can be replaced several times before the cost adds up to the original cost of wood furniture. But I would recommend cars and trucks be made of metal as the plastic ones have a disturbing habit of losing their wheels. Cars and trucks form the base for never-ending arrangements of roads, bridges, garages, and service stations, both inside and outside the house. A corner of the backyard left in a dirt or sand pile for such purposes will be the site of hours of creative building.

The last items I would add to the toys are a cash register and two toy telephones. A store can be put together from boxes, empty cans, and cereal boxes, but having a cash register really enhances the play. Toy telephones offer opportunity for conversation and an introduction to the use of a real telephone.

All these small toys have great value in vocabulary and language building for your hearing-impaired child, representing in miniature the important real life objects with which your child is surrounded. The variety of "life situations" that can be created with them for pleasure and for learning is infinite.

Some thoughts about the larger dolls girls first play with: I have come to the conclusion that a few select dolls are far better than a large host of dolls, some lying about in grotesque postures, undressed and ignored, and others minus arms and legs. Steer away from buying hollow dolls that mildew inside when wet, as "young mothers" will

214679

persist in bathing them. Baby dolls are endearing, but not versatile—most can't sit up for a tea party. Try to stand your ground against the pleading of a big-eyed little girl for a doll that eats, talks, crawls, wets, and develops diaper rash. No matter what its advertised feats, carefully examine the entire doll and be satisfied with its durability, especially its arms, legs, and hair.

A dancing doll, which unfortunately I haven't seen in toy stores lately, is excellent for auditory training. It is a big rag doll with long arms and legs, as tall as a child, with a piece of elastic sewn under each foot. The elastic straps slip over a child's shoes and the child can then dance with the doll attached. I made one for my granddaughter by elongating the arms and legs of a stuffed-doll pattern.

Allied to toys is a box of dress-up clothes that can be accumulated at no expense. These discarded clothes have many uses, both for play and playacting, and they come in handy when you are working with your child's language. Be sure there are clothes for both girls and boys. Girls' accessories can be high heels, jewelry, purse, and hat; and boys can use an old wallet, toy watch, tie, and hat. The most popular dress in my classroom playhouse was a very full skirt with elastic run through the waist to make it small enough for a child—it slipped on easily and didn't keep falling down.

For your older child who is reading, a painless way to learn the language of instructions is for him to assemble toys and models from kits. He will need your help at first, but after a while the repetitive structure of the language will become familiar and he will be able to follow the instructions himself with minimum help and maximum satisfaction.

BOOKS

Begin to introduce books to your hearing-impaired child at an early age. As soon as he is able to handle a book, he should be taught to respect and care for it, and to understand that it is something to be cherished. He shouldn't be allowed to write in a book or tear it; if treasured books become worn with age, help him to mend them. Teach him to look at a book, page by page, from the front of the book to the back.

To endear your child to books it helps for him to have a specific place to keep his books. A practical, inexpensive solution is to make a small bookcase from ½" × 10" wide boards of the desired length and supporting concrete blocks. Set firm rules regarding the care of books, and insist that he put them away when he is finished with them.

Following your lead, his early love and respect for books will develop into a personal desire, first to enjoy the pictures and later to read his books.

Books designed for preschoolers should have many brightly colored pictures, clear-cut and realistic. There need be little or no writing in them, as for some time your youngster's language will probably not be equal to the language of books. But, it is important that a child see a picture and relate it to ideas, his own person, and finally to words. Also, a book opens the way to new, oral vocabulary. And since a book is mainly for pleasure, it shouldn't contain concepts which are too difficult or be too long—understanding and attention span will develop gradually.

Children outgrow their first simple books very quickly. It is better to buy only a few, choosing large, colorful, and medium-priced books. I have in mind the Golden Book series, which include the beautiful Disney books based on films; the Mother Goose rhymes; timeless children's stories with colorful illustrations like Peter Rabbit; and a select group of variety store books.

Depend on the library for most of your children's books. They have a wealth of excellent books from which to choose. After some initial guidance, let your child choose his own books; it will be an opportunity for him to show independence by picking out the ones that strike his fancy. Give him time to browse, and respect what he chooses—out of three or four books, one or two will probably be really good choices. If he brings home a book that is obviously wrong—too difficult or uninteresting—never mind, he chose it and he will learn by doing.

In addition, learning the function of a library is good training in itself. Your child will soon understand that books are borrowed and must be cared for and returned in good condition. Let him have his own library card as soon as permitted. Presenting his card (with his very own name on it) for the librarian to stamp makes him feel important because he is doing something for himself.

Read to him often, but avoid reading word-for-word as he will soon lose interest unless his vocabulary and language perception are good and his attention span unusually long. It is best to paraphrase the story, or talk about a picture in the language he understands, slipping in a new word now and then. Looking at a book together affords you the opportunity to lengthen his attention span and improve his ability to speechread. By school age, if he can't listen attentively straight through to the end of a short story, he will also have difficulty holding his attention on the teacher through a lesson, and this is disastrous for a speechreader.

There is a bit of a trick to "reading" a story to a small hearing-impaired youngster. Place him facing you instead of at your side. Hold the book in front of you so he can't see the page while you say a few words enthusiastically about the picture. Then, playing to his anticipation, turn the book around dramatically for him to see. Let him study it as long as he likes, then catch his eye again and repeat or rephrase what you said before about the picture. Talk about it, add a little more language, and again, show it off as long as he is interested without hurrying him. If the book he has chosen has only a few pictures, you may improvise by drawing or finding other suitable pictures. A parent with an extensive picture file is prepared for these occasions.

RECORDS

Teaching your hearing-impaired child to listen is a slow but rewarding process. Although he may never "hear" a record quite like we do, he will love music as much as other children. You are dealing with a sense that is imperfect; you are helping to stimulate a small but very vital signal of sound for your child. Therefore, it is well to approach records selectively, knowing that if his loss is considerable, chances are he will not be able to understand speech on a record, tape, or television, or at the movies. But he can enjoy and benefit from the sound of music.

Choose records in which the music has a good, strong beat, like a dance rhythm or a catchy melody sung by a man's low voice or a woman's rich voice or a small chorus—in that order of preference. Your child will enjoy records to dance and clap to (for example, "Oh Susannah"; and simple songs that have a story he knows, "Hi Ho, Hi Ho," "Ten Little Indians," and Christmas songs). Records of familiar nursery rhymes are excellent when they are sung slowly and clearly. If there is too much narration between songs, these recorded rhymes are usually not understandable and always distracting. An impressive, relatively new teaching tool is the musical-story records with accompanying books, such as "Peter and the Wolf." Be wary of buying a record of a popular tune like "Jingle Bells" only to find it sung with the quacking voice of Donald Duck. Also, your child probably won't enjoy a record with music or a singing voice that is too fast, with shrill violin parts, or with complicated flutelike trills throughout.

In 1888, Thomas A. Edison, who had a total loss of hearing in one ear and limited hearing in the other, was improving his earlier invention, the phonograph, for recording quality on wax records with an eye toward mass production. According to biographer Matthew

Josephson, Edison, straining to hear, developed some decided opinions on the voices of the famous musical artists he was recording (Josephson, 1961). It is said that he detested Wagner, but loved Beethoven. Caruso he considered an indifferent singer. The tremolos of Italian tenors and the coloratura sopranos profoundly annoyed him. He also wrestled with the problem of a loud orchestral accompaniment that tended to sound like "booming the cannon around the cry of a mouse."

The safest way to judge a record before buying is to listen to it in the music store. Has it a basic, strong rhythm? Are the lyrics simple and the recording short? Does the song have a slow enough beat and some repetition? If there is a singing voice, is it clear and reasonably low?

I recently went hunting for children's records in Los Angeles and stopped in a huge, well-advertised store. I found only a small collection of cellophane-wrapped Disney records for children in a remote corner of the store. No facilities were available for listening, if one were allowed to unwrap a record in the first place. Then, I luckily stumbled upon a unique record store called the Children's Book & Music Center (5373 West Pico Boulevard, Los Angeles, California 90019). There they all were—the records I had found most useful for my needs, and more, like "Where Are Your Eyes?" and "Toys" that used to be on the old Pram label. These are still being produced on the CMS label with the full, rich voice of Tom Glazer. CMS also has activity and game songs, like "Skip to My Lou." Another label, Vocalion, has a fine "Child's First Record" with nursery songs, while Kimbo has good records for small children. The Educational Activities label—a difficult one to find—was there also. They had one record I consider priceless by a pair of young men under the Youngheart label titled, "We All Live Together." All were unwrapped, with a record player available on which to listen. This store has an extensive general catalog and a parents' catalog from which you can order records by mail. Either is available upon request for a small fee.

Supplement the playing of your child's records with a book, pictures, and real things; expect to play records often before seeing true signs of recognition of the sounds of music. Dance to his records, clap to his records, and swing and sway to them, being sure they are played loud enough for your child to hear.

A hearing-impaired child's record player need not be expensive, but essentially should have good volume and tone quality and be portable. It should be made of durable material with basic mechanical features, as your child will want to operate it. The record player needs only a manually operated arm that plays one record at a time, three speed settings, and a turntable that accommodates both large and small records.

GAMES AND PUZZLES

Your child can learn a lot from games. In fact, I can't think of a game that does not have some value in addition to the obvious one of encouraging good sportsmanship.

The stores are flooded with manipulative games made of light, plastic pieces molded into unending shapes that are great for small-motor and perceptual development. Games of cards and board games come in a myriad of types, colors, and sizes, and they are dressed up by subjects that tantalize children, from fairy tales to television favorites. Here is practice in concentrating, reading, language, matching, counting, and more; and these games are designed for children of all different ages. In buying more advanced games, look for those that challenge a child's memory and reasoning ability. Choose your games as carefully as your records, and your child will have hours of enjoyable practice in the very skills he needs.

Not only are the materials used in a game valuable aids for learning, but the playing of a game is a lesson as well. In the early years, finishing a game is an accomplishment in itself because the young child is still developing the required concentration and attention span. Later, the more opportunity the child has to experience competition, the better he will learn to lose as well as win gracefully. Learning to play a game in a sportsmanlike way will serve him throughout his life.

As children grow older, they get a kick out of making up and constructing their own games. Games can be copied successfully with very little time and expense. A large piece of cardboard will hold a very adequate homemade game; a few dice and a numbered spinner, left over from an old game, can complete the equipment.

Puzzles are especially valuable for eye and hand coordination. As your child grows older, keep challenging him with jigsaw puzzles that are progressively more complicated. You can make your own puzzles by mounting a pattern or picture on cardboard and cutting it into different shapes.

PARENTS' MATERIALS

First on my list of parents' materials is a blackboard. If possible, have two blackboards, one in your child's room and one in the kitchen, both hung at your child's eye level. The kitchen blackboard can become a focal point for quick explanations for all the children in the household. It will be especially good for your hearing-impaired child whose language improvement can't always wait until you have time to sit down with him for a lesson. If possible, you need to capture that exact moment when he wants to know something, and when intuition tells you he'll stand still and accept correction. Be sure your board is big enough for you to scan a sentence, show an accent, describe a pronunciation, and explain a meaning with a drawing. Often, your child may use the board to draw a picture of what he is trying to say when you can't for the life of you make it out. There was never an end in the use of our blackboard—it was covered with innumerable messages, games of Ticktacktoe and Hangman, and later, math and chemistry problems.

A parent should have on hand a good supply of blank paper. I found the most economical, useful types of paper were large-sized pads of newsprint and rolls of white shelf paper. The newsprint is large enough for a small child to color, cut, and paint on, and for you to draw and write on. It makes fine scrapbooks when folded in half and stapled down the middle. The shelf paper, because of its width and length, can be made into murals, streets for a toy village, and monthly calendars. Varicolored construction paper is nice to have stored away for special creative work—a red valentine or an orange pumpkin. Along with the different papers, provide a few blunt, loose-working scissors for the use of your hearing-impaired child and his friends.

Of course, have plenty of crayons, pencils, and chalk available for your child to use, but keep a close watch until he learns not to mark on anything but paper. Providing materials for painting at home is an elective matter, since he will have opportunities to paint in school. However, if he has coordination problems, he will benefit from added opportunities to improve his hand-eye coordination by painting with tempera watercolors. Three colors and long-handled brushes are enough for him to make a satisfying painting on newsprint or shelf paper. If your child is hyperactive or very tense, finger painting will channel his energy effectively, giving him freedom of movement and the soothing sensation of gooey paint on his hands. Buy a commercial paint set, or make your own, by putting a glob of liquid starch on a large piece of shelf paper and sprinkling it with his favorite color of dry tempera paint. Then, let him mix and spread it. It's messy, so be prepared by putting an old shirt on him backwards and by protecting nearby surfaces and the floor with newspapers. Finger painting brings to mind an incident that I witnessed, after a heavy rain, in the unpaved driveway of the bungalow that first housed the John Tracy Clinic. The teacher of a little boy had removed the boy's shoes and socks and was standing aside to watch as the boy squished his toes through the oozy mud.

For reinforcement in vocabulary and language building, build a picture file of magazine cutouts. Gather pictures of objects and people and also action pictures that stimulate conversation and provide new verbs and adjectives. (A beauty parlor operator or doctor's receptionist will often be willing to give you outdated magazines.) If you don't have a picture to fit the situation, draw something for your hearing-impaired child. Don't worry about your artistic prowess; your child won't be particular, he will delight in your efforts. Simply develop recognizable images and stick figures for certain familiar objects and people. (Try holding an object out in front of you, concentrate on its outline, and copy what you see; it will turn out amazingly well proportioned.)

A small hearing-impaired child usually welcomes a short lesson. Have a lesson plan in mind and maintain complete control of the activity. In a cupboard, beyond his reach, keep a bag of small items to be used only at lesson time. Proceed with the lesson by pulling items one at a time from the bag. The fact you are giving him your undivided attention, coupled with his anticipation, will assure his enthusiastic cooperation. This bag collection should include toys and real things that appeal to your child's particular interests. For instance, it could be comprised of: a bell and a clacker for auditory training; plastic spoons, sea shells, and varicolored cars for work on colors, matching, and counting; and a feather and a candle for speech training. Consider what you can use for a small reward now and then—it can be very simple, a gold star on his hand or a check after his name on the blackboard.

chapter 6

auditory training

There are very few children who do not have some residual hearing. Learning to use this hearing to its greatest potential is now a possibility with the advent of the modern hearing aid and continued improvement in its quality. The earlier your child begins to use the hearing he has, the more he will benefit from it, no matter how small the amount. Being able to hear the gross sounds—an airplane engine's drone, the hum of traffic, and the bustle of the household—and learning to distinguish between these sounds and knowing their sources, will make him feel more a part of the world around him. This is very important for his well-being. And, if a child's residual hearing is so slight that he still is unable to understand speech after training with amplification, he can nevertheless learn to supplement his speech-reading with his hearing when aided. In this case, his own speech will be better, even if he is able to hear only the timing, rhythm, and accent of speech.

As Doreen Pollack explained, "The main goal of educational audiology is the integration of hearing into the personality of the so-called deaf or hard-of-hearing child" (Pollack, 1970). Doreen Pollack is one of the auditory-verbal pioneers, and well known for her work in developing the Acoupedic approach. She was Director of Speech and Hearing Services at Porter Memorial Hospital in Denver, Colorado before her retirement. In order for a child to have a hearing personality, he must form a habit of continued listening. He must listen from habit as a normal person does, sorting out what he hears from its source. Your child will need your help to identify the sounds of the vacuum cleaner, washing machine, and automobile horn. Training him to listen must be continual, and his hearing aid must be worn every waking hour to take full advantage of amplification. The value of such training is inestimable to your child's developing personality— he will achieve a giant step toward overcoming his handicap when he forms the habit of listening.

It is possible that your introduction to auditory training will come about because of the need to condition your young hearing-impaired child for his first hearing test. In the beginning, he must be given a reason both to listen and to indicate when he hears a sound. To put a finger in the air to indicate he hears a small, insignificant audiometric tone is not meaningful enough to hold his attention until he is much older and able to concentrate on the task. Instead, the most proven method, play audiometry, is to use a toy consisting of multiple parts, where the child responds by putting a block into a hole, or a doughnut onto a post, or a marble into a box.

The procedure for preparing a small child at home for later testing by an audiologist should be in the form of a fun game, with the parent first setting an example for the child to imitate. You need marbles, a box, and a drum, or other instruments that he can hear, ones that are loud and low toned. Assuming you use a large pan, for want of a drum, have your child bang on it for you as you hold a marble in a listening attitude near your ear. When you hear the sound, show recognition and pleasure in your expression and put the marble in the box. Repeat this several times, then let your child play the same game. When he learns to respond in view of the noisemaker, then teach him to respond when his back is turned to the noisemaker. Take turns. After he learns to listen and respond to this gross sound, he will be ready to play a similar game with the audiologist.

My personal experience is that a child with a severe hearing loss who is asked to recognize very soft, nearly inaudible signals, sometimes only a few at the top volume setting of the audiometer, will be at least six or seven years old before he can give a reliable audiometer reading without the use of play audiometry by the audiologist. An experience with Linda illustrates this point: she was five years old when the process of enrolling her, for the following school year, in a hearing-impaired day class began. The class was in a school out of our district, but she was eligible through an agreement between adjacent school districts. However, our home district wanted their own audiometric reading of her hearing, and sent a school nurse to our house to give the test. She arrived at the door, an officious, middle-aged woman lugging a heavy audiometer, and having an air of competency. I established her with Linda at a card table and tried to be inconspicuous. With earphones positioned on Linda, she told her to indicate with her finger when she heard the tone, and proceeded to manipulate her machine. Very soon she became frustrated; Linda, even though she had had many tests before, did not respond to any sound at all, and the poor woman found herself staring at a blank page. It became obvious that she had never tested a child with so little hearing. At this point I stepped in, rushed to the toy chest, selected toys similar to those I had seen the audiologist use in previous play audiometry tests, and between us, by using these "indicators," she completed a reasonable reading of Linda's hearing.

CARING FOR A HEARING AID

When the aid (or aids) is being purchased for your child, insist that the dealer explain its operation to you in detail. Learn to know by its sound if it is in working order by putting the receiver next to the microphone and listening to the sound it makes; it should be a clear, loud, steady tone. If the tone, or feedback, is not clear and the volume is low, the battery power is probably running out. The life of a hearing aid battery will vary from child to child as it depends on the length of time the hearing aid is worn and the degree of amplification needed; a battery is made for a specific amount of power usage. If, on the other hand, the tone you hear cuts on and off, the trouble may be shorting due to a worn cord.

Some parents purchase an earmold for themselves to determine more accurately the working condition of their child's aid. Another valuable instrument available to monitor the performance of an aid is the binaural stereo listener. It looks like a doctor's stethoscope and is used in a similar way: an ear tube plugged into each ear with the main tube cupped to the hearing aid receiver.

Be fastidious about the working condition of your child's aid because he cannot take the responsibility himself for some time. Too many times I have seen pupils come to school with malfunctioning hearing aids. I want to emphasize that parents have to maintain their child's hearing aid on a regular basis if they expect their child to reach his full hearing potential.

It is difficult to make a good-fitting earmold for a small child.

First, his ears have the consistency of soft rubber, and it is hard to manufacture an earmold that fits firmly in a small, malleable aperture. Second, if the fit is not snug, there will be feedback from the mold caused by the short distance from the microphone on the chest to the receiver at the ear. Therefore, be sure the dealer, who makes the wax impression of your child's ear, has had ample experience in making children's earmolds, because his work is the key to a tight fitting, comfortable earmold.

If the mold hurts your child's ear or doesn't fit properly, take it out immediately and return it for adjustment or a new mold. The ear sore he can get from an ill-fitting mold is painful and takes more time to heal than adjustment of the mold. Wearing the hearing aid must be a pleasant experience for your child.

A well-fitted earmold will not give any feedback for some time, but as your child's ear grows he will outgrow his earmold as he does his clothes. The high-toned feedback squeak from a loose earmold is a nerve-wracking sound to people with normal hearing. This feedback squeak can only be corrected by having a fitting for a new mold, since lowering the volume to compensate for the squeak leaves your child with inadequate power to amplify his hearing.

An extra cord and good supply of batteries should be kept on hand. A mercury battery's volume tends to lower slightly toward the end of its life, then go dead very suddenly.

Although body heat does not hurt a hearing aid, even if worn in bed, it should not be left in very hot or humid places, such as in a car's glove compartment on a summer day. When a child wears a hearing aid all day, as almost an extension of his body, he may inadvertently still be wearing it when he goes into a shower or swimming pool. My best advice for coping with a wet hearing aid is to open the aid immediately and dry out the moisture as quickly as you can, putting it in front of a fan or blower or in a warm place to prevent rust. Besides that, take it to the dealer right away; internal parts can rust in spite of every precaution.

A body hearing aid for a young child has three parts that are liable, on occasion, to become lost: the cord, receiver button, and earmold. Especially in your child's active play, these parts, plugged into the hearing aid and into each other, can easily be pulled apart and single parts of the three-piece apparatus lost. Since these parts are expensive to replace, launch an exhaustive, organized search throughout the area where your child has been recently; near home, enlist the services of the whole neighborhood to hunt. (At one school where I taught, all work stopped and everyone, including the teachers and students of other classes, searched the schoolyard.)

When your child's hearing aid needs extensive repairs, it must generally be sent to a distant repair shop or the manufacturer. Repair may take several weeks. So that your child doesn't lose valuable listening time, arrange for a loaner from your hearing aid dealer or use one kept at home for such emergencies. Long periods without an aid are devastating to a child's progress. You may want to look into financial protection through insurance coverage on hearing aids and repairs.

Service is a much-needed area for improvement in the hearing aid industry. Dealers should never allow a child wearing one of their aids to be left unaided any length of time during repairs without furnishing a comparable, substitute aid. Parents, as concerned consumers, can help pressure the dealers to upgrade their service.

A CARRIER FOR THE HEARING AID

In spite of the relatively recent advent of strong-volumed, high fidelity, behind-the-ear aids, the body aid is still best for a growing child. The bone and cartilage structure of a young child's ear is too soft and small to hold a behind-the-ear aid in place, and the child is too active. There are numerous ways for a small child to carry his hearing aid. Most parents buy a commercially made harness that hooks into place, adjusting the straps to fit their child. Other parents sew pockets either inside or outside a child's clothing. Boys often attach a hearing aid to their belt, sometimes on the side or back. Some schools insist on an outer-jacket garment with pockets in order to avoid sound interference caused by the child's clothing rubbing against the aid's microphone.

Since there is a divergence of views on how best to carry a hearing aid, I would like to offer my ideas for your consideration. In my opinion, the hearing aid of a small child should be carried:

1. Inside a cloth pocket that fits skintight to the aid and is equipped with a buttoned closure, which is

2. Attached to an elastic harness without hooks, that is worn tight to the body, and

3. High on the chest and next to the skin, or at most, with only an undershirt between skin and carrier.

For maximum comfort and safety to the aid, the pocket should be tight around the aid to prevent it from sliding and shifting. There should be a hole made in the pocket for the microphone, unless the microphone is located at the top of the aid where the pocket is already open. The only way to keep an aid from falling out of the pocket of an active child, who is often upside down, is to button it in. (A snap or a safety pin can give way under the weight of the aid.)

When Linda was young, we made our own hearing aid pockets from strong, cotton material that was doubled and fitted tightly to the aid, with a buttoned flap to secure it. Later, I found I could buy a "pin-on pocket" from a hearing aid dealer. This type of pocket is designed to pin onto clothing by two small flaps at either side of the pocket. Cutting off the pin-on flaps and altering the top flap to close with a button instead of a snap, I then sewed the pocket onto a homemade elastic harness. For two aids, two pockets should be sewn on the harness, one to each side of the center.

As a teacher, I have, much to my dismay, rehooked dangling, ill-fitting commercially made harnesses on children many, many times a day, and this has made me appreciate the elastic harness more than ever. My homemade elastic harness follows the same design as commercial harnesses, but stretches to fit over the head and into place without hooks (Figure 2). It is made with soft, one-inch elastic, the kind sold for the top of pajama pants. The elastic clings to the body and is wide and soft enough not to chafe; the aid rides securely with a minimum of bobbing motion as your child runs, tumbles, and climbs. This homemade harness, being comfortable and well-fitting, soon makes the child forget it is there—when he wears it close to his body it becomes almost a part of him.

Even though hearing aids worn outside clothes may be free of clothing noise, they also come off when the clothes do. I have never felt from my own experience that the amount of noise caused by clothing was sufficient to warrant fighting the on-again off-again tactics with which children can try your patience. An outer jacket with a pocket to hold the aid is even more likely to be taken off, much like a sweater. All in all, an aid tucked away under the clothes is harder to take off at every opportunity; and, esthetically and psychologically, a hearing aid out of sight will make your child feel less conspicuous.

Gimmicks for carrying hearing aids on very small children don't always work, as I found out with our youngest, Leslie, who was fitted at two years of age with a very small, lightweight aid. In fact, the aid was so small that I put it on a barrette (made especially for a hearing aid) in her ponytail. It was no time at all before I abandoned this method because her little hand kept coming up and snatching it out of her hair.

When older sister Linda complained that the V-shaped harness (Figure 2) showed above her blouses, I remodeled it to lower the aid

figure 2. V-shaped harness.

below the neckline. This was accomplished by adding another horizontal body strap across the upper back of the pocket and connecting it with vertical shoulder straps in a square-necked design (Figure 3). This design better accommodates two hearing aids and does not pull as much on the shoulders as the V-shaped harness. The only minor disadvantage is that, being slightly lower, the microphone is further from the mouth.

The best way to position the cord is to run it over the shoulder and behind the back on the opposite side from the ear in which the earmold will be placed. After the mold is in place, turn the receiver button so the cord can be tucked in around the back of the ear with a minimum of slack. This way, the cord is out of the way and less likely to catch on things. If the cord is too long, entwine it loosely around the carrier's shoulder strap before running it across the back to the opposite ear.

For two aids, repeat the above procedure for each aid. In ac-

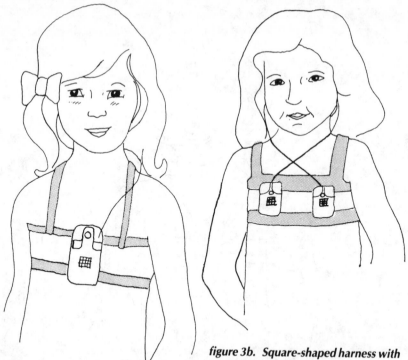

figure 3a. Square-shaped harness that we made for Linda.

figure 3b. Square-shaped harness with two aids worn by many children today, but often replaced by less conspicuous behind-the-ear aids.

cordance with Dr. Ciwa Griffiths' (HEAR Center, Pasadena, California) recommendation, when wearing two aids always put the earmold in the ear on the same side as its corresponding hearing aid, necessitating a double crossing of the cords behind the neck (Griffiths, 1976).

LEARNING TO WEAR A HEARING AID

Begin introducing a hearing aid to your child for only a short period of time each day; then increase the period as rapidly as he is able to tolerate it until he is wearing it all day every day. At first, be firm in insisting that he wear his aid for the designated periods—you know that his future is tied to acceptance of, and later dependence on, his aid. If you encounter either a prolonged, negative reaction in wearing the aid or annoying, attention-getting behavior (such as pulling the earmold and receiver out of the ear repeatedly and playing with the volume control), look into the principle of behavior management which is based on reward for good behavior rather than punishment for bad behavior. It works!

Body-type hearing aids are sturdier than they look. They can withstand considerable abuse by the most active child, with only a reasonable amount of repairs. Aids should not be removed before outdoor play as they withstand it well, and your child needs the hearing to relate to his friends. Hearing aids are as sturdy by night as by day—I discovered this fact when Leslie insisted on wearing her aid to bed every night, still in the "ON" position. She did this until junior high school, at which time she finally turned it off at night, while still wearing the aid and placing the cord-receiver-earmold close at hand on the night table. With this kind of usage, the aid needed no more repairs than normal. Of course, this was hard on batteries, but Leslie's satisfaction in knowing that she could hear if she awakened at night was worth the extra cost.

When your child puts on an aid for the first time, the volume should be set low enough to ensure that your child isn't frightened by a sudden blast of sound. After he has worn it for a day or two, cautiously begin to increase the volume until he shows a reaction to sound. A good rule to follow for a child with a profound loss, who needs all the volume he can stand, is to set the volume at its highest point, then back it off a point or two in order to get good sound quality—setting an aid at maximum volume distorts the sound.

Because the optimal setting will vary with the strength of the batteries, a child should be encouraged as soon as possible to take the responsibility for setting the volume of his aid. The setting will have to be changed several times as battery power wanes and also when a new battery is put in the aid. There is an extra bit of auxiliary power stored in a new battery that soon diminishes. For this reason, I would see Linda put her aid at 2 or 3 of a possible 0-to-7 volume setting after she had put in a replacement battery, then move it up after about an hour to 5, her usual setting. Again, toward the end of the battery's life, she would move it to 6 or 7 before it gave out.

As your child begins to take the responsibility for setting the volume by himself, and you sense that he is turning his aid too low, give him time to experiment. Do your part in making sound interesting enough that he will want to listen; one day you will see him fumbling around to turn it higher himself. Taking responsibility for his aid will encourage him to gauge its performance and to come to you when there is something wrong with its operation; as one of his first opportunities to make a decision, it will also give him a feeling of independence and pride of ownership.

SAFEGUARD YOUR CHILD'S HEARING

Although your child's hearing is already impaired, it is extremely important to protect the hearing he has left by providing the proper medical attention and home care. Infections, childhood diseases, and allergies affect the hearing of most children by making it drop slightly, then slowly return to normal. For a hearing child this temporary change is not enough to affect his schoolwork or his relationships with people. However, if your hearing-impaired child suffers even a small loss for a short time, it may be serious. His hearing may drop beyond the reach of the amplification he is accustomed to, thus hindering his schoolwork and social life, and more importantly, possibly causing a further permanent hearing loss.

Parents should take special care to guard against infections in their hearing-impaired child. Colds, influenza, other viruses, and bacterial infections of the throat can reach the middle ear through the eustachian tube. During and after any illness, check with the ear doctor for buildup of fluid behind the eardrum. Childhood diseases and high fevers can affect the hearing, as well as that baffling culprit, allergies. The more severe the case, the worse it is for your child's hearing.

There are several drugs that adversely affect hearing. Learn from your ear specialist which ones you should be on guard against in case your pediatrician or another doctor inadvertently prescribes one of these drugs. Also, have your child's ears checked regularly for earwax; this wax can build up and become compacted behind an earmold, causing a temporary hearing loss.

There is a tendency for the hearing of young children to be quite sensitive to infections, allergies, and temperature changes. Their reactions happen quickly and often suddenly, even overnight, and on occasion, seemingly without cause. Both our hearing-impaired children experienced drops in hearing from viral infections, and also had unexpected sudden drops. Leslie, who suffered from bronchial infections and allergies, had five or six significant drops in hearing between the ages of two and fifteen. After each drop, her hearing would slowly return, but not all the way back; there was always a further incremental and permanent loss. These drops in hearing were traumatic for her both academically and socially. She slowly learned to take preventive measures by staying out of drafts and covering her chest when riding a bike or traveling in a car with open windows. Her hearing loss of 35 dB at two years of age gradually slipped to a loss of 82 dB by the time she was a teenager.

My experience with Leslie, who was extremely prone to infection, has alerted me to the necessity of warning parents to watch for differences in their child's hearing acuity. Often you can prevent drops in hearing by taking precautions beforehand and providing good care when childhood illnesses strike.

Living day by day with your child, you become highly attuned to his listening ability and can become a very important monitor for him. You will know, if anyone will, if his hearing seems to be lower—or occasionally, higher—than usual, and you will probably be right. A hearing loss as shown by a child's first audiogram should not be considered absolute. Hearing losses do change, sometimes for obscure reasons. In fact, there is a certain type of hearing loss that progressively slips lower as time passes. Therefore, hearing tests of all hearing-impaired children should be taken at least once a year, and more often, if there is a question of change in either direction.

LEARNING TO LISTEN

At the present time there is a new emphasis on training a person to use his residual hearing, especially in the early years. Listening training has always been with us, but its importance was overshadowed by other communication methods, largely because the means for reaching the hearing-impaired person's residual hearing was not available or fully appreciated.

Twenty-eight years ago, Linda wore a large, heavy, boxlike aid (using two dry cell batteries) in order to receive all the amplification possible at that time. For five long years, the sound received was apparently not sufficient for her to care whether her aid was on or off. When they became available, we purchased a transistor aid for her, and at last at the age of nine she took a personal interest in her aid. Thereafter, she turned it on with purpose, and came to us when it was not functioning properly. This leads me to conclude that, for those with a profound hearing loss, the early aids did not have enough amplification to hold one's attention to sound.

The performance of a transistor hearing aid has already advanced a long way from Linda's first transistor aid, and with its steady improvement, listening has begun to receive more attention. What will follow in the future in the field of amplification can only be imagined. Providing your child's sensory ability to listen and to interpret what he hears is intact, he can benefit from the proper use of the equipment available today, and I believe he will have an opportunity to benefit even further from future technical advances.

For a normally hearing child, learning to listen meaningfully is acquired in the first years and taught most often by the mother who instinctively talks all the time to her baby. If the mother's voice is not heard at all or is so faint as to be meaningless, the baby will turn to his senses of touch and sight for comfort from his mother; the unimpaired senses will prevail and block out the imperfect sense. Why should the baby listen to a sound so weak? Even a hearing-impaired child that uses his residual hearing at first may later ignore this very small signal. In spite of concerted efforts to test infants' hearing, a child's hearing loss is often not discovered until he has already turned off this small signal in favor of his other more satisfying senses. Therefore, just as soon as it is determined, or even if there is the slightest suspicion, that a child may have a hearing loss, the process of stimulating his remaining hearing should be started, whatever the age.

Do not wait! Do not wait to start this process until your child can be fitted for a hearing aid, or until you can receive instructions, or for any reason at all. The earlier you can reach and stimulate his residual hearing by any means you can devise, the more likely he will want to hear, try to listen, and develop a listening attitude. While you are waiting out the days it takes for testing, evaluations, earmold and hearing aid fittings, and information on how to teach your small hearing-impaired child, you can be doing something constructive at home to bring his attention to the sounds he may be able to hear unaided.

Raise the level of sound around him immediately; project your voice and turn up the volume on the record player and television. Try to elicit a reaction to sound from him—any sound—to get him to begin to listen. Although he may not react at first, continue to try to stimulate him. Do not allow yourself ever to think, "He can't hear me, so why bother to talk to him." Even if you think you have been talking a lot to your baby or young child, talk to him more, sing to him more, more than ever before. Rock him and talk to him right into his ear, but don't talk loudly or shout at such close range. By cupping your hand to his ear and speaking in a normal voice directly into his ear, you raise the volume of your voice to a tolerable 100 decibels. And let him feel the vibration of your voice through your body as you hold him.

Even after your child wears a hearing aid, learn to use those moments when he doesn't have it on to stimulate his residual hearing. The limitations of a hearing aid will never cover the frequency range of sound in quite the same way and with quite the same quality as the natural ear. Encourage him to listen when and if he can with his ears, without amplification as well as with amplification. Try every method in training him to listen; let nothing go untried.

Bath time is one of the most valuable times for stimulating your young child's unaided hearing. Sounds between the close walls in a bathroom, often partially tiled, bounce back and forth with extra resonance. Just as it's pleasant for you to sing in the shower and have your voice reverberate in full, round tones, similar conditions exist for your hearing-impaired child in the bathtub. Your active child is happily corralled in one place by circumstances, affording a perfect opportunity to talk to him. An interesting aside concerning hearing ability in a swimming pool was brought to my attention by Leslie: she says when her ears are near or on the water level, sound is amplified to a degree where she can hear what people are saying around her. She finds this also holds true in a bathtub.

Still, bathrooms, halls, and tunnels do not have the same value for a child using his hearing aid. Sound that bounces from wall to wall distorts amplified speech. As soon as your child has been fitted with a hearing aid, lower your voice and the noise level to normal. The hearing aid is now compensating, and a loud voice or sound will only be distorted.

If your child has turned off sound, your challenge is to transform that child who has stopped listening into one who listens. Putting a hearing aid on him is not enough—he must learn to know what he hears. Sounds must be pointed out, experimented with, and felt as well as listened to by your child. Sound should be a pleasant experience, a wonderful discovery, and it must be brought to his attention often in conscious repetition until he has formed the habit of listening. When, for example, vacuuming a rug, tell him you hear the sound of the vacuum cleaner, putting your hand to your ear. Let him feel the vibration of the vacuum cleaner, and then encourage him to listen hard for its sound. You will know when he's listening for himself because he will tell you when he hears a sound.

The early years are the prime time to teach a child to listen to the small signal he receives and make it a regular part of his sensory being. Nevertheless, occasionally, a child will consciously reject sound for one reason or another. If not sufficiently motivated to listen or if he's more comfortable with other methods of communication and rebels against wearing a hearing aid, you may not be able to persuade him to listen. But if at any time he decides he really wants to listen, it is never too late to learn.

So, if and when this older child expresses a sincere desire to wear a hearing aid and to learn to use his latent residual hearing, grasp the opportunity to work with him and encourage and give him incentives to listen. Your help and his own desire will spur him on to find ways to practice listening by himself, as Linda, Leslie, and many others have done. As a teenager, Linda improved her discrimination of environmental and speech sounds by methods she devised herself. She continues to do so today. (Several methods are described in Chapter 17.)

Many hearing-impaired adults, born before the advent of the modern hearing aid, have learned to use a hearing aid in middle age. Learning to listen at any time follows the same pattern as for a child and begins by identifying the environmental sounds one hears. Learning to identify sounds again reoccurs when a person purchases a new, better aid and he suddenly hears many little sounds he didn't hear before. At first, they seem loud and annoying, like the squeak from a rocking chair or the hum of a refrigerator, until they are singled out, located, and identified. Then, these sounds are stored away for recognition later. Normally hearing people frequently assume that a person who wears a hearing aid and speechreads does not hear most sounds. Quite the opposite is true. Sounds are amplified so that hearing aid users hear many sounds; their problem lies in identifying them and later discriminating between them. Hearing people can actually give invaluable assistance to hearing-impaired persons by alerting them to the source and nature of the sounds around them.

Training to listen meaningfully is a long, slow process for a child with a severe loss. Dr. T. J. Watson of the University of Manchester, England, advocates that auditory training should continue all day, every day (Watson, 1961). I also maintain that listening has to be encouraged consistently throughout each day to be effective. The ability to refine listening to an ever-finer degree of discrimination is heightened by the child's growing desire to understand better whatever he hears.

Take every opportunity to use the sounds around your child and plan specific periods for listening, using games, musical instruments, and records. Games for practicing on-and-off, high-and-low, and other sound discriminations can be found in *Play It by Ear!*, written by Edgar L. Lowell and Marguerite Stoner and published for the John Tracy Clinic by Wolfer Publishing Company (1960). Also, the John Tracy Clinic Correspondence Course has auditory training suggestions, and with imagination and the help of these sources, it shouldn't be difficult to develop your own games.

Incidentally, it is wise to cultivate and learn to tolerate a noisy household. Your child needs to grow up with sound, lots of it, around him. He needs to learn, like normally hearing people, to differentiate between sounds, to ultimately tune in the sounds he wants to hear and tune out the sounds that are disturbing or distracting. A hearing-impaired child can learn to do this only if he has practice with all kinds of sound and recognizes what he hears. A severely hearing-impaired youngster learns to tolerate a lot of sound, and his hearing aid is designed to cut out peak sounds that may hurt his ear when amplified. But if a sound is so constant and loud as to be disturbing, he should learn to adjust his aid, as his environment will not change for him. He isn't going to be spared the combined traffic and motor noise on a bus or the hubbub of a room full of chattering people. Unfortunately rooms are rarely acoustically treated and some are veritable echo chambers.

When your child learns to recognize important sounds for his own well-being or for the convenience of others, begin to expect him to hear them—such sounds as his name, the doorbell, the telephone, an automobile horn, a siren, and certain words like *no, wait,* and *stop.*

I want to emphasize that you should teach your child as early as possible to turn to his name. Of all the reactions that will give him a hearing personality, this one will be the most significant. Of course, there are limitations in distance, background noise, and the performance of his aid, but even a profoundly hearing-impaired child can learn to turn most of the time to his name across the length of a quiet room. What a great pleasure it is to everyone around him when he responds to his name! If he doesn't respond, go to him and tell him you called him and let him listen for his name again. Insist that he pay attention. The constant repetition of the speech sounds of this particular word, his name, eventually will form a pattern to which he will respond, even though he may not yet respond to many other words.

If you are having a very hard time getting your child to respond to his name, keep trying, because the other options are poor substitutes:

1. You can wait for his eyes to come to you naturally, which is the best alternative, particularly in public places;
2. You can go to him and touch him gently on the arm, but most hearing-impaired people find this annoying when done too often;
3. You can stamp your foot on a resilient floor surface and the vibration will gain his attention; and
4. You can use other methods commonly used in the classroom like turning the lights on and off, ringing a cowbell, and banging a drum.

But nothing, absolutely nothing, can compare with the mutual satisfaction of having him turn to you when you call his name.

A word of caution to those parents who are not yet fully aware of how cleverly a hearing-impaired child uses his other senses to compensate for his hearing loss. Children with hearing losses are notorious for substituting another sense for hearing. In observing his child's listening ability, a parent can be confused by the child who seems to hear one minute and not hear the next. The bright eyes of a hearing-impaired child will soon learn to pick up the smallest clue to care for his daily needs. What he may seem to "hear" may be a slight visual clue that you have overlooked. Could he have seen a clue from the corner of his eye, or felt something, or smelled something? Analyze the situation before concluding positively that he heard you.

SPEECH DISCRIMINATION

Remarkable results are being realized today by some children through concentrated auditory training. For as long as twenty-five years, teachers scattered throughout the United States, Canada, and Europe have been utilizing an auditory approach that emphasizes the maximum use of residual hearing over any other mode of communication. The auditory approach advocates early detection, prompt use of a hearing aid (often binaural), and extensive work in developing the discrimination of speech through hearing alone. Speechreading is added incidentally, if at all, only after speech discrimination through hearing is well established. (For more information on this subject, refer to Doreen Pollack's book as listed in the references.)

For a child with a mild hearing loss, undoubtedly auditory training is most important and often sufficient, but for the profoundly hearing impaired, after establishing maximum use of residual hearing, training in speechreading often facilitates a child's understanding of speech. At the same time, I would not suggest that speechreading be foremost in early training until good listening habits have been developed. Because a person tends to use a whole, perfect sense and to neglect the imperfect one, very good speechreaders often prefer to rely on their speechreading and ignore their residual hearing. The visual approach sometimes leads a child to abandon his hearing altogether, which in the long run is to his disadvantage. Therefore, even for the profoundly hearing impaired, I agree with the basic tenet of the auditory approach, but would follow up with extensive speechreading training after the habit of listening and identifying sounds is formed by the constant use of a hearing aid.

When your child is listening attentively, give him numerous opportunities to hear speech when he's not watching you as well as when he's watching you. Opportunities arise when you tie a little girl's bow on the back of her dress, zip a zipper, and brush her hair; or when you tie a boy's shoe and tuck in his shirt. Casually talk to him and, if he looks around, repeat what you have said so he can see your face. Give him the chance to hear your conversation as well as speechread it and effectively combine the two; this will sharpen his ability to understand, through his hearing, some of what you say.

If your child is watching you talk but you lose his eyes before your sentence is finished, always finish your sentence in case he might hear you. Who knows what he may pick up in discrimination, timing, rhythm, and inflection from your speech? Stopping in the middle of a sentence because he turns his eyes away, or stopping and then starting again, chops up the rhythm into an unnatural speech pattern. It is always better to finish your full sentence in a normal rhythm, repeating it again when his eyes return to you.

In addition, give your child practice recognizing the names of familiar objects. A game can be devised with three objects whose names your child knows well. Place them in front of him and say, from behind his back, the name of one of the objects, or face him and put a piece of paper over your mouth so that he can't speechread you. Choose words of low frequency and strong volume, and at least one that has two syllables for variety and a possible clue; *ball, airplane,* and *mouse* are suggested words differing from each other in consonants and vowels. Speech discrimination is difficult enough without introducing words that are too much alike at the outset of speech discrimination practice. Never pursue this game to the point of frustrating your child. If he can't tell one word from another by hearing alone, let him see your face, speechread the word, and then hand you the correct object with a feeling of accomplishment. Show pleasure and try again another day. Learning to use his imperfect hearing sense to understand speech is the most difficult task you can ask of him. Be sure your relationship with your child is relaxed and happy during this game.

Above all, don't be discouraged; if your child's loss is great, he may not learn to pick up the correct object every time, but meanwhile he is gaining valuable exposure to differences between speech sounds and also practice in specific listening. When he is successful, vary the game with other words. Eventually, try a question when he can't see your face; answering correctly will be a significant breakthrough.

A point to remember about your child's hearing aid is that he receives the most gain and the best quality when speech comes from a distance of four to twelve inches in front of the microphone (Pollack, 1970). No one has more opportunity to speak at that distance and at microphone level than the parent who so frequently talks to his child on a close, one-to-one basis.

The further away the speaker the more distant the sound, based on an inversely squared ratio that decreases quickly to a volume too small for understanding. Sound drops twenty decibels in two feet (Ling, 1978)! In spite of this, a child with a profound loss can often learn to answer to his name in a room from a distance of six feet or more with consistent practice. The walls confine the sound, while in the open air he probably wouldn't be able to hear you.

Further, the frequency range that reaches the ear also shortens with distance, thus reducing the frequency range that the hearing aid is amplifying (Ling, 1978). A child who hears in the 3000 Hz frequency range at a distance of two feet only when the volume is turned very high may not hear the same frequency at six feet, since volume and frequency are both affected by distance.

Classroom distances vary so that speechreading is generally needed to supplement hearing, and there is an added variable of classroom noise with which to contend. Some classrooms are equipped with a loop system that allows the sound to enter the aid at the same gain no matter where the teacher is standing. When available, this has its advantages in the classroom, but it does not give a child the opportunity to adjust to different life situations. It is better if he is prepared to meet the hearing world as it is with the combination of as much listening and speech discrimination as possible and as much speechreading as necessary.

chapter **7**

speechreading

After your child has begun to listen and you are sure that the habit of listening is well established, begin to teach him to speechread. Your child should learn how to speechread and practice it even if he has a usable degree of hearing. Not only can he support his imperfect hearing with one more clue in everyday conversation, but speechreading can pull him through short, temporary periods of communication breakdown such as, emergencies, noisy circumstances, or if his hearing drops during an illness.

As you bring his attention to your face, continue with listening training. Talk to the side and back of him, stress household and environmental sounds, and call him often until he turns to his name. Never fail to try to reach what hearing he may have so that he combines his hearing with his speechreading. You will soon find that many things you do are interrelated, and that his senses complement each other.

I do not attempt here to outline a systematic course in speechreading as this is well explained and illustrated in the John Tracy Clinic Correspondence Course and other books and articles on the subject (many of which can be found in any recent Alexander Graham Bell Association for the Deaf publications' brochure). However, I will set forth some personal notes, hints, precautions, and comments on procedures about speechreading.

Children vary markedly in their ability to learn to speechread. In training an apparently slow speechreader, I would caution against giving up too soon. Parents have worked and despaired for as long as five years, when suddenly their child has begun to improve. Even if your child is not naturally gifted at speechreading, it stands to reason that he will improve with continual practice.

THE ART OF SPEECHREADING

Speechreading is not only the art of reading the lips, but also the art of interpreting speech from the muscles of the jaw, neck, and cheeks, and the expressions of the face, eyes, and eyebrows (how expressive are the eyebrows!). It can be thought of as a puzzle with the solution evolving from a combination of clues, of which only about twenty-five percent come from the mouth area. The speechreading puzzle also involves clues from: the posture of the body, like a shrug; the movement of the head, in a nod or shake; and the natural gesture of the hand, such as the open palm raised for *stop*. Good speechreaders are those who can combine successfully all clues with the partial hearing they may have into a meaningful message. Frequently, their quick decision on what has been said depends on a fortunate bit of guesswork. Realistically, if the guesswork is wrong, it can be embarrassing, but it's always worth the attempt as opposed to not trying at all. A good attitude toward others and a keen sense of humor can carry a hearing-impaired person through many uncertain situations.

Many unrelated words look alike on the lips. A classic example is the story the late, beloved Mrs. Harriet Montague of the John Tracy Clinic Correspondence Course told the parent classes at the clinic. Arriving at a couple's house on a warm day for the weekend, she and her friends went to the kitchen where the host opened the refrigerator door and said, "Do you want some beer?" Although she was very thirsty, Mrs. Montague didn't drink beer, and told her host, "No, thank you." Later she discovered that what he had really said was, "Do you want some milk?" Surprisingly, *beer* and *milk* look alike on the lips. Try it in the mirror!

Mrs. Montague worked for some years as a journalist on a newspaper. She often remarked that reporters are the most difficult people in the world to speechread—they have poker faces with absolutely no expression.

Researchers have had difficulty pinpointing why there is such a pronounced variation in hearing-impaired people's ability to speechread. The hearing-impaired themselves will tell you it is a God-given talent. It has long been suggested that the ability to speechread seems to be connected with a person's skill in synthesis, the ability to grasp a series of fragmentary parts and convert them into a unified whole.

An interesting study was made of this synthesizing skill by Dr. Jay W. Sanders and Janet E. Coscarelli (1970), when using tests consisting of the identification of incomplete pictures (line drawings with some lines missing), words lacking vowels (*h--l*), and sentences lacking consonants (*-o- a-e you?*), the researchers found definite correlations between good and poor speechreaders and their ability to score well on these tests. They wrote in summary:

> The major conclusion of the study was that lipreading ability is directly related to skill in visual synthesis. Not only were lipreading scores significantly correlated with visual scores, but also the better lipreaders, with or without training, were superior in visual synthesis to the poorer lipreaders. These results argue strongly for a synthesis approach to the teaching of lipreading and suggest a need for special procedures to develop and enhance visual synthesis skills in students of lipreading. (p. 26)

This study and its conclusions bring to mind numerous commercial and homemade puzzles and games, from jigsaws to crosswords, that can be used to sharpen a child's skill in synthesis. Remembering the television game "Concentration," you can devise a homemade game with a setup consisting of a large picture or handmade drawing on which are placed, at random and face down, cards from a deck of small playing cards to cover the entire picture. Then, play "Concentration," turning over one card and trying to pair it with another of the same kind from memory. If the second card you choose doesn't match the first, both are replaced face down, but if the cards are paired, they are removed from the picture. As portions of the picture are revealed, the person who identifies it first on his turn wins the game.

Later on when a child is reading, use such games as Hangman, Scrabble, and Anagrams for practicing the skill of visualizing a whole word by seeing only some of the letters.

Similarly, it takes a certain ability to think out the message from a multiplicity of clues for successful speechreading. According to Linda, this explains why there is often a noticeable time-lag between the spoken message and the reaction of the speechreader, even a skilled speechreader. To a normally hearing person, a pronounced hesitation before answering is unnatural. I have puzzled many times over this time-lag and wondered how the process could be speeded up to be less noticeable. Linda's explanation of what the mind goes through in translation suggests that the processes of understanding what is said and forming an answer are so complex that it is a wonder the lag is not greater. In fact, a skilled speechreader, given one subject for discussion, usually can carry on a natural, continuing conversation with very little lag. However, if you suddenly change the subject without notice, the speechreader will often flounder and ask for a repeat or a further explanation. Speechreaders need help and patience from the conversationalists when a new subject is introduced.

New vocabulary can also cause problems. The speechreader will not recognize a word he has never seen on the lips before. If he is having difficulty, the speaker should rephrase his sentence in familiar words, explaining the meaning of the new word and its correct pronunciation.

Linda feels that the added clues that hearing gives to speechreading are invaluable to the hearing impaired, no matter how small an amount of residual hearing one has. She herself has a 97 dB average loss through the speech range. Nevertheless, she has learned through long use and self-training to depend upon her hearing for perhaps one quarter of her understanding of speech, with the remaining three quarters dependent on speechreading. At an early age she relied almost entirely on speechreading, but with the improvement of hearing aids in quality and volume of sound, the clues she gains from her hearing have contributed immeasurably to her ability to speechread.

One evening when Linda and I were discussing the subject of speechreading, I asked her exactly what process she went through to understand what I was saying. She took a sentence at random out of our previous conversation, wrote it on the blackboard, and analyzed it. The sentence was: "That sounds really great."

"Let's see now," she said, "the *th* in *that* is easy to speechread because it is visible. The short *a* could be a short *e*, *i*, or long *e*, but with the short visible *t* sound on the end, I know it is *that*.

"In *sounds*, the *s* is visible and the *ou* is easy to hear and to see as it is a strong vowel sound. The *n* is not as visible as the *d* and *s*, but combined I can tell it is *sounds* by the small movement of the mouth as it changes to the *d* and *s*.

"The first syllable in *really* is strong enough to be a good clue for the rest of the word, and being a two-syllable word makes it easier to speechread. The *l* is very visible, a strong consonant to catch.

"*Great* has a combination of the guttural sounds of the *g* and the shape of the lips for the *r* that enables me to know it is a *gr*. The long vowel, *a* (or *ea* in this case), is an easier sound to hear than to see. It could look like a long *e* or a short *i* or short *e*, and might be taken for *grit*, but I can catch from hearing the prolonged nature of the vowel and know it is a long *a*. Seeing the short *t* at the end enables me to know the word is *great* instead of *grain* or *grade*.

"The content of the sentence also helps me to understand what has been said after I have some of the words and clues. By now, the word *great* makes more sense than the similar sounding words, *grain* and *grade*. The content fills in additional information that I might have missed during the time the sentence was spoken. Visibility, sound, and content, all three working together, help me catch the full meaning of the words. Sometimes, though, it takes me a couple of seconds after the sentence is completed to really understand what was said."

A further hearing clue, which Linda draws upon sometimes, is the ability to hear the first word of a sentence well enough to understand it before she has had time to raise her eyes and seek out a speaker's face. With this first word, she has an opportunity to fill in with speechreading more easily than if she had missed the first word altogether.

In group situations in classrooms or meetings, where a number of people are all contributing to a conversation, a normally hearing person finds the speaker through his hearing. He knows by loudness of voice and direction of sound which way to turn his head. A speech-reader must also rely on his aided residual hearing to find the speaker quickly. He usually can judge the distance to the speaker from the loudness of his voice, but the direction is more difficult. It is almost impossible to determine direction with one hearing aid, but a person wearing two hearing aids has, with practice, a much better chance of locating the direction of sound. When Linda was teaching at Cal Poly, she asked that her informal faculty meetings of eight teachers make it a policy to talk one at a time after raising a hand. It helped her immeasurably, and the teachers happily discovered that their meetings were more orderly and businesslike.

Another clue to the location of the speaker in a group is the pitch and quality of the speaker's voice. A hearing-impaired person using his residual hearing can learn to recognize a familiar voice, tell the difference in voice quality between speakers, and distinguish a man's from a woman's voice. Leslie says that in the classroom, "I was forever turning my head every which way to find the speaker. Often my only clue was elimination according to male or female voice; if it sounded male, I'd scan the male population to see whose lips were moving."

TEACHING YOUR CHILD TO SPEECHREAD

To begin with, your child must discover there is something of value to be learned from the face, and most particularly the mouth area. Be sure that you develop an expressive face as he will speechread all facial features. Speak a little slower than usual, but not unnaturally, and be forever watchful not to mouth your words. Exaggerated words are much more difficult to speechread and are not the typical type of speech that he will be called on to speechread throughout his life.

Curiously, it was only recently that I learned from Linda that it is easier for her to speechread a face turned slightly on an angle rather than one looking straight at her. This means that she is positioned to see important jaw and neck muscles that give further clues to certain sounds, such as *g* and *k*.

Be sure that your voice has inflection and accent. Even the most profoundly hearing impaired can learn to hear and discern accent in words and sentences as they become proficient speechreaders. Accent provides an added clue from which to catch the key words. As we know, meanings vary with accent, as in the sentence, "Please give me another cookie." Ordinarily, emphasis would be on the words *give* and *cookie*, but other times one might emphasize the word *please* if he wanted to plead for a cookie or the word *me* if he felt he was being left out. Such subtle differences in meaning caused by accent are too varied for any rule and are ultimately learned through usage.

Speak in complete sentences so the speechreader can gather the meaning from the full context. Always finish your sentence even though you have lost eye contact with your child and repeat it again when his eyes return to you, thereby retaining the rhythm and timing of the sentence. Short sentences about the subject at hand are more easily understood than a long, complex sentence combining several ideas. If what you say is not readily understandable, rephrase your sentence. This new approach often strikes a quick note of recognition from the speechreader.

When talking to your child, be sure to come down to his eye level whenever possible, or lift him up to yours. Imagine how high in the sky your face must seem to him, and at what an awkward angle! (When you visit a preschool hearing-impaired classroom, you will observe that the only grownup-size chairs in the room are those occupied by the guests.)

Lighting in a room is of great importance to a speechreader. Since this is not a factor to a normally hearing person, people around a hearing-impaired child must consider whether the speaker's face is illuminated. Learn to seat your child in a position that takes advantage of the best lighting in the room and to position yourself, the speaker, in the direct light, remembering that in daytime your face becomes a silhouette when a window is at your back. In our home, I discovered that in the kitchen, where my children usually found me, the light coming from the big corner windows in back of the sink was blinding my face. I had to learn to step aside before talking to allow the girls to see my face without interference from the outside light.

Some people are more difficult than others to speechread: those who have faces with small mouths, round cheeks, many wrinkles, or blank expressions; those wearing dark glasses, since the eyes are a very important clue; those who habitually look at the floor or cover their faces; and those with full-blown moustaches and scraggly beards. I am reminded of the Santa Claus we visited when the children were small. He had a beard that entirely covered his mouth, leaving no apparent opening; and he was talking to children from underneath it! He and I threw up our hands, as nothing he said came across to my speechreaders. After that I carefully chose the Santa we visited.

A normally hearing person can't always guess which people will be difficult to speechread. Generally speaking, someone with a mobile face and not too rapid speech will be understandable. However, speechreaders will amaze you. Often you will find your child at first having trouble speechreading a certain person, but after much exposure and concentrated practice, it might only be a matter of three or four weeks before he is able to speechread that individual remarkably well. Then again, there will be those few whom your child will always find almost impossible to speechread. In this case, it is best to take a philosophical view—*c'est la vie!*

For some reason, television programs are very difficult to speechread for all hearing-impaired people. (As a matter of interest, our girls say that the easiest television stars to speechread are Alan King and Carol Burnett.)

In sum, the major points to remember when talking to a speechreader are:

1. Have an expressive, open face when talking, and avoid covering any part of your face or having anything in your mouth.

2. Speak slightly slower than usual with accent and inflection and don't mouth your words.

3. Use complete sentences and finish them, even though you have lost eye contact.

4. Bend down to meet the eye level of your child.

5. Consider the lighting when you and others talk to your child.

SPEECHREADING FOR THE HARD-OF-HEARING CHILD

A hearing-impaired child usually uses speechreading only to the extent that he needs it. As a consequence, a child with considerable residual hearing who is using a hearing aid efficiently may need to draw very little on speechreading. However, it is a good idea that he learn speechreading as an auxiliary tool for those times when he will not have the full use of his aid; even a mild loss is a severe one without an aid. One must realize that the hard-of-hearing child will need speechreading in situations like the following:

1. When the aid needs repair and no replacement is available,
2. Special circumstances when he will not be wearing the aid (for example, around water or when he has a sore ear),
3. Times when he experiences a drop in his hearing,
4. When speech sound is too far away to reach the aid, and
5. When background noise drowns out speech.

To teach your hard-of-hearing child speechreading will take careful thought and ingenuity on your part. Initially, tell him about speechreading and how watching the face will be an added boost to him. Take advantage of situations, like those mentioned above, when he can't hear you to develop his awareness of the value of speechreading. Use opportunities such as when he is in the bathtub, around a swimming pool, or on the beach without his aid. Talk to him and tell him to watch your face. If he doesn't understand, repeat what you said and tell him to watch more carefully. Be persuasive and positive—with an air of expectancy—that he will understand if he tries. Give him a message through a closed window once in a while. Toss a few words to him over a distance too far for his hearing aid to reach. See if he can understand you in a noisy background, like on the bus.

Use natural opportunities that arise, but when he has his hearing aid on, don't turn it off to force the issue; it is too important, often frightening, for him to be without the aid even for a short period of time. It is also unwise to speak to him without voice in order to sharpen his speechreading ability. Few people can do this successfully without changing their own speech pattern in spite of their best intentions.

A knowledge of speechreading can fill in as a communication tool for the hard of hearing in countless unexpected circumstances. When seven-year-old Leslie's hearing dropped suddenly, we discovered that she had been depending solely on her hearing aid and didn't know how to speechread. She then had to start from the beginning to learn this skill, an experience we might have avoided had we given more emphasis to speechreading as a supplement to her hearing before it dropped.

NATURAL GESTURES

Occasionally parents become so engrossed in teaching their hearing-impaired child to listen and to speechread that they refrain from using natural gestures with their speech, for fear they will distract their child from using his hearing and watching the speaker's face. Indeed, elaborate gestures invented for the occasion are unnatural and distracting. But to refrain from using those natural gestures commonly used by your family in conversation is neither necessary nor desirable. Like facial and body expressions, some gestures are as much a part of conversation as colloquialisms and exclamations. Conversations in some ethnic groups and regional areas are laced with the gestures the people learned in childhood. If your child is to learn to communicate with his family, he should not be denied the color and subtle meanings that these gestures give to the conversation. And they are another clue for him.

Some specific gestures are aids to the parent of a small child with limited language. The crook of the hand in a gesture of "come on" can bring a child to you, bridging the length of a grocery store, playground, or park. I can't imagine surviving many harried occasions without the use of the index finger in the air that means "wait a minute." The palm thrust forward in a "stop" signal, like a policeman, can speak louder than words when your child is running full-tilt for the street. These gestures, however, should not be used without their accompanying word or words, because in due time you want your child to respond to the words as well as the corresponding gestures. If the moment is not an emergency, say the words and then follow with the gesture. When he learns the words, the gesture can be dropped (except when distance is a factor).

Often, a gesture may be the easiest, quickest, and the only way to explain the meaning of abstract words. Take the word *love* for instance; if you say the word in a sentence, then hug your child, or act out the gesture for a hug, the meaning will soon become clear to him.

One of my favorite gestures in class went with "Johnny brought cookies for *everybody!*" A sweep of my hand, encompassing the six little seated figures, was emphatic and fully understandable. Besides, it's a beautiful multisyllabled, rhythmic, roll-off-the-tongue variation of the word *all*.

THE COOKY JAR

This little story about Linda and me could be told anywhere in the first chapters of this book, but you will see why I picked the spot after discussing speechreading and gestures to make my point.

One day, I confronted Linda in the middle of the kitchen and said, "Do you want a cooky, Linda?" There was a pause, as Linda looked at me blankly. When I moved to the cooky jar and repeated, "Do you want a cooky, Linda?" She gave me her usual smile of recognition and turned toward the cooky jar this time. It was at this moment that I experienced my second shock: Linda not only didn't talk to me as a normal child would do by this age of two and one-half, she also didn't understand what I said!

How many times had we confronted the cooky jar together, Linda and I? "Do you want a cooky, Linda?" I had asked over and over, probably unconsciously pointing to or moving toward the cooky jar, and she had responded. Now I considered the phrase with vital interest in view of this second shock; the first shock being the previous week when the local ear, nose, and throat doctor with his tuning fork and the John Tracy Clinic using gross sound tests both told us that our daughter had a severe hearing loss. That first "Why me?" shock was still with me, but it was slowly spending itself. This second, cooky jar episode brought home the bone-chilling realization of how utterly lacking I was in comprehension of hearing problems.

I began to analyze the situation. Looking back before this incident, Linda always had smiled and hungrily greeted my words, but I hadn't noticed I was standing by the cooky jar and pointing to it. I realized parents with small children normally develop their children's language with such a show-and-tell communication system. Pointing and looking towards an object to draw attention to it are such natural movements that we hardly know we are doing them. But, for Linda, was I unconsciously prolonging her reaction to my gesture rather than to my words? What need would she ever have to try to understand the words I was saying when she understood me readily from my gesture or by following my eyes? This lesson was the first of many, but one of the most important, that I learned by trial and error in helping Linda develop her communication skills.

How many parents of hearing-imapired children continue the show-and-tell process from habit? How often does a mother, even after she is aware of the communication needs of her hearing-impaired child, continue to show and tell because it is easier during her busy days? Show and tell may be the beginnings of language for a normally hearing child, but for a hearing-impaired child, as soon as the realization of the problem is understood, and the "Why me?" dissolves into a resolve of "What can I do about it?", the first thing you can and should do is reverse the procedure to *tell and show*. Or better yet, to tell, then show, and tell again!

chapter 8

speech

It is in the area of their child's speech development that parents are inclined to feel most helpless. Without formal training, what can they do? Teachers often suggest that parents leave speech training to the experts. It's true that some of the methods and skills used by speech teachers in speech development and correction are indeed difficult for parents to learn and to use successfully, particularly with their own child. At the same time, this advice may turn parents off to all speech help at home, when in truth there is a great deal they can do!

A normally hearing infant listens to the speech around him and soon begins to vocalize consciously. He cries now with purpose and laughs in reaction to attention. He discovers the comfort and pleasure of the sounds other people make, and he begins to experiment. He enjoys the sound of hearing and feeling his own voice and begins to coo and babble. All the time he is absorbing and learning to interpret the meaning of the voices around him, and soon he tries to imitate what he hears. He plays with his voice, his tongue, and his mouth in a baby's universal language: "Bababa---mamama---googoogoo." Everyone is delighted and encourages him. From this play, he develops his voice quality and his facility in making speech sounds that imitate the words he hears.

Your hearing-impaired infant does the same thing. With a pleasant voice quality, he babbles and plays with his voice to the point where he should be imitating a few words; but, almost imperceptibly to a busy mother, he becomes silent. Later, when the silent child, through learning, begins to use his voice purposefully again, it takes on a certain quality associated with the hearing impaired.

What has happened? Why has the quality of the voice changed? Many people have pondered this phenomenon without reaching a satisfactory conclusion. Undoubtedly, one of the influencing factors is that the hearing-impaired child ceases to progress in speech production because he doesn't hear it precisely at the time when Nature intended him to develop his speech and provided him with the internal stimulus to do so. When this moment is lost, speech must then be motivated by introducing specific learning techniques, which are prone to cause stress and result in a strained voice quality.

No matter the causes of the hearing-impaired child's change in voice quality, from the time he becomes silent to the time he begins to talk again, we know that we want to avoid this period altogether or keep it as short as possible. The shorter the period between silence and reawakening speech, the more his voice quality will approximate what it was initially.

Today, with the new improvements in hearing aids and their early use, coupled with more intensive early auditory training, teachers and parents are helping hearing-impaired children to minimize this gap by keeping them vocalizing. Unfortunately, there are still too many children who are not fitted with an aid or stimulated to listen early enough. There are also those with significant hearing losses whose aids help, but don't bring a strong enough signal at an early age to keep the child vocal.

Therefore, one of the most important things parents can do on their own is keep a hearing aid on their child all day every day (even at night if the child desires it) and keep the aid in good working order. Encourage your child to become aware of the speech around him. His hearing aid is indispensable in not only bringing sound to his ears of sufficient volume to hear the speech of others, but also amplifying his own voice so as to hear himself speak. With guidance, hearing his own voice and feeling it internally enables him to establish a vocal quality, pitch, and volume that is pleasing to himself and those around him.

With respect to hearing one's own voice, the Ewings (of the University of Manchester, England) strongly recommend that the hearing aid microphone be four inches from the mouth or chin (Ewing & Ewing, 1964). Fortunately, the distance from the chin to the upper chest of a small child approximates that measurement. This is certainly a strong argument for rejecting a loose carrier with the hearing aid hanging nearly to the waist.

Summarizing this introduction to the subject of speech, it is worth every effort to stimulate sound at an early age to keep a child vocalizing, thereby retaining his natural voice quality. Thus, a parent's goals should be: that the child develop a clear, resonant voice that comes from the diaphragm at a comfortable pitch; that he speak in a pleasantly modified tone that is neither too loud nor too soft to a listener's ear; and that his speech be understandable. In practice, the child's speech should flow on a continuous breath with natural pauses in a relaxed manner, containing a reasonable facsimile of the vowels and consonants of speech as they are normally combined in a running sentence, with natural timing, rhythm, and inflection.

VOICE QUALITY

Several components add up to good, intelligible speech, not the least of which is a pleasant voice quality since the vehicle of speech is the voice. Hearing-impaired adults with high-pitched, nasal, thin, breathy, or otherwise unpleasant voices unfortunately make it uncomfortable for normally hearing people to listen very long to that type of voice. On the other hand, speech can have a "deaf quality" without being unpleasant. At the start, the setting of a child's voice in a pleasant range with good quality is more important than perfecting the individual speech sounds he produces. A child, up to the age of six, with a severe or profound hearing loss has a very tenuous voice that is not yet set in an habitual pattern; it can easily be "lost," even temporarily, if even one of two important ingredients is missing for any length of time:

1. He must have stimulation and a reason to use his voice all the time.
2. He must hear his own voice all the time.

With practice and encouragement he will locate the pitch, volume, and quality of his own voice by sound and feel, and will in time use it consistently.

During three-year-old Linda's first year at the John Tracy Clinic, her tutor said to me, "We have been so concerned about your daughter that she was the subject of our staff meeting yesterday afternoon. We don't understand why the happy babble of sound we were hearing from her has stopped."

I was dumbfounded. Living closely with her, I hadn't noticed. Sure enough, I observed that she was talking less, and as I thought about it I realized that I had not been stimulating her to talk. That omission was all it had taken to stop the flow of words. Family problems of moving to a new home and a very sick baby boy had diverted my attention from Linda. I had been only going through the motions of taking Linda to the Clinic and back at that crucial time when she was first attempting to speak. Within a few days of renewed stimulation at home, Linda was happily vocalizing again. These sudden reversals can happen so easily. While you think all is well, because your child continues to develop vocabulary, is he also continuing to express the words he knows?

This experience demonstrated to me the instability of the early voice and the young child's need to be constantly stimulated to vocalize.

In fact, in the same worrisome, fatiguing period, I again learned from experience about the second ingredient that has to be maintained to keep a child vocal. My husband and I took a two-week summer vacation, leaving a babysitter with the children. When we returned, we couldn't believe our ears; Linda had no voice at all, just a high, cracked squeak! After questioning the sitter, it developed Linda had rejected her hearing aid during the hot weather for most of our days away, and, when she was wearing it, there was no guarantee that it had been working properly. It was frightening to have left a hearing-impaired child with what we thought was an established, pleasant voice to come home to find it gone. After putting the hearing aid back on her and stimulating her to listen in every way possible, Linda's voice recovered its previous quality, but it took a month and a half. We never let this happen again, even though her voice needed our attention until she was about six years old to keep it stable.

As an amateur teacher of your hearing-impaired child's speech and an aid to his regular teacher, you should develop a listening ear and note any changes in the tonal quality of his voice. G. Sibley Haycock comments in his book, *The Teaching of Speech* (1961):

> It is imperative, therefore, that the teacher of speech to young deaf children should possess an ear which is sensitive to fine shades of difference in vocal tones—and be able, for example, to detect at once an element of strain intruding itself; any growing fault in resonance—a tendency, perhaps, towards too much or too little nasal resonance; or maybe early evidence that the pitch is changing—almost imperceptibly, getting higher or lower; or that the quality is become less clear, or tending to become thinner, or thicker, or hard or metallic; and so on. These, among other potential defects of voice, must be detected *before*

they become pronounced, and the only detector is a keenly active tone-perception or as we may say, a good phonetic ear. (p. 21)

Parents, as well as trained speech teachers, can develop a sensitivity to change in tonal quality by listening carefully and using their good ears as monitors for their child's voice.

You can also help by listening objectively to your own voice, remembering that your child will copy what he hears. He normally will pick up regional accents from you, such as the flat *a* of the Midwest and the long, soft vowels of the South, and in the same way, he will copy the tonal quality he hears. Determine if your own voice is too high pitched or nasal. If so, you should make a conscious effort to change it, although I appreciate the difficulty this may entail.

When you, yourself, are tense or when your child is tense, make it an absolute habit not to bring attention to an error in his speech, either in voice quality or specific speech sounds. This is considered one of the major reasons for the strained voices of hearing-impaired children after they begin to be taught specific language and speech. It isn't difficult to imagine how tense throat and tongue muscles and vocal cords can affect a young, undeveloped voice in a very short time. Catch yourself when you are either tired, tense, or nervous and try not to work on your child's speech improvement at those times. Your attitude and condition will be conveyed to your child and reflected in his speech.

Another point to remember is that it helps speech production as well as speechreading to come down to your child's height whenever possible. Not only can he see you better, but he can also speak to you better. On a family vacation with Linda when she was in college, I forcibly learned this lesson. Linda visited Mr. John Powell, a well-known track-and-field coach at the University of Guelph in Guelph, Ontario, Canada. She had studied his coaching techniques and read his book and was excited at the opportunity of meeting him. After a long conference with Linda, he came out to our car to meet us, a warm, exuberant man. In the course of our conversation, it was mentioned that Linda's voice quality was rather thin. "Of course," he said with certainty, "she is only five feet, two inches tall, and she has always had to look up to talk to other people, which strains her neck muscles."

Determining a child's best, personal voice quality depends upon the good ears of both his parents and his teachers. It is generally suggested that one listen for the tone of a small child's hearty laughter to gain a starting point for the natural pitch of his voice. A high-pitched voice is a common problem. Perhaps you can invent a home-made method to help your child gain practice in speaking at a desired pitch. Tried methods cover a range from expensive devices that register a high and low pitch electronically on a video screen, to a puppet with eyes that light up, to a simple light set in a box that can be turned on manually by a hidden switch when the pitch is right. This last method is very effective and can be homemade. Also, a child, once he has learned the sound and feel of his normal pitch, can be reminded by a hand signal indicating low or high. A piano or organ can demonstrate to a child the difference between a low and high pitch, as can two instruments of low and high frequency, such as a drum and bell. Be innovative! You can include these exercises in your everyday auditory training.

Another frequent obstacle for hearing-impaired children is a nasal tone to their speech. The only nasal speech sounds in the English language are the *m*, *n*, and *ng* formed by dropping the soft palate in the back of the mouth over the oral cavity, allowing the sound to flow out through the nose. All the rest of the English sounds are formed on a breath emitted through the mouth. A nasal tone results from a weak, pendant soft palate or by bunching up the tongue in the back of the mouth, closing off the oral cavity.

To encourage your child to bring the voice out through the mouth in full, round tones, you can try some of the methods used by voice teachers. Singers, speakers, and others who have had voice lessons tell me that their exercises include:

1. Singing out the vowels on a controlled stream of breath from the diaphragm,
2. Holding the tongue low and forward in the mouth to insure that the tongue does not spread and thicken in the back of the mouth, cutting off the entrance to the oral cavity; and
3. Keeping the neck, vocal cords, and mouth areas relaxed so that the sound can flow in a full and resonant tone.

Hearing-impaired children must be taught the difference between whispers, normal tones, and loud tones. It is very embarrassing for them to grow up unaware that their voice is not modulated to a whisper in such places as the library and church. Your child can hear a whisper close to his hearing aid microphone, and can learn with your help how, where, and when to whisper.

Particularly in the case of severe or profound hearing loss, children often have trouble breathing deeply and controlling their breath for speech. They find it difficult to breathe deeply enough, hard enough, and long enough to blow up a balloon. Usually, they have to be taught to blow out a birthday candle and blow a soap bubble. Therefore, opportunities for all kinds of blowing exercises should be presented often in a fun way, for relaxation, until your child can draw up a deep breath and, then, control its outward flow.Can he let it all out at once in a big blow, as would be necessary to blow out several candles? Can he let it out slowly but strongly in a steady stream, as for inflating a balloon? Can he let it out very gently to blow bubbles? Can he blow gently enough to blow a cotton ball across, but not off, a table; move a candle flame, but not put it out; ruffle a feather or a tissue? These exercises to develop breath control can all be done at home. Remember, the inability to hold one's breath long enough to reach natural pauses can cause choppy, nonrhythmic speech that is difficult to understand, and too much breath at the wrong places can make speech sound breathy.

You can also strengthen your small child's voice and prolong and control his breath by babbling with him. Sit him on your knees facing you and use voiced consonants and different vowels, letting him imitate you. Sing the babbling sounds up and down the scale to help him gain inflection in his voice, then make a rhythmic pattern of syllables that are stressed and unstressed.

You can see that it is essential to establish the good breathing habits of your child early. It is diffucult to change faulty breathing habits once they are established, as a child tends to compensate by correcting a fault with another fault. For instance. Linda had a noticeable, unnatural habit of panting for breath at the end of a sentence when she was excited. It was only after a speech-therapist friend remarked to her, "It seemed like you were holding your breath until you finished your sentence," that a clue to her reason for panting was discovered. Indeed, she was unconsciously trying to say all she had to say on one shallow breath, then panting to replace the depleted air in her lungs.

Linda had a similar problem when running in track competition. After she finished a 100-yard dash one day, someone told her it seemed as though she had held her breath the entire race. She realized this was true and spent many practice hours on the track learning to breathe deeper and in a regular rhythm as she ran. Running, jogging, and swimming undoubtedly help the hearing impaired develop better breathing habits.

The long hours you spend with your child at home, your good example, and your watchful monitoring of his voice will insure him a greater potential for having a pleasant voice quality.

ASSISTING IN EARLY SPEECH DEVELOPMENT

It is not recommended that the first speech of a hearing-impaired child be corrected before it even has a chance to develop naturally.

Only when you are sure that the flow of speech and the desire and need to talk is formulated, should you begin to consider the possibility of cautiously correcting your child's speech. Since speech training is technically oriented, arrange for your child to have speech lessons if a good speech teacher is available; the greater the loss, the greater the need. For a small child, speech lessons are inevitably tiring, dull, and repetitious. They should not last very long and should be preferably in the morning hours when your child is rested. Speech training is concentrated and there should be no tenseness and build-up of distaste for the lesson. Progress is often slow and frequent encouragement should be given, even when there is little improvement, with boosters like "that's a little better," "let's try again," or "once more."

If your child is having speech lessons, there are ways that you can help on your own, such as, but not limited to, the following:

1. Observe speech lessons—your own child's, other children's—every chance you can. You will pick up ideas to use at home to remind your child of correct speech and sharpen your ears for the fine differences in sounds. Ask the teacher for guidance in following up her speech work at home. The short time she spends with your child is not enough to sustain good speech unless you support and encourage him to use what he learns correctly.

2. Know the speech sounds yourself. Study, in a mirror, the manner in which you make speech sounds to become familiar with them. There are descriptions of individual sounds to be found in many speech books (for example, *The Teaching of Speech* by G. Sibley Haycock and *Speech and the Deaf Child* by Irene R. and A.W.G. Ewing, Washington, D.C.: The Volta Bureau, 1954). Included in these books are drawings showing the placement of the tongue and teeth for the various sounds. The knowledge you have of this material will be of value to you throughout the growing years of your child. You can then explain the proper way to produce a speech sound in a variety of ways (besides hearing, seeing, and feeling) by writing, drawing, using props, and whatever other means you may devise.

3. Increase your child's vocabulary by adding the words he needs to know for speech correction. If he knows the words that describe a speech sound, both the speech teacher and you can better explain how it is produced. Of prime importance are: *mouth, tongue, teeth, lips, breath,* and *voice.* Also, he should know: *up, down, through, front, back, top, bottom, middle, open,* and *closed.* You may want to add other pertinent words to this list.

Moreover, consider what a parent can do about corrections known to have been introduced by the speech teacher. It is valuable for the parent to follow up closely on these corrections so that they will be incorporated in the child's everyday speech.

When your child has learned to make a certain speech sound in isolation, then you can help him put that sound into his words correctly or say a sound correctly where it has been used incorrectly (for example, in substituting a *t* for a *k*).

A case in point: One day at the John Tracy Clinic, the tutor came out of the tutoring room with Linda in her arms. "Listen," she said joyfully, "Linda can say a *k!*—Linda, say a *k.*" Linda beamed and pronounced a fine *k* sound. This is a very difficult sound for a severely or profoundly hearing-impaired child to master as it is of low volume, thus difficult to hear, and made in back of the mouth where it is not visible. Linda was obviously as pleased with her accomplishment as we were. She could now make a *k* sound with ease and at will.

In a similar situation with your child, this would be the time to step in; show your pleasure and help him retain the ability to make this correct sound knowingly, and persist until you're sure it won't be lost. Then, begin the work of putting this sound in the words of his everyday speech. Just because the sound can be produced correctly in isolation does not mean it will automatically go into the words your child already knows.

Suppose that your child has now learned to make the *k* sound, but some time ago he learned to say the words *car, cooky, candy,* and *comb,* pronouncing them without the *k.* It is now necessary to break his habit of saying *-ar* and replace it with *car.* What is more, if he learns to put the *k* on *-ar,* this doesn't mean that he will necessarily put it on *-oo-ie.*

So, my method was to choose one well-known and frequently encountered *k,* like the word *car.* During the day correct your child and have him put the *k* in the word ten times, continuing each day in the same way with this single word. After a while you will find him putting it in the word himself, at first two times out of ten and then five times out of ten, until it becomes an unconscious habit. Then, go on to another word. Your concentration on one word at a time will set up a system to follow until he is putting the *k* in all the words he already knows. Still, this one-by-one progression does not preclude emphasizing the *k* in new words that he is learning.

There is a helpful signal for the consonant sound *k* that your child can learn quickly and that will serve as a reminder. It is a flick under your chin using your bent index finger and at the same time saying the word with the *k* sound (Figure 4). There are similar, re-

figure 4. Hand signal for k *sound. This reminds pupil/students how to form this sound.*

minding signals for some of the other consonants. Speech teachers often use them and they can be learned from observing speech lessons or in the literature. You can also invent signals. A signal or a correctional method can be meaningful to you and your child, but it does not necessarily have to be used by anyone else. Just be sure to drop it when it is no longer needed—you don't want it to become a crutch.

A word of caution merits repeating here: never correct your child's speech or language until he has finished his thought and you have responded to it.

SPEECH TRAINING AT HOME

It is usually recommended that a hearing-impaired child have speech lessons from a trained speech teacher, but, realistically, this is not always possible. Individual circumstances involving time, transportation, and cost can prohibit parents from arranging for lessons, or a competent teacher may not be available. If you are in such a position, you can train yourself, despite minor limitations, to monitor, develop, and correct the speech sounds in your child's speech. However, without a professional speech teacher taking the initiative, it will definitely mean more responsibility and work on your part, realizing that your goal for your child is the same.

I emphasize that, if you must assume the responsibility for speech training, you should follow the suggestions already given for assisting in early speech development, while simultaneously making more of an effort to improve your basic knowledge of the subject. Travel to a clinic or school where you can observe skilled teachers and watch carefully for teaching methods you can use at home. Study in more detail speech books like those mentioned earlier (by Haycock and the Ewings) and, also, Daniel Ling's (1976) book, *Speech and the Hearing-Impaired Child; Theory and Practice*, which incorporates modern techniques and the principles of the auditory approach to the teaching of speech.

The next step is to spend a few days listening to your child's speech, jotting down two lists: first, a list of the sounds he makes correctly and, then, a list of those that are incorrect or omitted. The list of good speech sounds may surprise you. A child in the process of listening and speechreading will use many, if not all, of the vowels and some consonants, depending on his hearing. The late Dr. Janet Jeffers, professor at California State University, Los Angeles, often said that if a child has enough residual hearing to hear a speech sound, why should we spend our energy trying to teach it by other means? Thus, concentrate on the sounds that you actually need to develop and correct.

Generally, any method that works can be employed to improve your child's articulation of a speech sound, short of manipulation. (An example of manipulation would be to put your finger or a tongue depressor into a child's mouth to control his tongue.) You should try to get the best possible results through means of imitation, description, and suggestion. Your nearness to your child affords the time and continuity in the development of new sounds and correction of old ones, giving you a good chance for success.

The *s* sound is one of the most difficult for the hearing impaired to perfect. In Linda's effort to improve her *s*'s, she used to try so hard she would jut out her lower jaw and emit a smothered *s*. This position brought the tongue forward into the front of the mouth where it bunched and impeded the normal flow of speech, not to mention a satisfactory *s*. She has recently learned to relax and produce a much better *s* by retracting her lower jaw so that the upper and lower teeth are separated slightly and the tip of the tongue is just behind the opening. In fact, relaxing and keeping the lower jaw back with the bulk of the tongue out of the way is the best basic position from which to start speech.

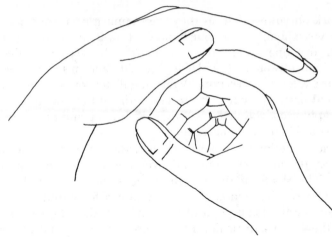

figure 5. Hand shape for k *and* g *sound demonstrates position of lips and tongue when making these sounds.*

A vivid method for describing the position of the tongue for the plosive consonant sounds (*p, t, k,* and *ch* and their counterparts *b, d, g,* and *j*) involves the hands. First, form an inverted cup of the left hand to represent the mouth. Then, using the back of the right hand to represent the tongue, flick it into the cup of the left hand. Varying the tongue shape and contact point, the hands illustrate how the different speech sounds are made. The Ewings' book has photographs of these hand shapes in various speech sound positions, while, here, Figure 5 illustrates the hand shape for the *k* and *g* sounds.

My good friend, Dr. James C. Marsters, a well-known deaf orthodontist, made me a set of plaster of Paris teeth like the molds he makes of his patients' teeth. In the classroom, I used this, with the addition of a thin piece of damp, pliable sponge cut in the shape of a tongue, to illustrate many speech sounds. The upper and lower teeth and the tongue were adjusted by hand to show the shape of the tongue and where the teeth and tongue should be positioned for a certain sound. The children were enthralled with these teaching aids.

Often, a child benefits from a large mirror in which he can see his face and yours at the same time. He will imitate what he sees on your face in the mirror, and being side by side he will see how the speech sound looks on his lips compared with yours. A child will delight in watching you write and draw on the mirror with a wax crayon. Write the letter for the sound, a word incorporating the sound, and a picture to illustrate the word. Motivate him by putting his name in the corner of the mirror and adding a check each time he makes the sound successfully. (A tissue will easily wipe off the crayon marks.)

Work on vowels first, as they are the meat of a word and the basis for voice quality. Use your hand or draw a line to differentiate a short from a long vowel. Vowels are more visible, have more decibel volume than consonants (see Table 2, p. 20), and in many cases do not require a lot of correction. Determine if the vowels sound right to you, and particularly if they are said with natural timing. But, try not to emphasize a vowel yourself by exaggerating and prolonging it because your child will imitate you.

Most of the long vowels are made with a relaxed tongue, with the breath flowing freely out and over the tongue from the diaphragm. The shape of the mouth changes with each of the long vowels. This can be seen easily, can be drawn for lesson purposes, and should be the main point of reference. Of the long vowels, the long *e* is the the most difficult for the severely and profoundly hearing impaired, as the tongue alters its position slightly and is more rigid. As for short vowels, they are all relatively more difficult because they have less duration, visibility, and volume.

One can feel the breath of an unvoiced sound on the hand and the vibration of a voiced sound through the chest and cheek. A blown-up balloon held between the two hands near the mouth will vibrate from a voiced sound, but not from an unvoiced sound. When demonstrating to your child the difference between unvoiced and voiced consonant sounds, the most dramatic aid is a lighted candle. Held in front of the lips when one says the unvoiced *p* sound, the flame will flicker. When one says the *b* sound, which is voiced and spoken in a continuing pattern like a babbled *bababa*, the flame will not move. Similarly, you can show the difference between a *p* and a *b* with a tissue, ball of cotton, or feather.

There are pros and cons to using the sense of touch to teach speech (by putting the child's hand on your face and, then, on his own face to feel the sound). One cannot argue away the value of touch when one knows that development of the remarkably intelligible speech of the deaf-blind is based almost solely on touching the face, often using both hands. On the other hand, it is claimed that excessive use of the hand on the cheek will draw attention to the nose area of the face, creating an inclination towards a nasal voice. I believe the most sensible approach is a middle course, using touch with discretion mostly for children who have severe or profound losses. Those who need considerable, specific speech work to perfect speech sounds will undoubtedly benefit from feeling the sound as well as seeing and hearing it. However, after the sound has been established, the touch method should be used for recall only.

Body contact during lessons is warm and good, and creates an atmosphere of closeness in this tedious and exacting work. A reassuring arm around the waist, a pat of pleasure, a warm smile, and bits of laughter will ease the tension for your small child and make him more responsive.

In working with individual sounds, never stray too far away from the word you are using to demonstrate the sound. If a sound is taken out of a word for corrective purposes, always put it back into the word again. Have your child repeat it, and then put the word into a sentence. You will note that subtle changes occur to speech sounds, both consonants and vowels, when they are spoken together in a sentence. You want your child to learn the smooth blending of one syllable into another that occurs in natural speech. Only constant usage will make this happen for a hearing-impaired child.

THE SPEECH SOUNDS

All hearing-impaired children should learn to recognize the speech sounds by sound (insofar as possible), through speechreading, and on the written page and in diagrams, regardless of their degree of hearing loss. Whether they can say a sound correctly or not, they should learn its proper structure. This knowledge will not only aid them in speech correction, but also give them a thorough background in phonics for sounding out words when reading.

Phonics is usually taught in kindergarten, first, and second grades in preparation for, and in conjunction with, reading. Unfortunately for the hearing impaired, it is taught in regular classes only through the hearing sense, frequently employing records and tapes. If your child is in regular school classes, he will need a more thorough grounding in phonics than he will receive by this method. He needs to supplement his hearing with knowledge of what a speech sound looks like both on the lips and in a drawing of the mouth area, how it feels, and how it relates to other speech sounds. He should learn the speech sounds like the multiplication tables, so that he can use them at will in both speech and reading.

There are also situations in classes solely for the hearing impaired where a child may not have the opportunity to learn this material well. The individual speech sounds may be only partially taught in the class, or started by one teacher and not continued by the next. If thoroughness or continuity is lacking, a parent can give valuable help in this area at home, even if limited to vacation times from a residential school.

Beginning when your child is becoming aware of the letters of the alphabet and his name in print, and is looking at words with interest, develop two notebooks with your child, one of vowels and one of consonants. Generally, a child is able to benefit from these notebooks by late preschool age—however, this may vary as each child's eye assimilation varies with maturity. These notebooks can be expanded as time passes and used to advantage thoughout the elementary school years.

The notebooks should devote a page for each sound, with a logical progression of the sounds in types and relations to each other so that your child can remember them. Refer to published speech books mentioned earlier in this chapter for exact descriptions and diagrams of the speech sounds and verify the positions of these speech sounds by reproducing them in front of a mirror.

The Vowel Notebook

The vowels are best divided into three groups: the long and short vowels and the diphthongs. Begin with long vowels as they are most visible and easiest to teach. To instruct, as well as to please your child, draw a face clearly showing the shape of the mouth for each vowel. Below are the principal vowels only; the more subtle, unaccented vowels can be added later:

Long vowels
    ä as in f*a*ther
    ô as in b*a*ll
    ü as in c*oo*l
    ē as in b*ee*t
Short vowels
    a as in b*a*t
    e as in b*e*t
    i as in b*i*t
    o as in c*o*t
    u as in b*u*tton
    u̇ as in c*oo*k
Diphthongs
    ā as in b*ai*t
    ī as in b*i*te
    ō as in g*o*
    ou as in h*ou*se
    oi as in b*oi*l

It is especially important to build the notebook with your child's help, since you want him to feel it is his property. Using a page for each vowel, write the vowel sound and its diacritical marking at the top of the page in bold manuscript printing. (Again, refer to the speech books to get a feel for handling these distinctive phonetic symbols.) Underline it in red crayon as all vowels are voiced sounds, and, by convention, red is the color code used for a voiced sound. Say the sound, then draw a picture of the front view of a face with the mouth in the shape of the vowel. Next, write down a word or two using this vowel, say them, then put them into a sentence with your child repeating them after you. Use simple words familiar to him, always underlining the vowels in the words in red. Use some two- or three-syllable words for contrast, and vary your consonants. After each word, add a pasted cut out picture or a drawing for illustration. If you can manage it, use the names of family members and friends, along with a photo or drawing, under the proper vowels; it will pique his interest. Whenever possible, paste in a real object, such as a button, feather, penny, flower, or piece of yarn or hair.

Don't be in a hurry—take at least a week for each speech sound, adding words slowly and reviewing often. Leave room for more words to be added later. It's always great if your child can contribute a word himself. Your role in this exercise is not primarily to correct speech, but to teach him to recognize and focus on the sounds and know how they are made, regardless of his ability to reproduce them.

The Consonant Notebook

The majority of consonants can be paired. Teach the pairs first in order to contrast them with each other. Put the pairs on facing pages in your consonant book; develop a pair at a time, contrasting as you go along. For example, *p* and *b* are a pair of sounds that are made alike but that are different in that the *p* is not voiced (and is called a breath sound), whereas the *b* is a voiced sound. Some of the most frequent speech mistakes of hearing-impaired children are made by not giving the proper voiced or unvoiced quality to a consonant. Hearing-impaired children should learn these differences, and be able to distinguish between voiced and unvoiced speech sounds.

Begin your list of these pairs with the consonant sounds that are the most visible, made in the front of the mouth, and progress to the sounds made in the back of the mouth. The consonant sounds are divided further into categories according to their other characteristics. The two most important categories for your small child are those sounds called "plosives" (they explode from the mouth) and those called "continuants" (they are actually continued sounds).

The paired *plosive* sounds, according to where they are made in the mouth, are:

unvoiced	voiced
p	b
t	d
k	g

The *p* and *b* are made by the momentary pressing of the lips together; the *t* and *d* are made a little further back by the flick of the tongue on the roof of the mouth just behind the upper teeth; and the *k* and *g* are made by the middle of the tongue rising and touching the central part of the roof of the mouth.

Write a *p* at the top of the first page of the notebook and underline it with a blue crayon (the color code for an unvoiced sound). The *b* should be opposite the *p* and underlined in red for voice. A drawing of the mouth with the proper placement of the tongue and teeth can be made to illustrate a speech sound. Draw a side view of a face with the lips, teeth, mouth, and tongue exposed, showing the overall position from which the sound emanates. (The speech book written by the Ewings will help you with these diagrams.) Then, begin to develop some familiar words with this speech sound, first choosing those with the sound starting the word. Later, you can add words with different vowels, and some words with two or three syllables. Underline the sound in the word with the proper color crayon (voiced or unvoiced). At this stage, avoid consonant blends, such as *pl*, *st*, and *br*. Illustrate the word with a picture, cutout, or real object. Teach your child to identify the blue for the unvoiced sounds and red for the voiced, and to tell the difference by feeling the contrast on the hand, or with a feather or tissue.

The *continuant* consonants, according to where they are made in the mouth are:

unvoiced	voiced
wh	w
f	v
th	TH
s	z
sh	zh

Show your child that these sounds are sustained in comparison to the plosive sounds by drawing your hands apart to show extension.

There is one more pair, the plosive *ch-j*, that is really made up of two consonants. These two sounds are more easily understood by children if they know that the *ch* is really a fast combination of *t* and *sh*, or *tsh*, and that the *j* is really a *dzh*. A child soon learns that the sound *ch* begins from the position of a *t* sound and quickly blends into a sharp explosion with *sh*.

There are a few sounds that are not paired: the *h* which is just a breath, hardly a sound, and *l*, *r*, and *y*, which are voiced. An *x*, like the *ch-j*, is a combination of *ks*, and *q* of *kwh*, both being unvoiced.

The last sounds to be added to the notebook are the nasal sounds, *m*, *n*, and *ng* (color-coded by the color brown). They are voiced sounds and can be felt on the upper cheek bones, where the sound vibrates because it is sent through the nose instead of the mouth.

TIMING AND RHYTHM

Many years ago, I heard a recording of an example of English spoken off-beat from its normal rhythmic pattern. The voice rambled on, completely incomprehensible, even though it was using the King's English with proper enunciation of the speech sounds. Only the rhythm of normal speech had been altered. This experience brought home to me, as nothing else could, the prominent role rhythm plays in speech and its comprehension. How much, then, of the speech of the hearing-impaired that seems so difficult for us to understand is due to improper speech timing and rhythm? Dr. Ciwa Griffiths of HEAR Foundation, estimates that 80 percent of the intelligibility of speech lies in its rate and rhythm.

Studies of visible speech patterns show the divergence in timing and rhythm patterns between the speech of the hearing impaired and normal speech. They show abnormally long, drawn-out vowels, and breath pauses in unnatural places. Hence, it is quite possible to teach a hearing-impaired child how to produce his speech sounds exactly, and still be unable to understand him altogether because his speech timing and rhythm are faulty.

Timing and rhythm are the areas in which residual hearing play the greatest part. Any gain in these areas is the argument to end all arguments for wearing a hearing aid, no matter how very slight the residual hearing may be. Through amplified sound, the hearing impaired have the chance to pick up a sense of the timing and rhythm of speech even though the speech they hear is otherwise not understandable.

Timing

Speech, if it is to sound natural, and therefore be readily understood by others, must be spoken in a normal time pattern. Timing should be practiced by hearing-impaired children early before the correction of individual sounds can possibly distort it. The opportunity to develop conversation at home and to hear normal speech constantly are the keys to developing natural timing. When your child is small, babble with him as rapidly as we talk normally, helping him to learn to speed up his tongue and mouth movements.

Frequently, a small hearing-impaired child does not have, for some time, enough language to put together more than a few words spontaneously. You can encourage your child to imitate sentence timing before he is expressing sentences by having him repeat a full sentence exactly as he hears and speechreads it, regardless of how imperfectly he pronounces the individual sounds. To work for sentence timing, play a game, use an experience, or engage in a conversation where he will be expected to repeat a full sentence as it is presented to him. Accept anything he says that approximates what you said if it's in a normal time span. Such an exercise develops not only your child's breathing and memory habits, but also his sense of timing and rhythm. Good breath control, with pauses for taking a breath in normal places in a sentence, is an essential part of timing.

On television, some time ago, a lesson in speech timing was demonstrated by a teacher and his small class of hearing-impaired six year olds. The teacher had a large box of dress-up clothes and from it he would take out a costume piece, hold it up, and say, "Who wants to wear this skirt?" When a hand went up, he would help the child with an answer ("I want to wear that skirt") and have the child repeat it after him. After everyone had an item, the teacher prolonged the lesson by asking each child if he wanted to trade what he had for something else. Each transaction included a repeat of a full sentence, with no attempt to correct the speech of the child. The resultant conversations between teacher and pupils helped the children sense the rate and duration of good speech.

I witnessed another instance of teaching speech timing in a class of preschoolers during an "experience" lesson where they were making candied apples. This example could well take place with your child at home. The teacher said, "Johnny, go wash your apple," and then helped Johnny answer, "Okay, I'm going to wash my apple." There are numerous rich, everyday experiences at home ideally suited to practicing sentence timing, which involve a series of steps, like setting the table, cooking, dressing, picking up toys, and making beds. Try to use as many of these opportunities as you can to develop good sentence timing for your child. But expect him to need a lot of help at first.

Rhythm

Tapping and dancing to music and rhymes will help your child gain a sense of rhythm. Using a drum beat, piano, organ, or any other instrument he can hear, let him copy various rhythm patterns that you play. Carry this over to speech by babbling together in a rhythmic pattern. Have him listen to and learn nursery rhymes and simple lyrics as well as listen to the rhythm of familiar speech phrases.

Some years ago, I watched a demonstration of five young adults being tutored by the late Mrs. Lucelia Moore at the University of Southern California. They all clasped hands in a chorus line and stepped out in rhythm as they recited together the nursery rhyme, "Baa, baa, black sheep, have you any wool? Yes, sir; yes, sir, three bags full." It seemed incongruous to see grown adults reciting a nursery rhyme, but they were serious and enthusiastic about performing the exercise in order to improve their speech rhythm. In fact, one pretty young woman had never used her voice before Mrs. Moore started tutoring her. The physical act of stepping to the rhythm and trying to stay together helped them keep their speech close to the normal rate and rhythm of the rhyme. Afterwards, Mrs. Moore would relate this exercise to everyday speech patterns.

To aid in explaining to your child the proper rhythm of a specific word or sentence, you can devise written rhythm signs, in a sentence scanning system, that show the metrical structure of a sentence. The method I used is a combination of a variety of scanning methods.

Even before a child can read, when he is in the reading-readiness stage, sentences can be presented to him in writing (complemented by relevant illustrations), especially when you want to motivate him to express an idea of his own, such as: "I have on a new shirt."

Write the sentence slowly and let him absorb it gradually; this is the introduction to reading. Now, underneath the sentence write your rhythm pattern. Following your signs, say the sentence and have him repeat:

I have on a new shirt.

Adjust your system for the moment's need. If your child is in the just-learning-two-syllables stage, it will help to see both syllables:

cooky

If he is into sentences, you can help the words flow better by putting phrases together:

I have on a new shirt.

Later when breathing, spacing, or timing is your concern, you can scan several sentences:

I have on a new shirt. / It has blue and red stripes.

Be sure your child does not learn to speak the words in a sentence in a pronounced one-by-one manner; often words flow into each other and should not be isolated in speech. Note above that "have on" is scanned in such a way as to suggest one word. There are many others that are actually spoken like one word. One doesn't say, "I have a ball,"

because it sounds unnatural. One says, "I have a ball." Writing it out and scanning it for rhythm can help your child see and hear how it should sound in everyday speech. The goal is for conversational speech rather than speech learned by rote. Too often a hearing-impaired child's speech sounds like it would in a reading lesson:

I have a new airplane. It is not a jet.

Another problem for the hearing impaired is that contractions like *isn't* and *it's* are not practiced enough for speech to sound conversational. The following sentences might be scanned like this for better rhythm:

I have a new airplane.

It isn't a jet. It has a propeller.

Let's go for a ride.

When it is necessary to take a long word apart to get a better articulation of one syllable, or to show the make-up of it more closely, such as:

tel e phone

put it back together again afterward and repeat it several times emphasizing the whole:

telephone

If attention is paid to developing a natural flow of conversation, the rhythm of speech should fall into place. It isn't always necessary to write the word or sentence; scan it in the air with your hand as you say it or sketch the scan itself on the blackboard. Whatever method you devise to help your child with rhythm at home will make his speech more intelligible and complement other speech instruction outside the home.

ACCENT AND INFLECTION

Accent, or emphasis, and inflection are the qualities that give speech its variety and color. They are prevalent in normal speech. For instance, an inflection like a rise in the voice at the end of a sentence indicates a question and a drop in the voice indicates the end of a sentence. And, accents often change the meaning of a sentence and give a word or set of words a further subtle connotation. Note how the change of accent on one of the words can change the meaning of this simple sentence:

> How do you DO that?
> How DO you do that?
> How do YOU do that?

Many times accents and inflections are interactive, as shown by the natural inflection of voice that frequently accompanies an accent, for example, birth´day.

Hearing-impaired children will develop speech in a flat monotone, bereft of color, if they are not encouraged to listen and incorporate into their own voice the accents and inflections that they hear. Like timing and rhythm, much depends on how much use a hearing-impaired child makes of his residual hearing. Even with a small amount of residual hearing, a child can learn to listen for and imitate the differences in accent and inflection in normal speech.

What can you do at home to develop accent and inflection in your child's voice?

Babble

When your child is small, babble with him in a rhythmic pattern with stress (baBAbabaBA). Also babble with him up and down the scale to develop voice inflection, and encourage him to imitate you.

By Example

Listen to your own voice. Be sure it has lots of accent and inflection when you talk.

Highs and Lows

Bring your child's attention to the inflections he hears. Begin with high and low sounds. With the aid of two instruments of high and low pitch, such as a drum and a bell, play a listening game of identification until he can tell the difference between the high and low sounds from his hearing alone. Use a piano or organ if available. Indicate high and low with your hand. Play the game with him by taking a turn yourself occasionally. Utilize music, singing, and any other opportunity for him to listen and become aware of variations in pitch.

The Scale

In Helen Heckman's book, *My Life Transformed*, which was written before the advent of the hearing aid, her mother taught her the scale on the stairs—one stair up for each note. With time and considerable effort, she learned to make her voice go up and down a complete octave. Practicing a shorter version of this will give your child greater facility in voice inflection. Each stair is a physical thrust upwards, giving a child the feeling he needs for raising his voice like his body.

Scanning

Show in writing with scanning the accents and inflections of voice in speech. Start with your child's name and write it like this:

Dan
   ny.

Write the names of other family members and friends. Use your hand to further demonstrate up and down voice sounds.

Write and scan words and phrases like:

Scan sentences to show the rise and drop for a sentence ending:

How are you?
I'm fine.

Write a short sentence showing up and down inflections:

I want a coo ky.

In a well-known lyric the scanning could look like this:

Baa, baa, black sheep,

Have you any w o o l?

Yes, yes, sir, sir,

Three bags full.

In showing accent and inflection, use your own ideas of how they should be marked—they change meanings and vary between households, ethnic groups, and areas.

Bring your child's attention often to accent and inflection. The more your child is encouraged to listen and carry on conversations with normally hearing people the more he will use normal-sounding accents and inflections in his own speech.

chapter 9

communication

With the tools of hearing, speechreading, and speech, plus the language of signs and fingerspelling if used, our hearing-impaired child learns to communicate. Each child will use these tools in different proportions, according to his training and needs, to communicate through conversation.

Conversation with everyone is your ultimate goal for your child, and conversation as it is used within your family is the first stepping stone. In this respect, parents are in a unique position because they have the opportunity to do what a teacher can't do in a school day; they can bring to their hearing-impaired child the natural language of their daily life at home. The Reverend Anthony van Uden, internationally known educator and author from the Netherlands, calls this the development of an oral mother tongue (van Uden, 1968).

Conversation, as we know it, is oral communication between two or more people. As you help your child to build his vocabulary and language, the conversation between the two of you should grow in diversity and length. If he is not encouraged to use the vocabulary he understands to converse with you—answering questions and volunteering ideas—one day you will find that you are conducting a monologue. Once a child begins to use the words he knows spontaneously, expect him to do so; otherwise, he'll let you do all the talking. He should be able to carry on a one-on-one conversation consisting of a few words at first, gradually using sentences that slowly grow longer.

Since questions are a very important part of conversation, pose questions over and over to your child so that he becomes accustomed to them. He should be expected to answer a question he understands with at least an audible "yes" or "no." As a teacher, on Monday morning I could tell quickly if there had been any attempts to encourage conversation at home over the weekend. All too frequently, I couldn't even get a "yes" or "no" answer to: "Are you going to buy your lunch today?" If parents and others at home are not expecting the hearing-impaired child to answer questions and express ideas, the child will not bother to do so. Lacking motivation at home, school will be doubly hard for him with his handicap. When he learns to reply to others and express his ideas, he will soon discover the social pleasures of conversation, and, later on, reading and writing will come more easily.

To carry on a conversation, there are two language skills that hearing-impaired children need to learn. One is how to ask and answer questions and the other is the art of keeping a conversation going with standard fill-in phrases that normally hearing people learn subconsciously. With respect to this second skill, we automatically fill in conversational pauses with small talk: "You don't say! Isn't that interesting. Is that right? Wonderful! How nice." Silence between expressed thoughts, especially over the telephone where you have only sound to depend on, is so awkward that it frequently ends a conversation before it gets started. Teach your hearing-impaired child to practice often the art of keeping a conversation going.

Your communication goal, then, is that your hearing-impaired child understand what is being said to him and around him and that he have the ability and the desire to express himself in conversation. You have a singular opportunity to help your child develop these skills. Conversation is a basis for learning, a basis for sociability, and becoming skillful in it will enhance his chances for a happy, well-adjusted adult life. The amount of influence you can exert towards this particular goal at home should never be underestimated.

BUILDING VOCABULARY

In the early years, it is crucial that you have a vocabulary-building plan for your hearing-impaired child. Without a plan, your work may take a shotgun approach, with dozens of shots going every which way but only a few hitting the mark.

I remember a mother at the John Tracy Clinic who conscientiously worked with her son, and he seemed to be progressing. He was intelligent and had an endearing personality that made him a favorite. However, the teachers came to realize after working with him for some time that even though he seemed to understand what was said to him, when pinned down, he didn't know specific words. His attractiveness had, at first, camouflaged his lack of understanding. Actually, with more intensive testing, it was obvious that he knew very few words. His mother hadn't kept a vocabulary list and was teaching him everyday phrases without emphasizing specific words.

True, these everyday phrases are important, but they are not enough because a child should also be building vocabulary, word upon word upon word. The best way to remain alert and move ahead with your child's vocabulary is to keep a current list of the words you are teaching him. Besides, keep a running list of the words he knows until the words are coming so fast that your list of mastered words becomes unwieldy. When your list is beyond counting, all will seem worthwhile.

Your hearing-impaired child's first words will come very slowly, which entails repeating one word thousands of times (accompanied by the various grades of discouragement) to get the ball rolling. A hearing-impaired child may learn vocabulary: through speechreading; partly through hearing and partly through speechreading; entirely through aided hearing; or through the language of signs. Moreover, situations may evolve in time where an individual uses a combination of these means.

When your child begins building a vocabulary later than a normally hearing child would, his advancement depends on a definite building process, coupling your support and encouragement with detailed planning, to the point where his vocabulary is large enough to compete with normally hearing children. I do not say equal to the vocabulary of hearing children, because I don't think this is necessary for your child to be successful in school, but the vocabulary should not be so far behind as to handicap his comprehension of the speech around him.

It is difficult, if not impossible, to judge at home how extensive a child's vocabulary should be upon entering kindergarten. With my daughter, Leslie, it was especially challenging to make the correct decision as to placement in school. She was hard of hearing, but was not fitted with a hearing aid until she was two years old (principally due to recommended medical care). Therefore, she was late in beginning to build a vocabulary and extra effort was needed on everybody's part to keep her vocabulary climbing before age five. Despite all our efforts, in comparing her vocabulary with that of my older hearing children upon entering kindergarten, I felt it was still below average. Since there were no hard-of-hearing classes in our public schools and she was too advanced for the "deaf" classes, I had to take the responsibility of entering her in a regular kindergarten. How many mothers have in the past been, and are still today, obliged to make this same decision with only a minimum of guidance?

Wanting to find a preschool oral vocabulary list that would guide me in what I should expect Leslie to know by kindergarten, I asked Miss Marguerite Stoner, supervising teacher of the hearing impaired at John Tracy Clinic, if she had such a list. Her answer was revealing: in this age of television, it is not practicable to compile a representative vocabulary list. Today, the average child's vocabulary by school age has mushroomed from exposure to the television medium, and it's impossible to make a simple, useful list. Furthermore, the differences in known words vary from child to child to the point where a general list would not fit any one child. Upon reflection, I recalled with amusement that Leslie called a hot dog an "Oscar Mayer" for many months.

As it turned out, Leslie's vocabulary was indeed behind the other children that first year of school, but it was adequate, and continued to expand with exposure to the teacher and to other children. Besides vocabulary, her measure of success that year depended equally on other positive factors such as her readiness, personality, social behavior, and attention span.

THE VOCABULARY LIST

Begin with one word, and choose that word with care. Write it down, say it to yourself in front of a mirror, and test it with the following questions, the last two being most important:

1. Is it visible?
2. Has it one or two syllables?
3. Does its major vowel and major consonant have good volume and low frequency?
4. Does it resemble any other word on the lips?
5. Is it a word in which your child is interested?
6. Is it a word that can be used many times each day in a natural way?

This word will be your child's first vocabulary word. You will use it in sentences over and over (employing methods described by such sources as the John Tracy Clinic Correspondence Course or those suggested by your child's teacher) to bring him to the realization that your voice, mouth, and face are saying something meaningful. Generally, the first word is a noun, but it need not be. The action verbs, such as *jump, walk, run,* and *bounce,* are possible. A first word more often may be one of these: *boy, shoe, car, baby,* or *airplane.*

The word you choose should be continually kept in mind, and you should surround yourself with variations of it in objects and pictures. Contrive many ways to use it until you are fully satisfied that your child responds to the word as relating to a particular object or action. Then, at last, the word can be entered on your vocabulary list as "No. 1."

Don't be discouraged at the length of time it takes to get that first word listed. Much depends on the readiness of your child to learn, as well as other personality factors. The second word will be slow to learn also, and the third and fourth; but after a while each additional word will be assimilated somewhat faster, and you and your child will find life much smoother and exciting with this first bit of communication. As the list grows longer, you can perhaps work on two or three words at any one time rather than one. Don't hesitate to drop an ill-chosen word and substitute another; you can come back to it later when your child is ready.

Build the vocabulary list word by word, forming an upside-down pyramid, until the words come too fast to write down. The list should be based on the communication needs of your child, your own, and those of your family, always working towards two-way conversation. The words you choose for your child will differ from those another child may learn, just as families vary in their communication needs and in the particular pattern of conversation used among themselves.

The vast majority of first words generally are nouns; everything bears a name, including people, so nouns and proper nouns are most common. But mix into your list other parts of speech because sentences must have verbs (*walk, run, stop, go*) and descriptive words (*hot, cold, big, little*). Also, introduce early descriptive words for feelings (*happy, sad, crying, mad, laughing*) to avert your child's frustration from being unable to understand and express these feelings. It will help to draw little faces showing these moods, and when he has learned them his emotional problems can be relieved, having an outlet in language.

Keeping a vocabulary list for your child will help you see where you are, how far you have come, and where you want to go. Remember that if a newly learned word is not repeated again and again and integrated into everyday use, it eventually will have to be relearned. Repeatedly going back over your child's vocabulary will help him retain the words he has learned.

One excellent way to enhance the recall of learned vocabulary is to make a scrapbook. Put your list on the front page and on successive pages mount or draw pictures of each word for you and your child to review frequently. Write the word under the picture in lowercase, manuscript-style printing (the style used in early primary grades before script). It is never too early to expose your child to the written word. Your goal is to help him add to his "mind pictures" the words that correspond to those pictures, orally at first, and later through writing. Then, he will be thinking verbally, forming his thoughts into words that he must use to speak and write creatively.

We have been discussing building a vocabulary of specific words. This should not suggest that with your usual, everyday talk you should not try to teach him common phrases. Learning directional phrases and question forms (*wash your hands, come to dinner, where are your shoes?*) should continue naturally as well as other language that fits into a given situation.

Your vocabulary list is as much for you as for your child. It gives you concrete, visible proof of your child's progress, and keeps you both motivated.

EXPANDING VOCABULARY

There comes a time when your upside-down pyramid has grown to unbelievable proportions compared to the void with which you began. Now your child knows not a few, but hundreds of words. They are essentially made up of nouns, verbs, and descriptive words, and, what is more, he is beginning to use many of them spontaneously. In fact, you can communicate with each other using this vocabulary in nearly all aspects of family life.

When, with your own brand of Basic English, you have reached the point where you don't need to teach him more vocabulary to communicate adequately at home, you may feel satisfied remaining on this plateau. This is dangerous for your child's future! At this time take stock and consider your goals. It is all too easy to become complacent. Therefore, make every effort to continue climbing beyond this plateau by expanding your child's vocabulary in all directions during the years before formal schooling begins.

Concerning vocabulary building, some years ago a kindergarten teacher of the hearing impaired aired her lament to parents. She wrote that she was spending many school hours teaching vocabulary that parents could have taught at home. She felt these valuable hours would have been better spent teaching the complicated and difficult language principles that baffle hearing-impaired children.

So, once adequate home vocabulary and communication have been achieved, it is time to progress to planned vocabulary expansion. Begin by using different words that have the same meaning, as well as other words with similar meanings but slight variations in usage. To teach your child the concept of time, using past and future tenses, make a calendar for him and refer to it daily. As he progresses, work on words by categories and fill in many of the words he doesn't yet know that are akin to words he already knows.

Simple examples of words with the same meaning are *big* and *large* and *little* and *small*. If you have been in the habit of using *big* and *little* exclusively, now start using *large* and *small* part of the time. They will be important later when the first arithmetic workbook says, "Color the large triangle blue." Teach the similarity of other sets of words: *mother* and *mama, father* and *daddy, automobile* and *car,* and *home* and *house,* to mention a few.

The English language is laced with descriptive words that are related in meaning but slightly different in usage. They add color to our language, but are difficult for hearing-impaired children to learn to use in their proper context. For instance, the word *pretty* can be expanded to *beautiful* and *handsome,* but unless a child frequently hears them used properly in a sentence, you are likely to see a "handsome girl" or a "pretty boy" appear later in his writing.

Time is an abstract concept that is learned slowly by a hearing-impaired child through daily observation. To make time meaningful and to teach related words, make a homemade calendar for your child each month, with his help. On white shelf paper, draw squares ample enough to hold both the date in large numerals and a small drawing. Now, you have the basis for his learning *yesterday, today, tomorrow,* days of the week, numbers, names of months, and, most important of all for you, a sense of when he will do something like visiting Grandmother or going to school. Draw pictures or paste photos or cutouts in the squares to represent important family events and holidays. The problem of explaining a family event to him in a certain time frame will become easier. At this preschool age, birthdays and holidays offer new vocabulary and language when interest in such events is highest.

In addition, the calendar gives you an ideal opportunity to use the past and future tenses in natural situations. On a large pad of paper, write a short sentence about what happened or is going to happen and illustrate it with a simple drawing. These pages can be put into a folder in the form of a journal, to be read and reread.

Another way to check and keep expanding your child's vocabulary is by categories. For instance, consider parts of the head; surely he knows the words *eyes, ears, nose, mouth, teeth,* and *hair.* Now, see if he also knows *cheeks, jaw, eyebrows, eyelashes,* and *forehead.* Perhaps he knows the words for what a little boy wears but not what a little girl wears. If your child is in a preschool class the teacher may be teaching categories of words and you can follow that pattern at home; if not, make up your own categories. Some that quickly come to mind are: body, clothes, toys, vehicles (*cars, trucks, boats, trains, airplanes*), colors, numbers, table settings, food, houses, furniture, family, and animals. Other categories to work on are: words for craft materials (*paper, paint, glue, scissors*), what things are made of, the five senses, shapes, comparative sizes (*larger than, smallest, heavier*), and prepositions (*in, on, under, behind, through*).

Many of the categories mentioned above fit well into the seasons and holidays, and a wealth of other words can be developed using the calendar year as a guide.

In January, in the northern climes, weather is predominant. It is a natural opportunity to teach the words connected with snow, ice, wind, rain, winter play, and warm clothes.

February is the month for Valentine's Day. Here is a golden opportunity to teach the abstract word *love;* play it up, with a heart and the color *red.* Talk about the mailman, mailbox, stamps, envelopes, and make valentines. Conversation of all kinds come from the valentines themselves—their illustrations are ideal for using action verbs and descriptive words.

Easter emphasizes rabbits, chickens, ducks, and eggs, and includes such verbs as *hunt* and *find.* Basic colors can be repeated again and again while coloring Easter eggs, and *gray* and *pink* can be added to the color chart. Spring brings talk of farm products, machinery, buildings, and animals. This leads into zoo animals, and from there to small creatures that inhabit the forest, including squirrels, frogs, fish, birds, and insects. Gather up a pollywog in a glass bowl and let it grow into a tiny frog; put a caterpillar in a jar and wait for it to spin its cocoon.

Renew the old May Day custom of making a basket of flowers. Hang it on a neighbor's doorknob, ring the bell, and run and hide. In the process you will have talked about flowers, hiding, and made a new friend for your child. Watch the way a plant grows from a seed, by putting a bean in a small pot of soil. Also, a sweet potato with one end immersed in a glass of water will sprout roots and leaves. Show your child different kinds of plants around your neighborhood and in the park.

When summer is emerging, words for the outdoors are boundless. Summer is that special time when the park, beach, lake, and mountains are accessible, calling up their own distinct words, including words for traveling. The Fourth of July is for the flag, parades, musical instruments, and fireworks.

October brings Halloween, next to Christmas the most exciting of all events for children, with wonderful new words such as *witch, pumpkin, skeleton,* and *ghost.* This is also an excellent opportunity to go over the words for the body, clothes, and costumes.

November can be spent on food of all kinds, leading up to Thanksgiving. Don't forget associated verbs again: *eat, drink, set* the table, please *pass* the jam, and *thank* you.

Christmas, of course, is the time to learn the word *toys* and review them as a category. Before our children could read they enjoyed cutting out pictures of toys from a catalog and pasting them into their very own book entitled, "What I want for Christmas." The poem, " 'Twas The Night Before Christmas," by Clement Clark Moore, can be dissected into its delightful details, from the exact color and make of Santa's clothes to the presents under the Christmas tree and the reindeer on the roof.

Being mindful of the calendar as you work with your child on categories and related words will greatly expand his vocabulary. Be sure to catch the moments offered around holidays and special events when your child's interest peaks.

LANGUAGE

Language can be described as the process of expressing words in a meaningful combination, or as Edward J. Linehan, who has studied the language of dolphins, explains, "Broadly speaking, language implies an ability to convey thoughts by using arbitrary symbols—words—in proper syntax" (Linehan, 1979).

Assuming that your child knows many words and is using some of them independently, it is now time to take into account that sentences are made up of subjects and verbs, as well as modifying and descriptive words, all in their proper sequence. Suddenly, you may feel that the prospect of your hearing-impaired child learning this vastly complicated structure is overwhelming; it is amazing, after all, that normally hearing children learn it at such an early age. But, your hearing-impaired child can also learn to use proper language structure (for example, adjectives preceding nouns), albeit not quite so quickly. Although reading will supplement his oral language, he will need in-depth lessons in grammar from a teacher and continual reinforcement from you.

If you are receiving many one-word expressions from a large vocabulary of words your child understands, his next step will be two-word expressions—a noun with a descriptive word (*big* ball) or a verb (Michael *mad*). Expand his vocabulary to include the words that will enable him to form a proper sentence. Consider what your child may mean when he runs to you with a book in his hand and says loud and clear, "Book!" Does he mean: read me a story, look at the book I found, or see this picture? What words does he need in order to say what he means?

It is essential to encourage his efforts to talk. If his speech is poor, it will often take a concerted effort on your part to understand what he says. Try in every way you can devise to make out his imperfect speech, as his pleasure at being understood will keep him talking. Drop whatever you are doing (I have pulled the car safely to the side of the road on more than one occasion) and try to decipher what he said; have him draw or act out his thoughts if necessary, until his idea is clear to you.

As soon as you begin to receive spontaneous, expressive speech from your child in a one-word or two-word pattern, return his expressive attempt immediately with the correct language structure he should have used and have him repeat it. Your repetition of the right structure will, in time, expand and correct his language. If you do not detain him long enough to have him repeat his phrase correctly, because in your judgment it was not a proper moment to do so, he will still absorb your language pattern, to some extent, and gradually incorporate it into his conversation.

In your speech, use contractions and everyday language as you do at home. For example, you generally say informally, "Who's at the door?" "Daddy's home!" "Let's go for a ride." You want your child to talk in the same way. The more he is exposed to natural oral language, the more normal his speech will sound in usage, rhythm, timing, and inflection. Later, his schooling will add the formal language forms of reading and writing to your conversational oral base.

When you have your youngster's attention in a relaxed moment, you can further expand his awareness of the small words he probably does not hear and see by writing and scanning next to a picture, even if he isn't reading yet. You are not asking him to "read" at this stage, but to observe the writing in connection with the picture and follow the scanning rhythm, which he can generally hear when aided. For instance, if he comes to you pointing out the window at Daddy driving a truck, he might first say, "Daddy truck," while you respond, "Yes, Daddy drives a truck." When he is able to add the word *drive,* he will probably put the sentence together as, "Daddy drive truck." The soft, high tone of the final *s* on *drives,* may be lost to his hearing and speechreading, along with the unaccented sound of the article *a.* Here, it will be helpful to draw a picture of Daddy driving the truck, writing underneath the correct sentence and scanning it to enable him to see the *s* sound and the word *a*. The picture can be pinned on the wall or put in a scrapbook where it can be referred to again. This type of correction will slowly build good oral language.

If your child doesn't receive consistent help with his oral language, he is very likely to continue to use the same incorrect patterns. And, as an adult, such usage will appear unusual and quite noticeable to normally hearing people. Children who neither hear a complete language pattern nor see a complete pattern through speechreading can, and do, correct their oral language in time through constant usage, reading, grammar lessons, and reinforcement at home.

For children in a total communication program I might mention that those who use the language of signs will learn straight English language more thoroughly if they are taught by the Signing Exact English, or SEE, signs, which employ a sign for every word and verb tense in proper sequence. Also, their parents should use these signs in preference to the American Sign Language, or Ameslan, signs during the child's formative years. Nevertheless, speech that is spoken simultaneously with the SEE signs will suffer in rate and rhythm, because it takes longer to sign a sentence than it does to say it orally.

CONVERSATION

It has often been noted that hearing-impaired adults, at their own social gatherings and no matter what language skills and habits they have at their command, love to talk. Conversation flows thick and fast, and their get-togethers last far into the night; they seem reluctant to break up a party. But, when with normally hearing adults, they frequently appear shy, unsure of themselves, and less talkative. It is self-evident that talking with other hearing impaired is less difficult and they are more relaxed than when talking with hearing people. Much of this conversational strain between hearing-impaired and hearing people can be alleviated if a child is a part of a constant, free flow of conversation at home during his growing years.

From the earliest communication between you and your child, ply him with questions. The structure of a sentence involving a question is very different from a positive statement. It takes a great deal of repetition before your hearing-impaired child understands questions well enough to give an independent answer, and poses questions himself. Regrettably, the importance of the area of questions and answers was not brought to my attention when my hearing-impaired children were small. I want to stress its importance, as you and your child begin talking together.

The average American takes his first trip to Europe with no foreign language background other than high-school French or Spanish. Basically, he manages in the foreign countries he visits by learning words for *thank you, please,* and *good morning,* and soon discovers that he can do quite well by adding the question marks of conversation, *who, what, how, where, when,* and *why.* Realizing one can manage in a foreign country with *where* and *when* in the railroad station, *who* and *what* in the museum, *how much* and *how many* in the shops and restaurants, how important these words must be to the vocabulary of our hearing-impaired children!

In order to carry on a conversation, these question forms are imperative. Present them early, and use them at every opportunity. Ask questions that are pertinent to the occasion—dressing time is a wonderful time for questions, like "*Where* are your shoes?" and "*What* color bow goes with your dress?" and while in the kitchen ask, "*How many* cookies do you want?" In the beginning, you may stand there expecting an answer for some time; it helps to enlist a third party to prompt your child until he learns how to answer.

Use all six of the question forms, but sometimes in a game emphasize only one at a time. For example, devise a game for *what* with a book of pictures, asking, "*What* is the man doing?" A photograph album brings up *who,* and a game of hide-and-seek uses *where.*

Give your child as many opportunities as possible to make choices between two or more alternatives. At the shoe store, you decide he should have tennis shoes, but let him choose the color: "Do you want red or blue tennis shoes?" and "What color socks do you want?" Circumstances where he can choose for himself, like what to wear, what to play with, and what book to borrow from the library, are excellent times to initiate his independence.

He may not be able to ask a proper question for a while, but as he sees and hears the question forms many times, he will, as a normally hearing child does, learn them from repetition. Encourage him to ask questions himself as well as answer them, and see how long you can keep a conversation going.

Remember that class discussions are a form of conversation, and you are now preparing your child to participate actively, not passively, in them later on in school.

As mentioned earlier in this chapter, there is another area of conversation that is difficult for hearing-impaired children to develop and use effectively. This is the ability to keep conversation open and moving along with the small fill-in phrases that we use automatically to keep people aware of our interest. It is most noticeable on the telephone where nothing holds two people together at the opposite ends of the line except speech. Telephone conversation is glued together with small talk: "Okay! How neat! That's great! How come? Yes, I understand." So, when hearing-impaired children meet a friend

walking home from school or at the store, they have this same difficulty supplying small talk; they get along fine for a few sentences, but
then in many instances the conversation dies. Give your child plenty
of practice keeping a conversation moving so that he will know how
to use these phrases when he sorely needs them in a social situation.
This skill will help him to meet and keep friends, and, eventually, to
obtain a good job.

COMMANDS AND DIRECTIONS

Another area of language building that should be developed early is
commands and directions. For his own safety, your child should respond promptly to commands; and for his future success in school
and in business, he should learn to understand and respond accurately
to directions.

When your child is small, you should be in control of the situation
at all times for his safety. He needs limits and discipline to enforce
them; certain rules and regulations have to be followed strictly, and
in such cases he must respond to his parents' and teachers' commands.
He should know when you say, "Do not cross the street," that he
should not do so; when you say, "Stop, wait!" he should react immediately. If not, his safety will be at risk, and he will try the soul of
his teachers and everyone else. Occasional compromises are permis-
sible on less stringent rules so that life is not a continual flood of
commands.

It will be apparent, upon entering school for the first time, that
a child who does what he is told not to do as soon as one's back is
turned has not had consistent training at home. Habits such as this
are common with hearing-impaired children indulged by frustrated
parents who do not understand that their hearing-impaired child can
learn to respond to commands as well as any other child. I would
bring to your attention that the hearing-impaired child who does not
follow rules is found so frequently on the integrated school playground that it reflects on all hearing-impaired children. Why should
Johnny swing after the bell rings? He may not hear the bell, but he
certainly can see all the other children stop. Too often, he goes on
swinging just long enough to exasperate the teacher in charge. This
damages the image of the hearing-impaired child; it sets him further
apart from the normally hearing children, and it can be avoided with
proper early discipline.

Directions are a type of command. Think how often in his future
a child will be called upon to carefully follow directions in school.

Begin early. Give him small chores to do around the house; ask him to take out the trash, set the table, and bring the napkins from the top drawer of the chest. Invent games that include directions. In the classroom, I used to put some items in a drawer across the room (distance added the requirement to remember longer) and said, "Bring me the chalk (or pencil, or eraser)." The children loved the game, and, as an added bonus, learned to look and listen longer in order to understand the full instruction. To improve concentration, vary the request, making the sentences a little longer each time by adding different colors and more than one item. A child's mind will start to function, his attention span will increase, and there will be satisfaction in accomplishment. Be sure he succeeds easily some of the time, but is also challenged.

Another variation of a directional game has to do with the prepositions *in, on, under, over, behind,* and *through.* Give him directions and demonstrate all the prepositions with props, such as a miniature car with a road, bridge, and tunnel, or a chair with a ball.

Later he will have more particular directions from the teacher, who might say, "Put your name in the upper right-hand corner of the paper," and "Put a circle around the correct answers, and when you've finished, put your test on my desk." And when he eventually goes to work, his immediate boss and other senior employees will be bombarding him with complicated directions, such as "Tighten the safety bolt each time you finish work on this machine," and "When you're finished, go upstairs to Room 313 and bring me the materials the secretary has saved for me."

SENSE TRAINING

Since a hearing-impaired child is deficient in one of his senses, his other senses should be trained to the utmost to compensate. We know that a handicapped child unconsciously becomes more acute in his normally functioning senses when we observe the brightness of the eyes of the hearing impaired and the sharpness of the hearing of the sight impaired. You can help to develop your child's senses further with exercises and games at home. Children learn to be more efficient in the combined use of their senses if each sense is occasionally given individual attention. Training the sense of residual hearing and the sense of sight for speechreading in isolation have been discussed, but it will be of value here to touch upon training the other senses as well.

A favorite game for encouraging the conscious sense of touch is to place some dissimilar objects in a laundry bag that has a drawstring. Open the bag only wide enough for your child to put his hand into the bag, feel the objects there, select one, and then tell you what it is before drawing it out. The bag should contain familiar toys and small objects such as a car, airplane, square block, ball, and blunt pencil. This game can be played with speechreading, and, later, when you talk about blocks in shapes of squares, triangles, and circles, identifying by touch in the bag gives him added perception.

Take up the feel of things as a vocabulary category. Collect a group of items that are soft, hard, rough, smooth, and so on. The two of you can feel them together and he can learn the words at the same time. The category of "what things are made of" can be introduced, including leather, wood, metal, plastic, and cloth materials.

Smell and taste can be treated in the same way. Bring his attention to the diverse smells of the kitchen. Have him smell perfume, flowers, and new shoes that have a nice leathery smell, and include things that smell bad, like marigolds and fertilizer. For their contrast, let him taste foods that are sweet and sour and those that are mild and hot.

As your child becomes aware of all his senses, he will show more sensitivity to the world around him and his curiosity will be aroused.

chapter *10*

preparing your child
for school

Aside from ongoing concern for continual advancement in vocabulary, language, auditory training, and speech, there are other areas that will help prepare your child for a successful first year at school.

It must not be presumed that he will naturally be ready by virtue of maturity alone to accomplish the skills for kindergarten. Today, kindergarten is far more than the preschool-first grade interim for art-play that it used to be. Activities are carefully structured and aimed at preparing a pupil for later work in the basics of reading, writing, arithmetic, and reasoning. During kindergarten, there is work toward reading in phonics, the alphabet, and word and thought retention; toward arithmetic in numbers, shapes, and comparative concepts; and in thinking and forming thoughts into words, there is an emphasis on oral skills. In many schools, a serious attempt is made at the end of kindergarten to evaluate a pupil's readiness for learning to read, to write, and do arithmetic in order to assure that the child will be successful in first grade.

All children vary in their ability to master the different skills presented to them at school. Since your child already has a hearing handicap to overcome, it is advisable to prepare him in the other skills, besides communication, that he will need. Advance preparation will preclude awkwardness in these areas when he attends school.

A PREPLANNED STRATEGY: NINE SUGGESTIONS

Now is the time to form a preplanned strategy to help your child be accepted at school by his teacher and the other children in his class. Be mindful that his relationship to his peers will become increasingly important to him after he starts school, and that what you, as a parent, do now in preparation for fitting him into a happy situation at school will more than pay dividends. "Fitting in" implies that he will readily make friends and gain immeasurably from them in everyday exchanges in language, speech, and activities. These early childhood friends can be some of the most influential and enduring.

So, before your child enters school, prepare him along the lines of the following suggestions.

Manners

Insist that he have good manners at home, for his handicap is no excuse. He can learn *thank you* and *please* as well as the next child, and should use them spontaneously. He should know how to eat properly, stand in line to wait his turn, and start and stop what he is doing when he is told by an appropriate authority to do so. This background training will carry over and make him more acceptable at school.

Play

Give him every opportunity to learn to play with children his own age. If he has children in the neighborhood to play with, fine; if not, consider enrolling him in a regular nursery school where he can gain this play experience. Don't worry if he watches or plays apart from the other children at first. This is not unusual, as some normally hearing children are still at this stage in kindergarten and even later.

Physical Skills

Let him have advance experience with the body skills he will need in school rather than expect the teacher to develop them. If he can do something just a little better than some of the other children, he is succeeding, and these physical skills count big with children!

There are both large motor and small motor body skills. Those used on the school playground—with the climbing apparatus, slide, swing, tricycle, and ball—are the large motor skills. Give him comparable experience on equipment at a local park until he can compete with reasonable skill, and let him experiment with a jump rope.

Manual skills—handling a pair of scissors, crayon, large pencil, and paste or glue—are the small motor skills. Practice these skills at home and he will gain the admiration of his peers and build confidence. How satisfying for him to cut out a pattern more easily than his neighbor!

Experiences

Expose him to as many and varied experiences as possible. These need be neither complicated nor expensive. They will help him approach the reading materials presented in school with a background in real-life situations.

Writing

Form the habit of exposing him to your writing early, including numerals. Learn to print in the manuscript style used at school—don't confuse him with different styles of printing. His eye-and-mind coordination has its own maturity rate, so don't hurry him. Write simple words and sentences slowly as he watches. Let him absorb the letters until his curiosity tells you he is ready to differentiate between them and wants to know what they mean. Hopefully, he can learn to read and write his name before school begins, and to read the words on public restroom doors as well as *walk* and *don't walk* at street corners and crosswalks.

Numbers, Colors, and Shapes

Help him learn his numbers and colors. Count everything around you, and let him count with you. Even though he has matched objects and colors in his early sense training, don't neglect the names of the primary colors and brown, black, and white. Knowing them before school begins will be to his advantage. Besides, numbers and colors are great language-stretchers when inserted before the name of things, as in "Where are your *two brown* socks?" Children vary greatly in their ability to learn the concepts of numbers and colors, so don't be discouraged if your child is slow. If there seems to be a genuine mental block, have tests done to determine if your child has problems in color coding or in perceptual understanding.

Also, acquaint your child with the basic shapes of the square, circle, triangle, and rectangle. Compare differences in size, weight, length, width, and height of items, using comparative and superlative adjectives, for example, "Daddy is *taller* than Uncle John," and "Daddy is *tallest* of all."

Stories

Give him the opportunity to know and enjoy traditional children's stories and nursery rhymes. He should know how to put a story in sequence by school age. Cut up pictures of a story familiar to him, like *The Three Bears.* Paste these on cards with simple captions, mix them, and then guide him to place them in the proper sequence from left to right according to the story line. He must be able to tell left from right, learn that words are read from left to right, and recognize that pages are turned one by one from the front to the back of a book.

Thinking

Continually urge him to think out problems, follow directions, and answer and ask questions—it cannot be presumed that a hearing-impaired child will learn these skills without help. Because of the volume of vocabulary and language poured into a hearing-impaired child by school age, he frequently has not had sufficient opportunities to think for himself and be responsive.

Perceptual Skills

Watch for problems in his perceptual skills. As defined in the Encyclopedia Americana, "perceiving is the recognizing of objects and aspects of the environment in such ways as to prepare one for their appropriate utilization" (Dashiell, 1979, p. 569).* In education, we are particularly interested in the perceptual skills as they affect a student's understanding of words in order to read with proficiency.

Initially, perception begins very early, with the motor skills: the ability to balance, relate the body to space, and recognize the place objects have in space as to size, direction, and distance from the body. When a baby first reaches for a toy, he is experimenting with the relationship between his body and an object in space. He tries to coordinate his arm movement with what he perceives as the toy's shape, size, direction, and distance from him. If there is a snag in a

---

*Reprinted with permission of the *Encyclopedia Americana*, copyright 1981, Grolier, Inc.

child's orderly development of those interrelated motor skills, there may be problems later in accurately perceiving the shapes of letters and numerals, and this will, in turn, deter him in other educational pursuits. A perceptual problem may first show up when a child has trouble drawing a line from one point to another on the blackboard. For instance, at five years old, he may have difficulty drawing a square or a triangle, and eventually this may carry over to an inability to perceive the difference between the letters *b* and *d* or *b* and *p*.

To help children who are lagging in their perceptual development, educators have recently thought it wise to establish special learning-disability classes. Children go to these classes from their regular classes for a short period each day to concentrate on the skills they need to improve, and with this extra practice they show positive results. At home, if your child is having difficulty putting together puzzles and block patterns, have him practice these patterns many, many times. If he has difficulty drawing figures like a square, have him walk a square, trace a square cutout with his finger, and draw a square repeatedly on the blackboard and on paper. Secure manipulative toys of all kinds, including a pegboard and building blocks, with which he can practice hand-eye coordination. When a child starts using a pencil, you can find perception-oriented workbooks available at educational materials supply or variety stores.

Perception is such a complex subject that I have only touched the surface. Providing your child has persisting problems, he will need your further study and help at home as well as guidance from others. A psychologist can test perceptual skills, and in some schools the classroom teacher or the special learning-disability teacher is equipped to make adequate tests. Sometimes, a child's perceptual problem can be related to his eyes (Liepmann, 1973). In this case, one should consult an optometrist who is trained to test the child's visual function to determine whether or not the visual mechanics he uses to explore and orient himself in his environment are effective. The optometrist may prescribe corrective lenses or a series of visual training exercises to be practiced at his office and followed up at home. A few optometrists specialize in children's problems in this field.

In general, have your child as ready for school as possible. Ease his transition into this new environment where his handicap will be more noticeable and where it will take more effort on his part to compete and succeed. Be sure he looks forward to attending school and visits the school grounds in advance. Avoid the shock of the unexpected just as much as you can, as a child of limited language can be quite overwhelmed in a situation that does not include his mother.

NURSERY SCHOOL

A hearing-impaired child can gain valuable experiences, learn new skills, and have an opportunity to play with children his own age by going to regular nursery school. However, in the preschool years you should weigh how much of your child's valuable learning time should be spent in this way. One child may not need nursery school because he has ample opportunity to play with the other children his own age in his immediate neighborhood. Another one who is shy may not be ready for nursery school—he misses home so much that he pouts, stands around, and absorbs nothing—and is better off at home. On the other hand, the regimen and structure of a nursery school can calm down a hyperactive child and channel the energies of one who has aggressive tendencies. For your hearing-impaired child who has had extensive personal help from you in auditory training, language, and speech, there is a distinct benefit in sending him to nursery school to give him contact with other people, without you being present. This experience will lead him toward being comfortable with others and feeling independent.

Still, what is appropriate for one child may not be applicable for another. Since nursery schools generally take children for parts of a week and even half days, their flexibility allows you to enter your child for the length of time you think best at his age level.

Schools vary considerably in quality, so visit several before choosing one. For nursery schools that have never had or seen a hearing-impaired child, approach them positively, minimizing the problems and accentuating the advantages for both your child and their total program. Your pride and pleasant optimism should go a long way in chasing away any fears they have about handling a hearing-impaired child.

EXPERIENCES

Next to building a satisfactory communication link with your hearing-impaired child, the most helpful thing you can do for him is to give him a variety of experiences. Of course, he can have useful experiences in the home while you go about your daily routine, but let us discuss the broader experiences you should provide him outside the home. Quoting from Arthur I. Gates' book, *The Improvement of Reading* (1947):

> There can be little doubt that, other things being equal, the wider and richer a child's experiences and the greater his range of information,

the better he is equipped to learn to read. The underprivileged child is not only a less experienced learner but he may lack the concepts essential for full and clear understanding of much that he reads. (p. 147)

How can a child visualize the experiences, not to mention identify with the reading and related learning given in school, if he has not been away from home to see the city stores, park, zoo, mountains, and the seashore? A child starved for experiences in the world around him will often be slow to learn to read with comprehension and, in some cases, may falsely appear to have lower than normal intelligence. How much more, then, does your child, who necessarily requires extra help in learning language, need to relate that language to real things in the real world? The answer is "a lot more": not only will he benefit from experiences in themselves, but they will add to his vocabulary and open his mind's eye.

Experiences don't have to be expensive. A walk around the block opens up unbelievable avenues in new language. There are sidewalks, front doors, street numbers, mailboxes, cars, driveways, chimneys, roads, bushes, grass, trashcans, and dogs and cats; and these are only a beginning. When my class of hearing-impaired five year olds was studying cars and trucks, we went to a busy corner and watched and identified the different kinds of vehicles going by.

Somewhat further away, there will be a grocery store, drug store, shoe repair shop, and gasoline station. A trip to the store can bring up possibilities for learning about food, clothing, toys, money values, and much more. If it is not practical for you to shop when your child is along, take him when you have little shopping to do and just browse a bit. Walking along two blocks of storefronts can open up a Pandora's box of interesting items for conversation.

Taking your child to the park is an absolute must. There are butterflies, birds, and bugs to inspect; swings that you push to go high and slides that you go up and down; people to watch; and all sorts of other real things not found at home. You can take other short trips via bus to the airport and the train station, and stop sometime to visit a fire station.

Time and money allowing, plan short, weekend trips and a more extensive vacation trip with the whole family to places that your child hasn't yet encountered. If you plan ahead, you will really enjoy the outing as you watch your child light up with enthusiasm and learn new words and concepts beyond everybody's expectations.

In preparing for a trip, cut out pictures from magazines and travel folders representative of where you are going and what you will see. If you are going on a Sunday drive to the mountains, find pictures of a mountain, a stream, trees, rocks, and birds. Make a book of these pictures as you present them to your child, labeling it "The Mountains"; then write suitable picture captions as he watches. On the calendar, show him when you will go, and next to the date draw a picture of the car, the mountains, and stick figures of the people going. For later use, leave several blank pages in the back of the book. Review the book with him just before the trip. Then, on the trip, take pictures or buy postcards, and by all means bring home some mementos from nature—a smooth, thin rock from the stream, a pretty leaf, a unique piece of wood—preferably items small enough to mount with the pictures on the empty pages in "his" book. Now you have a remembrance of the trip that you can look at again and again, recalling together the experience and the new words he learned.

Indeed, there is a new set of vocabulary connected with each type of trip. At the lake or the beach you'll have water, waves, sand, shells, seaweed, and a pail and shovel—and be sure to take along something for collecting mementos. His experience books from outings such as these will be treasured.

An unexpected byproduct of family trips is your own relaxed attitude when you are with your child on an outing, however short. When a mother is at home and her child comes to her with a question and her errands or chores are still unfinished, any mother will, in spite of herself, grow tense because she's torn between his needs and her need to get her work done. But, on an outing, you and your husband have left the work behind, leaving you both free to devote your full time and attention to your child. You will feel the difference, and he will respond eagerly.

MOTHER GOOSE
AND TRADITIONAL CHILDREN'S STORIES

Nothing brings me more personal pleasure than discussing the valuable contribution *Mother Goose* rhymes and traditional children's stories bring to your child's understanding and enjoyment. Most of these stories are timeless, akin to the ballad, authorless, and delightful. Moreover, allusions to them crop up throughout one's life. If your child is acquainted with these rhymes and stories, as a grownup he will understand the many references made to them and be able to hand them down to his own children. Also, I happily discovered that their lyrical quality was better appreciated by my hearing-impaired children than I had hoped.

Don't depend on your child's teachers to introduce *Mother Goose* because they may not have enough time to do justice to the wonderful possibilities inherent in these rhymes. Have on hand a good *Mother Goose* book that has colorful, lifelike pictures. Introduce its rhymes at home one at a time, and consider each one's potential as a learning tool from every possible angle.

In addition, acquire a few inexpensive *Mother Goose* picture books that can be cut up and used on a flannel board, creating an excellent means for acting out a rhyme. To make your own flannel board, staple a good-sized piece of flannel to a comparable piece of plywood or heavy cardboard. Then, back each picture with flannel, pelon, or sandpaper. The two pieces of material will adhere to each other and allow you to tell the story graphically by moving the pictures or characters around on the upright backing. Your own hand drawings or pictures from magazines may be needed to supplement the book's illustrations.

After your child has become acquainted with the nursery rhyme you are presenting in the *Mother Goose* book and you have both acted it out with the aid of the flannel board, it is time to play-act the story with real props.

Start with a simple rhyme:

Jack be nimble,
Jack be quick,
Jack jump over the candlestick.

The key words are *jump* and *candlestick*, while the remainder upholds the lilt and swing of the rhyme. Recite the rhyme and have your child act on cue. Actually provide a candlestick and have him pretend he is Jack jumping over the candlestick on the word *jump* (he can easily do this from a low step).

Of added value will be your insistence that he speechread the rhyme as you recite and he acts. Making this a speechreading game requires that he look longer, concentrate, and follow directions; thereby, the nursery rhyme becomes a tool for several simultaneous learning lessons. Most nursery rhymes can be adapted in this same way.

For a next step in playacting with speechreading, use children in the family and neighborhood for the additional actors and the audience. "The Queen of Hearts" would be an excellent choice for this expanded production. Make real tarts, which is a learning experience in itself, or roll and cut clay tarts. Children love to wear paper crowns; make one for the King and one for the Queen. Pin a big, red heart on the chest of the Knave. It isn't necessary to explain a knave—don't spoil the poetry and rhythm of the original rhyme by changing the word, the children will soon glean from the story something of his character. As you recite the rhyme, have them act it out, letting each child have a turn playing all three characters.

You will find that archaic language is not a stumbling block to the understanding and enjoyment of the rhymes. "Little Miss Muffet" is an example of how the actual words are less important than the action and rhythm. "Curds and whey" can be quickly described as cottage cheese and "tuffet" as a pillow—then, on with the rhyme. A toy rubber spider on a string, a low stool or pillow, and a plastic bowl and spoon need be the only props for playacting this rhyme. The cue is the word *spider*, at which point Miss Muffet drops her dish and spoon and runs away, looking extremely frightened. The more dramatic the better, but make Miss Muffet wait for the word *spider* and the child working the spider watch for his cue, "along came a spider."

For sheer suspense, nothing compares to playing "Humpty Dumpty." Use a real, raw egg; draw a face on him, and even dress him, to the delight of the children. Make the wall of building blocks and use pictures or toys for the king's men and horses. Humpty Dumpty *sits* on the wall and, at the proper moment in the rhyme, has a *great fall* (into a shallow pan at the base of the wall). Enjoy the children's faces and give them ample time to discover that an egg can't be put back together again.

The traditional, much-loved children's stories can be approached in a like manner. If the story has been animated and includes such well-known, catchy tunes as Walt Disney Productions' "Who's Afraid of the Big Bad Wolf?" or "Hi Ho, Hi Ho, It's Off to Work We Go," rhythm work can be incorporated in the storytelling.

Many of the stories have a repetitive series of lines within the pattern of the plot. This simplifies the language for your hearing-impaired child. What is more, when you act out the story, the short, simple sentences are easier to repeat for your young child. The best examples of these stories are: *The Three Little Pigs, Goldilocks and the Three Bears,* and *Little Red Ridinghood.*

Our family and my classroom favorite was *The Three Little Pigs.* No matter how often we acted it out the children never grew tired of it. Our version went like this:

> *Scene:* Kitchen
> *Props:* A kitchen table to represent the big, solid brick house, and two high stools for the other two houses.
> *Players:* Three children as the three little pigs and a Big Bad Wolf (largely played by me).
> *Action:* The little pigs scurry under the stools and the table into their own houses and the Big Bad Wolf knocks on top of each one in turn. Each little pig responds, "Who's there?" and "No, no!" to the wolf's query, "May I come in?" Chances are that even the most reticent, speech-shy child will find his tongue. After the Big Bad Wolf has huffed and puffed and carefully knocked down the two chair-houses and each

little pig has run to safety in the big brick house under the table, the Big Bad Wolf huffs and puffs at it, and when he can't blow it down, he says, "I'll come down your chimney!" Whereupon, he climbs over the table, down the other side and plays dead. The lack of a chimney doesn't phase the children.

Finale: All join hands in a circle and dance around, singing "Who's Afraid of the Big Bad Wolf?"

To my knowledge, the fantasy stories filmed by Disney and presented in Golden Books, many pictures of which are made from the movie drawings, can't be surpassed for the combination of color, detail, and price. *Bambi* excellently pictures many of the forest animals. *Frosty the Snowman* and *Rudolph the Red-Nosed Reindeer* are seasonal favorites, and *Snow White and the Seven Dwarfs*, surprisingly enough, makes good reading at Halloween because of the witch in the scary, black costume. Look into all of them for material you can use at appropriate times. This reminds me of an amusing incident Leslie was involved in. One Halloween she duplicated the witch's costume in *Snow White*, even down to carrying a basket of shiny red apples. At one door, her expression changed to shock when, after saying "Trick or Treat," the man who answered her knock replied, "Why, thank you," took one of her apples, and started eating it!

One of the most delightful and beautifully written children's stories of all time is *The Tale of Peter Rabbit*, by Beatrix Potter. The language may seem complicated for a small hearing-impaired child, but if you pick and choose and don't read it word for word, the story itself is simple and engrossing. The basic plot and the moods and feelings described are a perfect miniature of an action-packed suspense novel. At first, simplify the book's detail to fit your child's language level, but keep expanding it as his comprehension grows.

Few new children's stories can match the old classics. They are a part of one's childhood, and all children should have the opportunity to enjoy the classics as often and for as long as they continue to find pleasure in them. As folk tales, they grow better with repetition and with the warmth and love of the storyteller and the home.

STIMULATING VERBAL THINKING AND MEMORY PROCESSES

Hearing-impaired children who are late in gaining verbal language tend also to lag in their ability to think in this language with the same facility as normally hearing children. Why is this? Can it be that the readiness to think verbally coincides with the period, in the very early years, when a normally hearing child builds up language and begins to express himself (from one to three years of age)? In other words, is this process stimulated at this time by nature's own growth patterns, patterns which have been interrupted for hearing-impaired children? Or can it be that our method of "pouring in" language for a hearing-impaired child (without expecting a comparable "pouring out" from him) is not adequate to stimulate his thinking process?

Whatever the cause, this ability to think verbally (in words) to the point of orally expressing an opinion or answering a question is a continuing problem with the hearing impaired. Later on, it hinders reading and writing, the comprehension of mathematical word problems, and subjects like history. Granted, the problem is, no doubt, confounded by the lag between the speechreader's reception of language and his ability to decipher it. Still this does not fully explain the often painful process entailed in getting a hearing-impaired child to think for himself in verbal language.

Clearly, the need is great to give your hearing-impaired child many reasons to use his thinking processes. Be sure to wait and insist upon answers to questions. Don't be reluctant to challenge him. Give him time to work out in his mind a word pattern to express his ideas. And, develop in yourself a patient, listening attitude.

Work with numbers and colors to help him see relationships in beginning arithmetic word problems: if this car in my hand is yellow and the car you are holding is yellow, how many yellow cars are there? I have spent weeks working on similar concepts in the classroom with a child who had a large vocabulary and knew his numbers and colors, but who had never been challenged to exercise his mind to think out such a problem.

Also, a hearing-impaired child requires practice in learning to remember what he hears and what he sees. Memorizing short phrases and lyrics will strengthen his memory skills. Has he forgotten the beginning of a sentence by the time you have come to the end of it? Especially, in directions, can he remember a direction well enough to carry it through? Certain games will strengthen a child's memory span; you can devise exercises for following directions, memorizing short limericks, and learning patterns such as parts of a folk dance.

I recall a memory game I played with my father. He would gather children together and open a book to a full-page, colorful, very busy picture. Our favorite was a children's geography book with pictures of faraway lands, many people, colorful costumes, and unusual animals. He would give us a few minutes to look at the picture in silence, then, turn it toward himself and ask us questions about it: How many children are there in the picture? Name all the colors you saw. What is the color of the camel rider's shirt? Name two animals in the picture.

This type of game is always excellent for training a person to remember detail in what he sees.

Give your hearing-impaired child cause to think in words and to stretch his memory.

chapter *11*

choosing a school

The solution to finding the right school for your hearing-impaired child varies from child to child, family to family, and area to area. Factors that might influence any advice I might give on this subject are of uncertain value without knowing the particulars. Above all, face it as a family problem. This is the time not to lose sight of what is best for the whole family for the sake of one of its members.

BACKGROUND

The U.S. population figure for hearing-impaired children, particularly the profoundly hearing impaired, is a very small portion of the entire U.S. population. It is possible that the parents of a hearing-impaired child will find themselves living in an area or small community with no other similarly handicapped children. If this is so, it is only realistic to anticipate that forming a special class in a small school district where there are only one or two hearing-impaired children is impractical. Usually your principal options are: integrating your child into the existing classes without professional help; sending him away to school, which is heart-rending; or moving near a school with hearing-impaired classes, which is rarely practical and always disturbing.

On the other hand, in a large city there are so many different kinds of schools that choosing the right one for your child can be confusing. And frequently, you don't have a choice when district rules and regulations for city public schools remain rigid. Often in placing a child, administrators and city officials are, for all intents and purposes, considering the child's hearing loss instead of the whole child. Hearing-impaired children of the same age can vary in readiness by as much as one to four years. For a school system to insist on placing a child in a special class that is working at a slower pace than he is capable of is as great a mistake as placing a very slow child in a class far beyond his potential.

Unfortunately, there are areas in our country where only one educational option is available for the hearing impaired. If the particular method is not what you feel is best for your child, do you move, do you send him to a private school, or, regardless of your better judgment, do you succumb to the inevitable by placing him in the only class situation available to you?

To answer this question you should undertake an objective evaluation to determine the best educational placement for your hearing-impaired child. You can seek assistance from those experts who have helped you thus far, but the evaluation should be made primarily by you and your family. The knowledge you have gained of hearing impairment and children's growth patterns will aid you in reassessing your goals for your child and predicting what he is capable of achieving in the light of his many variables (see Chapter 3 on evaluating your child). Always, your ultimate goal is to see him learning at his highest potential.

It takes careful thought and courage to make a final decision. But once parents have thoroughly thought through their various options on school placement, an amenable solution can be found. At this time, parents are awakening to all the possibilities they can pursue toward realizing their hearing-impaired child's future. They are exploring new educational avenues and helping to open new programs that are better suited for their child's needs. Integration into regular classes, even for the profoundly hearing impaired, is proving successful more often than not; and more parents are arranging for outside help to complement schooling through the "buddy system," tutors, interpreters, notetakers, and speech teachers.

Know your strength as a parent. Take what you think will be effective action. Most educators will listen to a parent of a child with a special educational problem and work out something for the good of the child. Don't accept a flat "No." Compromise, and get the educational system to bend a little to come up with a mutually acceptable answer. At the very least, work around to "We'll try it for a while." Any administrator who refuses a child's entry into his school solely on the basis of the child's hearing impairment should be confronted and challenged.

Moreover, there is federal legislation on your side. The Education of All Handicapped Children Act (P.L. 94–142), enacted November 29, 1975, gives legal clout to the right of each handicapped child to be educated according to his individual needs. The important and innovative requirement in this public law states that each handicapped child must be evaluated individually by a panel that includes his parents as well as educators, before a placement decision is made. This is the first time the parents have been given, by law, a voice in determining their child's school placement. This is not a cure-all—a governmental dictum will not solve every problem—and, since people of all backgrounds are involved in interpreting and ruling on the law, misconceptions and prejudices will still exist. However, it's to the distinct benefit of the child if all parties employ logical reasoning and cooperation and do not resort to time-consuming, expensive legal means.

Many service organizations have taken up the cause of parents who are finding difficulty arranging for the best schooling for their hearing-impaired children, offering support and information on what you can do about the problem. One such organization is the Alexander Graham Bell Association for the Deaf: write to it regarding its Children's Rights Program and its group of advisors available for consultation throughout the country (3417 Volta Place, N.W., Washington, DC 20007).

Above all, you cannot afford to be uninformed on any aspect of hearing impairment and the education of the hearing impaired. For further reading on this subject, consult the following books:

1. *The Rights of Parents,* by David Schimmel and Louis Fischer, 1977, published by The National Committee for Citizens in Education, 410 Wilde Lake Village Green, Columbia, Maryland 21044. Cost is $2.95 plus 55¢ for mailing.

2. *The Rights of Hearing-Impaired Children,* edited by Gary W. Nix, the September, 1977 Monograph issue of *The Volta Review,* published by the Alexander Graham Bell Association for the Deaf. Total price is $3.95 plus 75¢ for handling.

It stands to reason that each case history on school placement is individual. It is hoped that the majority of cases will be less complex than this example of a family in a very large city who had their hearing-impaired boy in an excellent oral preschool program for four years. Now, when he is ready for school at age six, the parents discover their family home is in a district where the only special public school class available to their child uses the total communication method. This family has already decided that their boy should have an oral education. A move is impractical: the hearing-impaired boy is the youngest of four normally hearing children who are doing very well in the district schools, and the father has a well-established professional career in the immediate vicinity of his home. Possible private oral schools which the child could attend are many heavy-traffic miles away and provide no transportation. For the sake of the mother, who is exhausted from commuting to and participating in a nursery school for four long years, while simultaneously keeping up with the activities of her other children, the answer would seem to be a good oral boarding school away from home. But the father was raised in private schools with little or no family life, and he refuses to allow his son to go to school away from home for any reason.

A tough decision, but let's consider a way out. The parents might:

1) Employ a tutor to help the child so that he can be placed on a trial basis in a regular classroom in his designated neighborhood school.

2) Enroll him in a local private oral school, and reach an agreement with other parents for transportation by carpool, taxi, or small bus.

3) Through a panel set up for evaluation under P.L. 94–142, receive permission to enroll him in an oral school outside his district.

In a quite different case, a pupil in a small oral day school in a surburban town did not learn to speechread, speak, or use his residual hearing in spite of the valiant efforts of his parents and teachers over a period of some four years. The family turned, with some success, to the language of signs for a method of communication with the boy at home. But, at that time, there was no school program using signs in his district. Again, the family was adamantly against sending their child away to school where he might have had the opportunity for better testing and observation and the option of several teaching methods. Since there was no acceptable alternative, the boy continued for a time with oral training at school and signs at home, a situation that satisfied neither the teacher nor the parents. Subsequently, for this child and others, a second area program was developed in which children were instructed by the total communication method. I believe that in a day-school situation set up to serve a well-populated rural and suburban area, possibly including several neighboring school districts, both methods of instruction should be available. And if the overall district is large enough, additional classes should be offered to the slow learners, as well as multihandicapped and aphasic children.

Generally speaking, a self-contained school designed for the hearing impaired, whether public or private, boarding or by-the-day, has the advantage of competent supervision, permanent staff, and a curriculum that ensures continuity in learning from class to class. Still, this is a sheltered situation where there is less opportunity to interact with normally hearing children. In contrast, a day-school program for hearing-impaired children contained within the structure of a regular hearing school frequently suffers from poor supervision, staff turnover, and the lack of curriculum continuity. However, it does offer the advantage of whole or partial integration and interaction with the normally hearing children at lunchtime and on the playground. Regarding small day-school programs, then, they should be assessed annually by parents, as the loss of one excellent teacher can suddenly change the quality of a program.

Realizing that there are almost as many individual answers to school placement as there are hearing-impaired children, you, as a parent who knows your child best, must consider all the options and exert every effort to ensure him the type of education you feel he needs.

PREPARING THE SCHOOL FOR YOUR CHILD

After your child is placed in a school, you have to continue practicing diplomacy and salesmanship throughout his school years. For the next ten to fifteen years you will have occasion to use these skills in your relationship with school personnel, time and again. In preparing a school for your child, his characteristics, personality, and abilities should be made known to the school authorities in advance. Ideally, this should be done in person in the spring, prior to the fall semester when a child usually enters school.

Besides his primary concern with children, the educational administrator has not only a complicated school system of classes in every grade, but also teachers with which to relate. He has regard for your child and wants your approval and cooperation, but he also must adjust his facilities to accommodate all pupils' needs. As a parent, as concerned as you are, you are still in the position of standing on the outside looking in. Given this setting, be reasonable for the sake of your child, and not overdemanding. Try to appreciate what the administrator is doing, offer compliments where due, and be considerate of his time. Be as pleasant and attentive as you would be when applying for a job—in short, be the diplomat. Present your child and yourself in the best light possible so that his educational experience will start in an understanding and receptive atmosphere.

If your child is going into a regular school, preparation is even more necessary. Numerous times the principal never has had contact with a hearing-impaired child and may hold unfavorable, preconceived ideas. Above all, you don't want to come across as exerting undue pressure, worrying him by spelling out the details of this handicap, its educational implications, and your child's needs item by item. Some educators don't relish "one more problem"; try to assure the principal that your child will not be an added burden.

Therefore, when you approach the principal, have clearly in mind only the most important requirements for your child for the coming school year. Your primary concerns with the principal at this time are: 1) to make him generally aware of the nature of your child's hearing loss, and 2) to have him do his best, when appraising his staff, to choose a teacher who will consider your child a challenge rather than a liability. If the teacher has empathy and enthusiasm, the chance for your child's success increases. Also, a teacher who has a mobile, expressive face and clear, not-too-rapid speech will be a definite plus for your child.

Before completing your discussion with the school principal, you will want to be assured that he will tell the assigned teacher in advance of the first day of school about your child so that neither of them will encounter a totally unanticipated situation. Other school personnel who should know right away are the school nurse and the office secretary. Subsequently, it would be well to inform the special playground aids, the librarian, the cafeteria cashier, the custodian, and any others on the staff with whom your child may come in contact.

When you speak to the teacher before school opens in the fall, be brief. At this time of year, many teachers feel most apprehensive, their class seems large and the problems overwhelming. Diplomatically, reassure the teacher that your child is really not going to be a big problem and that you want mainly to discuss seating him in the classroom where he can see and hear well. In this first meeting, it is not wise to go into the details of hearing aids, speechreading, and imperfect speech. Assure the teacher that you will cooperate in every way you can and take your leave.

At first, then, the only special need for your hearing-impaired child concerns the teacher's arrangement for his seating. The best seat for speechreading and listening is in the second row rather than the first, and two or three seats in from any windows. Sitting in the first row, for a hearing-impaired child who has to keep his eyes continually on the teacher, forces him to crane his neck upward in a strained position (this awkward position tightens the throat muscles, which tends to cause a thin voice). Being in front of the class also isolates him from his classmates, when group discussions will prove to be the most difficult part of school for him. Thus, from the second row he is close enough to see and hear the teacher and yet in a slightly better position to see and hear the other children in order to follow class discussions. Off-center seating is preferred because it gives the child a clear view of the front of the class by looking between heads in the first row. Sitting near windows, at one side of the room, affords your child the optimum, side-angle, speechreading viewpoint and puts the teacher's face in the full light.

On the first day of school, having shown the school to your child in advance and prepared him and the school for the experience, don't linger at the door—leave him gently, but leave him. In the next few weeks, if your child seems to be happy, let well enough alone, unless the teacher calls you. Give the teacher time to get oriented, organize the class, and get acquainted with the personalities and abilities of the children under his or her charge; hurrying the teacher might be more annoying than helpful. In about two weeks, if you haven't had any word, schedule a conference with the teacher and talk over your child's situation more fully.

In this longer conference, among other things, go into detail on the importance of seating and lighting. Some teachers may let a child move his seat temporarily if the teacher is apt to change position from one side of the room to another during the day. Check the seating of your child in the reading group. Assuming it is arranged in a semicircle, the teacher may intend to shelter him by placing him in an adjacent seat, whereas a seat slightly to one side of center would enable your child to follow the lesson better.

In addition, the teacher should be told about the workings of your child's hearing aid, its limitations as well as its advantages, so that he or she can explain it intelligently to the other children. Be positive in your presentation of the hearing aid. Explain that it is a well-made, sturdy instrument, invaluable to your child, and something to be prized like a miniature radio or speaker system. Although its monetary value is considerable, the teacher needn't always look to protect it because it can stand up to a child's active play. However, other children should not be allowed to play with it or damage it deliberately. And, a parent should leave extra batteries with the teacher in case of a sudden battery failure.

In turn, the teacher should explain the hearing aid to the class, letting them see it, feel it, and listen to it, thereby making it a familiar necessity and not a curious, unexplored object. He or she should also give a short demonstration of speechreading to the class by talking to your child without voice. This will interest and intrigue the other children—enough so that, later on, the teacher may see glimpses of silent messages floating across the classroom between your child and his friends.

The teacher should set the tone of the class by limiting the special privileges to your hearing-impaired child to only the few that are absolutely necessary, and not allowing him to use his hearing loss as an excuse. Teachers who give oral tests should think of providing your child with the same test in writing (except spelling tests). Promote to the teacher the idea of repetition in making important points and announcements. Also, suggest that he write homework and test assignments on the blackboard. There is nothing more discouraging for a hearing-impaired child than to arrive in class to find there was an earlier assignment he could have prepared in advance, but instead missed because it was tossed in the air orally as the class adjourned. It can't be taken for granted that the hearing-impaired child knows about an assignment, unless it is written, and then he has no excuse.

Finally, keeping up with vocabulary is always difficult for the hearing impaired. As the teacher introduces new subjects during the year, ask that you periodically be sent class related vocabulary words, enabling you to help your child learn the words and practice them at home.

After this longer interview, follow up only as needed, showing interest by visiting occasionally with advance notice.

MULTIHANDICAPPED CHILDREN

In 1971, a representative of the Special Education Department of the State of California told me that sixty percent of the hearing-impaired children in California were multihandicapped. The children in the classes I taught bore this statistic out. At that time, even if the percentage in the country at large were fifty percent, it would be a sobering figure.

The periodic occurrence of rubella (German measles) epidemics is the cause of a large proportion of multihandicapped children. These children can be afflicted with combinations and various degrees of: hearing impairment, sight impairment, heart problems, cerebral palsy, atrophy of one kind or another, and brain damage. Priority given to the treatment of another handicap may delay beginning remedial work on a hearing problem. If the child has cerebral palsy, for instance, it is essential that he have extensive physical therapy to learn to walk and care for himself before attention is turned to his hearing loss. A number of eye problems result in partial sight, and in most of these cases the "also hearing-impaired" child must be treated and fitted with glasses before he can be expected to speechread, if at all.

Some children have handicaps that are not detectable until their schooling begins. Six-year-old Joan with a severe hearing loss was in one of my classes. The year before, her teacher had noted that she had learned to speechread no more than two or three words, while the rest of her class had progressed well. She was a friendly, bright, attractive girl, and physically strong with excellent coordination (no one could swing better on the bars than Joan). She had no apparent emotional problems. Still, during the following school year, in spite of every effort, I couldn't be sure she learned to speechread one word. She showed no response to sound, although she faithfully wore a set of strong, binaural aids daily; neither did she show any ability to imitate speech or use it spontaneously. By the middle of the year, I began seeking a diagnostic clinic that could explain her learning disability. None being available close by, her mother consented to take her to a well-staffed, diagnostic clinic in a large city. This plan was interrupted by the family making a permanent move to a different part of the state so I lost contact and, with it, any future reports on her problem.

There seemed to be a child like Joan in my classroom every year, none of whom had ever been properly diagnosed. As a teacher, the failure of these children to learn still greatly disturbs me, and the question naturally arises in my mind: would the addition of signs for such a child be the answer? Recently I asked a respected teacher who several years ago moved from the oral to the total communication method of teaching. Her reply was, "No, it might help, but it isn't the overall answer for this child's communication and learning problems." It comes down to the fact that a complete, early diagnosis might have uncovered the problem and directed proper treatment and school placement.

Teachers cannot and should not be expected to diagnose the problems of a child. They may suspect and they may be able to see progress through specific teaching methods, but they are not qualified in the various fields of exceptional children to give an expert's diagnosis, nor do they have the necessary equipment. A teacher of the hearing impaired may often know little about impaired eyesight, cerebral palsy, or aphasia, much less obscure handicaps like Joan's.

Indeed, hearing-impaired children with impaired vision passed through my classes yearly. My training had never included study materials or analyses that would aid me in determining what amount of vision a child must have to speechread. Trial-and-error teaching for these children is a deplorable way to determine whether a child will ever see well enough to speechread. Several years of valuable educational training can be lost by the teacher not having sufficient information as well as through misplacement of partially-sighted, hearing-impaired children.

Therefore, the greatest single need for multihandicapped children is thorough, expert diagnosis. The best clinics are the ones connected with a university or hospital, where experts in diverse fields are available to test children, consult, and reach specific conclusions on the nature and extent of their handicaps. A clinic should see the child long enough to test him completely, even though it takes a week or more, and the child's parents should be willing to accede to the clinic's requirements. I can't express strongly enough the need in the field of exceptional children for more good diagnostic clinics, and also for better publicity to point the way to these services.

The new law, P.L. 94-142, holds the greatest promise for the multihandicapped. It calls for the educators to study each child individually, which must of necessity include adequate diagnosis, and, then, to find the best possible schooling for him. It is fair to neither the child nor the teacher to place a child in a class where he does not learn by the method used in that class and where the teacher lacks training and information from an expert on his other handicaps. By the same token, it is not right to place him in a hearing-impaired class and then expect the teacher to give him extra time for his special learning problems over and above that needed by the rest of the class. The teacher may not have the time to do justice to both this child and the other children.

Once I had a small boy in my class whom I suspected might be aphasic as well as severely hearing impaired. Conscientiously, I studied Mildred A. McGinnis' book explaining her method of teaching aphasic children (McGinnis, 1963). This involved an entirely different educational approach from the one I was using and to which my pupils were responding. I set aside a half hour every day to teach this child following McGinnis' method, but soon it became apparent that that short length of time wasn't sufficient for him to retain the material. At the same time, the other chidren were losing valuable classroom time. If he would, indeed, respond to the McGinnis method of teaching aphasic children, he should be taught by this method full time.

It is hoped that this new legislation, emphasizing placing children with special problems in classes according to their needs, will foster more and better diagnostic centers for the multihandicapped and the ways and means for forming the specialized classes in which to teach them.

part III

the elementary school years

"One has to keep one's eye in harmony. I go often to the temples to look at the flowers, to remember their colors exactly."

Kakko Hisamatsu,
A Japanese Artist

chapter 12

school days

School—that magical time that allows a parent an extra cup of coffee, a clean sink, beds made before noon, and time to reconnoiter; and the time when a teacher comes along to take your child in hand and instruct him in reading, writing, and arithmetic. As a parent, your role becomes more supportive than instructive while you continue to build, and never stop building, vocabulary and language and to help where you can with your child's school subjects. New words and concepts become easier for your child to learn as he matures and develops a vocabulary base on which to build. Now, as he begins school, watch progress carefully and keep a good rapport with his teacher. A parent should not hover over the teacher's shoulder, yet not be a stranger—strike a happy medium. Your child should go forward steadily both in learning and independence with the teacher's instruction and your full support.

This is a Pollyanna outlook, I suppose—there are stumbling blocks. Even though you may have chosen his school with the utmost care, programs can deteriorate and teachers change. One year with an excellent teacher could give your child the momentum to sail through the next year despite drawing a mediocre teacher. One very bad teacher, however, can impede his progress for an indeterminate time.

If his progress stops and he actually is going backward, you may find it necessary to step in and do something about it. If so, then I would suggest that you arm yourself with plenty of good reasons, put on your diplomat's hat, and go right to the top, to the administrator in charge. Administrators often have a healthier respect for parents' opinions than is generally realized by passive parents who are reluctant to interfere. I would not advocate this action unless the situation is grave; it is always better to work things out with the teacher if possible. Providing that the whole program slips, parents can be more effective as a group.

If and when such recourse is taken, a child will sometimes pick up and begin to progress again almost immediately with a minor adjustment, such as being placed one step below or above the previous level or with another teacher at the same level.

THE PARENT'S ROLE

Some parents feel that school is school, and home is home, and that the gap between the two environments should not be bridged. I'm sure parents with this attitude are in the minority, but one parent I know went so far as to say, "I pay my taxes for you to educate my hearing-impaired child. I don't intend to help. That is your job." Today, that parent's hearing-impaired daughter is entering the adult world with a faulty oral speech structure, unable to write a grammatically correct sentence. If she had had parents who took the responsibility of supplementing her learning at home with corrections, additions, and practice, she would be much better prepared today.

Of course, parents are as individually different as their children. For purposes of broad generalizations, they can be divided into two predominate groups: those who teach their child skillfully with personal satisfaction, and those who do so reluctantly, their interest lying elsewhere or thinking themselves incapable of helping their children. To this latter group, having a hearing-impaired child who needs special support is an unwelcome burden. But, I maintain that you don't have to give up many precious hours of your day or go back to school to learn modern teaching methods to help your school-age child. If you will just become aware of his educational needs and give him help along the way when you can and when his interest is high, you will be supporting him more than you realize. Be willing to complement at home, from your own knowledge and background, what he is doing at school. It can be done in a casual manner so that neither of you feels it to be a task.

To give examples of how you can help in the area of practical math: Does he know how much money he will need for a show and a snack? How much tax will be added to a certain purchase? How many weeks, days, and hours before you go on a trip? How far is your destination? Also, try dividing a cooking recipe in half. Using all the subjects that occur around home, the possible list of examples is endless. Ask any teacher how much your support from home benefits his work at school, and meanwhile notice how much it increases your child's confidence in handling himself in everyday situations. Give him your taste of life as it is and his mind will become sharper and he will grow in maturity.

Evaluate his needs for independence as well as his needs for knowledge. You must determine for yourself that fine line between helping him when he needs it and encouraging him to do his own work when he is able. Keep sight of your objective, always reaching for more independence on his part in learning and social relationships.

INTEGRATION

At the present time, the trend is toward placing hearing-impaired children in regular classrooms whenever they can manage it academically. There is no doubt that the incentive to try harder is there, and learning generally moves at a faster pace than in a contained hearing-impaired classroom. While the regular classroom isn't the place for every hearing-impaired child, and each child is unique in his readiness to learn, generally speaking, in the past too few children have been given the opportunity to integrate at all. If you are wavering in your decision whether to integrate your child or not, give him the benefit of the doubt and enter him in the integrated situation. Providing you honestly think your child can keep up in a regular classroom and you are willing to do all you can to help him, you should not have any qualms about integrating him because chances are he will succeed.

On the other hand, if you are reluctant about making a firm commitment to enter him in a full-time regular class now, consider an interim answer:

1. Wait a few grades until you and your child are ready for full-time integration, or

2. Place him in a special class in a school where the option exists for part-time integration into regular classes.

If your child is enrolled in a special hearing-impaired class and begins to integrate into a regular class part of the day, see that the time allotted is long enough to be of value. One of the few times I stepped in as a complaining parent was when Linda, as a second grader, was scheduled to spend twenty minutes in a regular class. The time taken to leave one class, walk to the other, figure out what they were doing, and settle down to become a participating member of the new class just about used the full twenty minutes, and then it was time to go back. The minimum time spent in a regular class should be at least forty minutes, or preferably the full period between recesses for regular classes.

Ideally, to attain the social value intended, it would be best to place only one hearing-impaired child in each regular classroom. Hearing-impaired children have the tendency to play with their hearing-impaired friends almost exclusively and not mix into activities with normally hearing children. Yet I recognize that in a small school this ideal situation is difficult to arrange.

When your child starts full-time integration, you should try to see that he soon achieves some measure of success, so as to set the right tone. That first impression will carry him a long way through other difficult times. A talent above the average is likely to catch the eye of both the teacher and pupils, make him new friends, and assure him a position of esteem in the classroom, overshadowing his hearing loss. If there is anything for which he has talent—science, athletics, dancing, or artwork—capitalize on it, encouraging him to develop it further at home.

A bright hearing-impaired child can, with your guidance, prepare so well for a test that his grade will give him initial status in the class. I experienced this with Linda when she entered regular school for the first time in fifth grade. She had never had a report card, or a test of any dimension, or any homework. Her first assignment was to study for the next day's test on the world globe. She had absolutely no background for this, not knowing a hemisphere from the Tropic of Cancer. I shall never forget her first pronunciation of Panama Canal, it sounded like Pun-am´-a Can´-el.

So we sat down at the kitchen table and I taught her how to study for a test, and she went over and over the parts of the globe she was required to learn. I didn't know too much about the globe myself, but we studied together, long past her bedtime until we felt she knew the material. The next day she took the test and received the best grade in the class. After that her position in the class was assured, hearing aid and all.

This may seem an unusual procedure, but hearing-impaired children are special in this way; they need extra, intense help at certain times. The reward in prestige and success is a satisfaction to both of you and hard to describe unless experienced.

Once, the mother of a young, profoundly hearing-impaired boy came to me about the prospect of placing him in a full-time fifth-grade regular class. I felt that since his speech was reasonably good, his intelligence average, his athletic ability outstanding, and his work in the special class advanced, that he should be given the chance. There was opposition, but after convincing the administrators, he was placed with an excellent teacher. The next time I saw the boy's mother she told me she was working hard with him at home to help him learn the names of a list of rocks and minerals the class was studying for geology. I remembered my experience with Linda and thought to myself, "He's getting the help he needs, this boy will make it." The last I heard he was doing well academically in high school and playing on the football team.

Enough cannot be said of the merits of integration. From my husband's and my experience and those of increasing numbers of parents of hearing-impaired children, like the boy just mentioned, integration has been a blessing. Integration is seldom easy for a hearing-impaired child, but if you give him your support, develop his talents, and encourage his social relationships, integration is well worth the effort. Realistically, it won't always work exactly the way we want it to, but it should be tried, and as soon as the parents and child feel ready. Nothing can be lost by trying and much can be gained.

NOTHING SHOULD BE TAKEN FOR GRANTED

By third grade, Leslie had been in the same regular school since kindergarten. The kindergarten teacher, with admirable tact, had oriented the children to the small hearing aid Leslie wore and to her speechreading and speech difficulties. She did fairly well in first grade, and even in second grade the same children who had been introduced to her hearing aid were in her class. However, several weeks into third grade, Leslie confessed unhappily to me that most of the children were new to her and didn't understand her inability to always hear her name or completely understand speech. I hadn't realized this, thinking all the children around her age at school were now familiar with her hearing loss. Now, with many new children in her class her disability had to be discussed again—it couldn't be taken for granted.

The third-grade teacher was understanding, but knew little about hearing problems. I suggested that she introduce Leslie's hearing aid to everyone, perhaps now in a more scientific manner, building it up as an interesting, technical instrument that she must wear to compensate for her hearing loss. She could also show an example of speechreading, extolling it as an art that only Leslie knew.

The teacher was most cooperative and wisely chose a moment when the children were clustered closely around her to tell them about Leslie. They were curious. She let them listen through the hearing aid, explained how it worked, and how Leslie had to speechread as well as listen with her hearing aid. From that day on, Leslie was a true part of her class. And it had taken so little effort to make such a big difference in the life of one hearing-impaired child.

KEEPING IN HARMONY WITH NORMAL SPEECH

Like the Japanese artist who introduced Part III and who frequently renews his color sense, a hearing-impaired person needs to renew his hearing sense all his life. Regardless of the amount of his hearing loss, he must keep in touch with the harmony of normal speech in order to absorb its timing, cadence, and inflection. Many a time, after a hearing-impaired child has been integrated into a classroom of normally hearing children for a year, he will astound everyone with his improved speech and vocabulary, gained solely through association with the hearing. If one of your goals for your hearing-impaired child is to have him follow conversational speech with relative ease and to produce speech that is intelligible to others, then plan on making a special effort to ensure that he is around normally hearing people as much as possible, particularly children his own age, so that he can hear and see normal speech.

The neighborhood children are a good start in this direction, and whenever you can, you should plan experiences with other normally hearing people. This is especially important for a child attending contained classes or a boarding school for the hearing impaired. For such a child, you can provide valuable contact with normal speech by thoughtful planning for after-school hours, weekends, and holidays.

Plan to devote at least some portion of your summers to giving your child the opportunity to relate to normally hearing people, joining in their communication, absorbing their vocabulary, and listening to their speech. Consider sending him to a regular camp instead of one for hearing-impaired children. You might initiate him with a day camp in the local park or have him participate in "Y," church activities, or Red Cross swimming lessons. Usually, there are summer classes in art, dancing, and athletics sponsored by the local recreation department or other citizen groups.

A hearing-impaired child may seem relatively quiet in a normally hearing group, relying, as he does, on one-on-one or two-on-one conversations. As long as he seems to be comfortable, even though he's not mixing very well, don't worry; he is, in his own way, renewing his hearing sense and absorbing the harmony of normal speech around him.

chapter *13*

continuing communication skills

The key word through the elementary years is *continuity*. If you drew upon your fund of patience during the preschool years, now you may find that you need the patience of Job.

Recently I read that most children, both normally hearing and hearing impaired, have poor diction until they reach their teens. During the elementary school years, children are developing many skills and expanding their knowledge about many tangible things. Their attention is focused on body energy, fun and games, exploration, experimentation, and social relationships with other children who are similarly motivated. They aren't willing to take the time, nor do they have the interest, to stop and perfect their communication skills.

Your child's ability to speak and speechread improves and his vocabulary and language expand during these years, but with a carelessness that is sometimes exasperating. He is often too busy to stop for the instructions to watch and listen carefully, impatient to be on his way. In his haste, the words tumble out in disarray, one speech sound slurring into another. He doesn't care as long as he is understood by his family and friends who have become accustomed to his speech. It is discouraging, but keep plugging; surround him with new vocabulary, straight language, and proper speech. Before you know it, he will be on the threshold of his teen years, and almost overnight he will exhibit a new desire for better communication and more understandable speech. From this time on, his personal motivation to be socially accepted will keep him improving his communication skills.

SPEECHREADING

In the elementary years, it is best not to coddle your hearing-impaired child when he speechreads you, as he must learn to understand many different faces and to speechread at various angles and under poor lighting conditions. It is harder to speechread some people than others, just as it is harder to hear some people than others; family members, particularly the mother, are naturally more easily understood. A child often looks at his mother for interpretation when an outsider speaks to him—at first, because he knows Mother will help him, but then, because it has become a habit. On this subject, Dr. H. Latham Breunig has observed that "when I attempt to speak with a young deaf person, it is often the parent who answers. Here we see the parent's failure to cultivate the independence that the deaf child will so sorely need if he is to make his way in the world" (Breunig, 1978).

Is this happening at your house? If so, tell your child to look at the speaker again in hopes the speaker will voluntarily repeat himself—if he doesn't, your child should ask him to repeat or rephrase his sentence. After many incidents of this kind, he will learn to handle a speaker's conversation on his own. Help him develop polite phrasing for his request, together with a pleasant manner. Using this approach, he will avoid many future awkward moments when he is unable to understand the speaker the first time.

For your hearing-impaired child, life is not and never will be a straight-on, one-to-one relationship with perfect lighting. In order to build up his confidence in handling speechreading under less than perfect conditions, sometimes toss speech to him that's not easy to understand. Say something to him over your shoulder when working at the kitchen sink. You may have to turn around and repeat it, but you force him to try to understand with only an off-angle look at your face.

At elementary school, the rather sheltered arrangement of the contained classroom with one teacher to speechread seems enough of a challenge for a hearing-impaired child. However, these days one teacher per class is often not the rule. Innovative programs include open classrooms with teacher's aides, team teaching, and the platoon system, in which children are expected to relate to anywhere from two to four or more different teachers each day. By fourth grade, for example, Leslie was not only attending her regular classroom, but also went to one teacher for reading and another for mathematics, while a teacher came once a week for Spanish lessons, a different one supervised the outdoor games, and frequently a teacher who was more proficient in science or art took over the class in those subjects. In another instance, when I substituted in an elementary-level program employing the platoon system, the children were moving from teacher to teacher for each subject all day long.

Clearly, it's a good idea to have your child learn to speechread many different faces by bringing him in contact with the conversation of people from diverse walks of life. Give him practice by sending him on errands to the store and to homes in the neighborhood. This contact outside of school will not only give him the preparation he needs for handling situations in and out of school, but also bolster his independence.

SPEECH

Although your hearing-impaired child, at this age, will pay little attention to how his own conversational speech sounds, he will still progress in perfecting his speech. His knowledge of the speech sounds will grow and his facility in using his vocal cords, breath, tongue, teeth, and lips will improve, provided he is getting continuous help from someone with a good ear who monitors and corrects his speech. With a severe or profound hearing loss, it is hoped a child would receive speech lessons from an experienced teacher throughout his elementary years. Gradually, he will be able to produce a word or a phrase correctly in a lesson situation, even though he's pouring out sloppy conversational speech elsewhere. For now, it is important that he keep talking with good timing and rhythm and that he really knows how the sounds should be made. With reasonable help and correction from you at home, you can keep him on this track.

As he begins to read, add to the two speech books that you made earlier for him spellings that sound the same. For example, in the vowel book, add the spellings *ea, ee, ei,* and *ie* that all sound a long *e* in words; and in the consonant book, add the *c* that sounds like an *s,* the *c* like a *k,* and the *s* like a *z.* Also, add unaccented vowels in the vowel book, like *er* in *father,* and some consonant blends to his consonant book, such as *pl, br, cl,* and so forth. Dramatize with your hands how closely the consonants follow each other in the blends, and how to form the first consonant on the lips, only to fuse immediately into the second. A particularly hard blend for a hearing-impaired child to say is *x* (write it *eks*); it will crop up amazingly often in the word *except.* Equally difficult seems to be its reverse with the *s* in front of the *k,* as in *skip.*

There are a series of words, like *picture,* in which the *t* is a *ch* (write it *pikcher*). Leslie, even with her good speech, didn't realize this until her early teens. Linda still works on it. Similarly, just the other day I explained to one of them that *cello* is pronounced *chello.*

Many words end in a very small plosive sound that is made by a flick of the tongue. Write the sound as a small *t* above the line at the end of the word. It is frequently a blend at the end of a verb in the past tense, like *worked* (*work^t*). A special stumbling block is the word *asked*—it sounds infinitely better when written *as^t*.

Then, there are those pesky words that end in a stop consonant, such as *stop* itself. You can observe in a mirror the parting of the lips after the plosive *p,* which makes the word look like there is another syllable, or *stop-a. Home,* looking like *hom-a,* is another good example. Hearing-impaired children "say it as they see it" and they must learn the ends of these words are closed. To show how a word stops at the end, imitate the action of the mouth by closing the fingers of your hand down on the thumb as you say the word. Your child will have to develop a memory bank in which to store these differences.

As schoolwork progresses and your child's reading improves and vocabulary grows, so will his requirement for help in pronunciation. All children have problems with pronunciation as they become familiar with new words, principally through reading. I still remember making an obvious error as a teenager when I pronounced *reality* as reel-ity, and the embarrassment I felt when everyone laughed.

I asked Linda's teacher how Linda, with her profound loss, could ever learn where the accent should be on a word. Her teacher assured me that, even with her loss, Linda could hear the accent if she listened carefully through her hearing aid, and that she also could gain some clues from seeing the accent through speechreading. This encouraged me, and I found the teacher to be right. But, pronunciation remains a problem for the hearing impaired as long as their vocabulary is expanding.

Keep using the blackboard or anything handy to write the word as it sounds, showing the placement of the accent. If it is a long word, scan the syllables. If you take a word apart to practice a sound, always put it together again and emphasize the rhythm of the word.

You can help your child's pronunciation through his vocabulary work in school. It will benefit him if you start a casual conversation on new subject matter like science or history and, as he talks, correct any glaring mistakes in pronunciation. Proper names are especially difficult to speechread and pronounce. When he is expected to learn the states and their capitals, help him find them on the map, memorize them, and also pronounce them correctly.

Generally, spelling lists are sent home for additional preparation for the weekly oral test. It is as important for your child to practice hearing and seeing the words on his spelling list as it is to practice the spelling. He must be able to understand the word when the teacher says it on the oral test. It will help immeasurably to go over the list with him, saying the word for him to speechread and hear, putting it into a sentence, and then having him repeat it for pronunciation.

English spellings are notoriously nonphonetic. The word *says* may be spelled this way, but it is pronounced *sez* (which is how it is often written in dialect). Another similar type of word is *because*, pronounced *becuz*. Words taken from foreign languages, principally those from French and Spanish, are difficult for the hearing impaired to learn to pronounce correctly. The various endings of words are a constant irritation in that they follow no consistent rule. Examples are: *compare*, which becomes *com´-parable* with a different ending, and *abolish*, which changes to *aboli´-tion*. Some words change accent with different meanings, like *invalid*, which when pronounced *in´-valid* means a person who is ill, but when pronounced *inval´-id* means of no force or weight as when a ballot is voided because it is improperly filled out. Look what happens to the word *perfect:* as an adjective it's *per´-fect*, and as a verb it's *per-fect´*. These stumbling blocks continue to confound the hearing impaired well into adulthood, and a hearing-impaired adult who is anxious to continue learning will be grateful to be shown these differences when they arise.

Your child will now be expanding his sentences in complexity and length. To keep them flowing in a natural, rhythmic pattern, it would be wise to review material on breathing, timing, rhythm, and inflection. Continue to use the approach of: writing it, scanning it, explaining it, drawing it, and phonetically signaling it until his sentences sound right to you.

Since you are constantly with your child, you may accept what you hear from him because you are used to his speech, forgetting that he may not be as understandable to others as he is to you. It will take disciplined listening to be sure you are not in a speech rut. Change your surroundings for a while—a short vacation will bring you back home better able to judge his speech. On occasion, carefully watch when he talks to others to see that he is understood by them. Have him read aloud to you. Imperfect speech patterns become more noticeable when you can listen objectively.

VOCABULARY

As school progresses, a normally hearing child will expand his vocabulary at an ever-increasing rate. A hearing-impaired child's vocabulary will also expand noticeably but, due to his handicap, at a slower pace. Through elementary school, the gap in vocabulary between these two children will become wider and wider, effectively decreasing the hearing-impaired child's ability to keep up academically with his normally hearing peers. A hearing-impaired child placed in a regular classroom has a better chance of keeping his vocabulary within a reasonable distance of the normally hearing children's because of the faster pace of study in the class and the incentive to try harder. Nevertheless, no matter what school setting your hearing-impaired child is in, his lag in vocabulary will be such that he will need continual reinforcement at home.

One way to expand vocabulary is through weekly spelling lists. Be sure your child knows the meaning as well as the pronunciation and spelling of the words. The meanings can slip by easily at school. He can memorize the spelling without knowing how a word is used in context, although he studied it in a spelling workbook; worse, he may even have copied or guessed the answer. It will definitely take more repeating and explaining for him to learn a word than a normally hearing student, whose vocabulary is more advanced and who has probably heard the word before.

Work at home in your own way on the new vocabulary being introduced at school, always defining, repeating, and explaining. Watch for words he has somehow missed; the simplest words that you thought he knew will surface. About this time, abstract words will need explaining; repeated use in their proper context will be the only answer to comprehending most of these.

I well remember one incident when Linda, in a fifth-grade regular classroom, brought me an issue of *Weekly Reader,* a popular children's magazine used by the schools. She had underlined the words she didn't know in a half-page article, and I was surprised that there were twenty-five. I had thought she had a fair vocabulary, but this woke me up. She was able to get the gist of the article, but running into that many strange words left her understanding of it cloudy.

What is the answer to this differential in vocabulary for our hearing-impaired children? I firmly believe that vocabulary must be continually built at home as well as in school. When a new word comes up, it should be explained immediately—on the spot! Don't send him to the dictionary or put it off to another day. Explain the meaning of the word as best you can orally, in language he can understand, while his interest is high. If the word is new to both of you, consult the dictionary together. Your child will have to learn to use the dictionary, but, for a hearing-impaired child right now, time is of the essence. There are too many words he doesn't know, and the dictionary's definitions often include more new words. The on-the-spot help you can give your hearing-impaired child to learn new words and their meanings will narrow his gap in vocabulary when compared to a normally hearing child's, and a good vocabulary is crucial for your child's progress.

My opinion is further strengthened by reflecting upon another incident when Linda was about six years old. I had been chosen to be on a panel of parents of hearing-impaired children ranging from preschoolers to a high school student.

I recall that the high schooler's mother was tense as she related the utter frustration she felt with the work her son was facing in regular high school: "Take, for example, his homework assignment last night. He was supposed to read a chapter in his history book on life in Mexico. It was about the home life there and was entitled 'The Hacienda.' As he proceeded with the first paragraph, he kept coming to me, first for the meaning of *hacienda,* then further for *patio* and *adobe arches.* I forget what-all in the life of the hacienda he didn't know. I kept telling him to look the words up in the dictionary. By the time he had read one paragraph, he had been to the dictionary three or four times, half an hour had passed, and he had barely started his reading assignment."

As the mother of a six year old, I pondered this problem with little understanding, but somehow felt there was a fallacy in her story. Years later I understood what was wrong: the boy's vocabulary was too small to rely altogether on a dictionary. He needed oral explanations right then in his vocabulary range that would allow him to pursue his lesson with understanding at a faster pace. Continually having to break into his thought process was a sure way for him to lose interest in the subject altogether.

STRAIGHT LANGUAGE

Words do not make a meaningful sentence unless they are used in sequence in accordance with good English usage. It is disconcerting to witness your hearing-impaired child develop an extensive vocabulary only to fail to put the words together in correct order or with the right meaning. The greater the hearing loss and dependence on speechreading and/or the language of signs, the more glaring are the errors in the sentence structure (syntax) of a child's speech. The most common mistakes will include words out of place, wrong verb tenses, substitutions, omitted words, and words added unnecessarily. These problems first show up in oral expression and later in written expression.

The incomplete code that a hearing-handicapped person receives, the many idioms in the English language, and the incomprehensible vagaries of pronunciation team together to make learning straight language a tough hurdle. Your child can conquer that hurdle, but will need help—sometimes extensive help—from a special teacher of the deaf or an English teacher or a tutor who is versed in English grammar and the ways to teach it. Your child must not only learn the rules of grammar, but also have disciplined drill and a great deal of conversational practice. And most parents are not equipped to give their hearing-impaired child this intensive work in grammatical structure.

What then can you do at home to be helpful?

Proper Language Structure

You can give your child proper language structure, using your own ear for the good, straight language you have developed through long usage. Every time he uses an improper language structure, repeat for him what he's said using the correct arrangement of words. If time allows, have him repeat it correctly after you. When you are both relaxed and unhurried, write and scan it on the blackboard.

Take care how often you correct him lest it be every time he opens his mouth. You want to present proper English syntax for him to absorb while making it as little like a correction as possible. A repeated mistake, like leaving out *a, an,* or *the* or using the wrong verb tense, can be treated like the letter *k* in *car* (described earlier in Chapter 8). This method will provide him the necessary repetition of correct syntax to continually improve his language.

Reading

You can encourage him to read. Reading gives him another source of straight language to relate to. Through his reading, he will have the opportunity to correct his language usage by comparing some of his own language to that in print.

Writing

You can instill in him the confidence he needs to write. Develop the habit of correcting his writing; then, have him copy it over correctly so that it leaves an indelible and favorable impression as he rewrites it.

CHILDREN WHO LOSE HEARING AFTER LANGUAGE IS DEVELOPED

Mrs. Harriet Montague, for many years Coordinator of the Correspondence Course at the John Tracy Clinic, used to tell the story of how she began to lose her hearing in her teen years. It was a progressive loss that finally became serious enough for her parents to enlist the help of Miss Mary New of The Clarke School for the Deaf in Northampton, Massachusetts, who insisted that the teenager read aloud for long periods of time. Only in her later years did she realize the value of this therapy; Miss New was forcing her to use her voice, even when she could no longer hear it—to use it and use it, and engrave in her memory the feel of her voice so that she would retain her normal voice quality, timing, and rhythm.

When my daughter, Leslie, suddenly began to lose her hearing, I recalled Mrs. Montague's story, and I credit it for the success Leslie has had in retaining her voice quality. If your child's hearing ability has suddenly dropped, by all means encourage, insist, indeed demand that your child continue to speak.

Leslie's hearing nearly disappeared overnight at seven years of age. (Previously, she had had a mild loss and had developed good speech and language through her usable hearing, aided by the constant use of a hearing aid.) When this happened, she had to depend on speechreading for the first time, and she floundered for months while learning to communicate all over again. But she never stopped talking because we wouldn't let her. Time and again, I vividly remember stamping my foot on the floor and insisting to little Leslie, "Talk! I can hear you! Talk, talk!"

After Leslie's hearing had fluctuated up and down several times, it settled at an 82 dB average in her mid-teens, and since then hasn't varied much from that level. Today, she retains a good natural voice quality and normal flow of speech, despite certain high speech sounds she no longer can hear. I am sure her voice quality would not have been as good as it is today if we hadn't heeded Miss New's example and made her continue to talk after her sharp drop in hearing.

The most importance advice I can give a parent of a suddenly deafened child is to keep him talking. This, combined with large portions of love, understanding, and positive attitudes, will produce results. Sympathy will never help; a child must almost immediately learn to get along by means other than hearing. However, he still has the advantage of having his memory of how speech sounds, which a child born without adequate hearing will never have.

chapter 14

support for school subjects

The teacher will teach your child to read, write, and do arithmetic, and give him the beginnings of knowledge in geography, history, and science during the elementary grades. For your hearing-impaired child, the success or failure of the teaching may depend upon your supplemental support at home. True, this support would benefit any child, but it means much more to your hearing-impaired child.

If, in reading, you can bring him in contact with books to read; in writing, good practical reasons to write; in mathematics, everyday use of figures; in geography, history, and science, experiences that will make these subjects come alive for him; then, his chances for academic success will multiply. These things a teacher can't do all alone. The teacher is limited to working within the four walls of a classroom with what is at hand: books, illustrations, movies and slides, some props, and the dynamics of his or her own personality. It remains for you, at home, to bring these subjects to life.

You can help stimulate motivation and make learning a pleasure, if you:

1. See that he does his homework. Help him develop good study habits by setting aside the time and place for his quiet work without upsetting your family. If he is floundering in one subject and needs assistance that you can't give him, seek help through a special teacher or a tutor. A bright youngster a few years ahead of him in school can be helpful. Learn to judge how much help to give your child, because, as soon as possible, you want him to have the will and the ability to do his own homework.

2. Help with new vocabulary, as discussed earlier.

3. A hearing-impaired child greatly benefits from knowing something of a new subject before it is introduced at school. In the first class discussion of any new subject, a child can easily become confused. Therefore, ask the teacher to write you a note prior to a change in subject matter so that you can prepare your child for what to expect.

4. Relate the material your child is learning in school to life situations. Open up experiences for him that will give his school subjects new dimensions.

READING

Reading is of such paramount importance to the future of your hearing-impaired child that you should stimulate his interest in as many imaginative ways as you can devise. The oral language that he will miss can be compensated for if he is a good and enthusiastic reader, if he likes to read. Reading will serve to fill the holes in his vocabulary, language, and knowledge left by his imperfect hearing and speech-reading.

Many books on the subject of developing a good reader have been written, and many different teaching methods have been tried. The consensus of opinion, as far as I can determine, is that one or two methods may work well for any individual child, but no one method works for every child. A good teacher fits the method to the child. But, whatever method used, you can always help at home. So, here are several suggestions for encouraging your child to read for knowledge and pleasure.

Introducing Books

The single, most important thing you can do for your child is to bring books to his attention early. According to a 1975 Associated

Press news report, twenty top British educators came to the conclusion after three years of investigation that:

> the best way to prepare the very young child for reading is to . . . read aloud to him stories he likes—over and over. The printed page, the physical comfort and security, the reassuring voice, the fascination of the story—all these combine in the child's mind to identify books as something which hold great pleasure. (p. 10)

As you read to your child, stop occasionally to talk about what you have read, making sure he understands the story. Stimulate his imagination by guessing with him what may come next in the plot.

It isn't necessary to spend a large amount of money on children's books. But buying some of the more advanced classics for children is recommended, as they can become part of a person's library all his life. *Winnie the Pooh, Alice in Wonderland, The Wizard of Oz, Treasure Island,* and *Tom Sawyer* are examples. Use the library frequently for the bulk of books that will satisfy your child. Teach him to choose his own books for pleasure reading that are not beyond his ability, but rather just below his ability (so that frustration does not become synonymous with the experience of reading). The more he chooses his own books the better he will enjoy them.

Still, if a difficult library book excites his fancy and he insists on checking it out, let him do so and help him enjoy it; finding out for himself that he can sound out some of the harder words and understand their meaning will keep him reading and coming back for more. In some cases, the pictures alone may suffice for the value of the book. It's interesting to note that Arthur Gates in his book, *The Improvement of Reading,* lists among the reading-readiness skills the ability to interpret pictures, both still and moving. They are, he says, extremely fruitful sources of new ideas and experiences. Further, the skillful interpretation of pictures is a great help in learning to read since the illustrations often supplement the words of the book; and conversely, the words add to the interpretation of the picture (Gates, 1947).

Offering Experiences

Continue offering him experiences to build up a background of knowledge for his reading. Widen his vocabulary in many directions. If Dick and Jane go on an airplane ride, your child will read the story with better understanding after watching a real airplane taking off at the airport.

Aiding Memory

Encourage him to develop memory retention; he needs to store in his mind the written words he learns if he is to read easily. At first, help him remember by choosing books with simple words and phrases that are repeated many times. Show him words, the same ones he sees in his reading book, on cereal boxes, signs, TV, and in magazines until they are familiar to him and he recognizes them wherever they appear.

Practicing Phonics

It is imperative that your child develop confidence in his ability to sound out unfamiliar words for himself. This takes practice in phonics. Although most schools teach phonics, the teaching methods in the main depend on children hearing normally. Your child, being deficient in this sense, and likely in vocabulary also, can use all the extra help he can get. Your earlier work on speech sounds can be referred to and expanded (see Chapter 8). In conjunction with a review of your speech books, play a game in which you find small objects whose names start with the same sound and display them on a shelf. For the *p* sound, collect, among others, a picture of a puppy, a penny, and a pencil. Then print the letter *p* on a card and stand it on the shelf. For another display, use the diphthong *ou* with a small paper house, a toy mouse, and a towel.

Explaining Vocabulary, Setting Examples, and Building Confidence

When new vocabulary words come to light, promptly explain them in everyday language that he can understand. Continue to use these words as often as possible for a week or so afterward.

America is a nation of readers. A 1978 study of readers by the Book Industry Study Group indicated that a surprising 55 percent of Americans are book readers. Nonbook readers (those who read newspapers and magazines but rarely books) number 39 percent, while nonreaders form only 6 percent of the population (Kirsch, 1978). This is certainly an encouraging sign, and suggests the doomsday prediction that television would replace reading is not materializing. A parent who reads extensively will set a good example for his children.

One approach to beginning reading that teachers find successful is to spend a few months, before a standard reader is introduced, writing a series of short, three-sentence experience stories. The teacher, collaborating with the pupils, writes the stories on the blackboard.

Children like to read stories about themselves, so they read and copy these with enthusiasm, gaining confidence to begin reading printed material in books. At home, your journal (discussed later in this chapter) is the same idea—use it for practice in reading as well as for development of language.

Keeping Up

Don't let your child's reading level fall too far behind his class level. It's important to keep his reading level close to his age level, because the material available to him at his reading level may no longer interest him. An example is a story in a first-grade reader about a little boy riding a tricycle; for your older slow reader, say two grades behind his age group, such reading material may be on his level, but the subject matter is not. In fact, this story about a tricycle is old hat and almost insulting to an eight year old. If you are the parent of a slow reader, consult his teacher and the librarian. There are books to solve his problem, books with simple vocabulary on more mature subjects. Also, some low-level reading material is available at educational supply stores. If slow reading persists, consult a reading specialist.

By all means do all you can to aid the teacher in keeping his reading and vocabulary moving forward fast enough for him to be able, in due time, to read from standard textbooks. This is no small achievement, as teachers of the hearing impaired will tell you. They are often forced to rewrite material for the level of the reading vocabulary of their pupils. The longer your child depends on such spoon-fed material, the more difficult it will be for him to understand a standard text when it's presented. Since school texts are carefully written in graded steps of difficulty for language, vocabulary, and meaning, entering into this regular, step-by-step sequence as soon as possible, and getting away from dependence on specially prepared reading material, is advisable.

In this technological age in which we live, new electronic instruments are continually becoming available to us in the home, some of which, with ingenuity, can be additional, valuable learning tools. One of these is the television adapter that now brings a host of captioned programs and tapes to the hearing impaired. Further experiments are going on in real-time captioned television, such as the first-ever captioning of a presidential inauguration, other important news, and sports events. Spanish-language captioning is also steadily expanding its coverage.

I watched skilled editors captioning television programs recently at the Hollywood branch of the National Captioning Institute (NCI), the nonprofit organization formed to caption ABC, NBC, and PBS programs, as well as Department of Education and syndicated shows. Their procedure is to place a brief, printed version of the soundtrack on the screen in such a way as not to disturb the picture but still retain most of the original language and vocabulary. Skillful juggling of allotted viewing time and screen space for the caption are required so as not to exceed a target reading speed of 120 words per minute.

TV is such a popular, motivating medium that schools and programs for the hearing impaired have already recognized that captioning can greatly increase reading skills. Some children's programs like "Sesame Street" are already being captioned, and highly rated programs are also coming on the videodisc market. Principally, these are being introduced in the schools, but parents should, if possible, through the purchase of an adapter for closed captions, offer their hearing-impaired children extra reading time by this means. In addition, if you are fortunate enough to own a videorecorder, besides recording father's coveted sports events for later viewing, your child's favorite captioned programs can be recorded and played back as often as desired for review of language, vocabulary, and speed in reading.

WRITING

"Learning to write is the hardest, most important thing any child does," says Carlos Baker, Chairman of the English Department at Princeton University and author of a best-selling biography of Ernest Hemingway. "Learning to write is learning to think" (Sheils, 1975, p. 61).

If writing is difficult for the normally hearing child, it can be the despair of both the parents and teachers of the hearing-impaired child. For the hearing impaired, it is not only a sign of being educated, but also a medium of communication that fills in when oral communication breaks down. And now, with the advent of the teletypewriter as a popular telephone communication instrument for the hearing impaired, to be able to write what you want to say in straight, comprehensible language becomes doubly important.

A hearing-impaired child must learn to write the same language structure that he reads, but unfortunately this is usually not the same as he hears, speechreads, or signs. Speechreading, together with partial hearing, does not give a severely hearing-handicapped child a full picture of straight language. He loses the small words, the unaccented endings, and is forced to determine the meaning from an incomplete picture. Neither is the language of signs straight language, being made up of abbreviations, short cuts, and grammatical inversions. The new

Signing Exact English (SEE) sign language has been created in the hope of alleviating these shortcomings and it does, to some extent, in the classroom.

If your child is small and you have had little contact with hearing-impaired adults, it may come as a shock to you to learn that many of these adults have great difficulty writing an intelligent sentence. My first encounter with this was when I received a note from a hearing-impaired mother asking Linda to her house to play with her daughter after school. I found, after reading the note carefully, that all the necessary words were there, yet it was barely understandable. An adequate vocabulary alone isn't the answer if the words are not placed in their proper order according to English usage. Where grammar and syntax have been neglected in the growing years of a hearing-impaired child, you will find a resultant written language meager in quantity and riddled with errors.

Parents of hearing-impaired children often do not know of this writing problem until valuable time has elapsed during which they could have done something constructive about it. I want you to know it now when your child is young, and not when he begins to write garbled compositions. Study the two papers in Figure 6, which were written by children at sixth-grade level attending an oral day school. Check the language and note the words that are left out, unnecessary words, modifying words in the wrong places, and improper verb tenses.

A hearing-impaired child need not be burdened with a writing handicap when he is older if his parents follow a three-point program at home while he's young.

First, encourage his reading. "There is no question in the minds of educators that a student who cannot read with true comprehension will never learn to write well," reports Merrill Sheils in "Why Johnny Can't Write," *Newsweek* (Sheils, 1975, p. 59). Reading, then, should be your primary concern if you aim to do something at home about your child's writing ability. His reading should become both a discipline for learning and a diversion for pleasure.

Second, consistently correct his oral language. A pattern of thinking lucidly in words in their proper sequence must be established in order for them to be recalled for writing. All the more reason for you to encourage your child to talk, engage in frequent conversation, and for you to follow up by consistently correcting his language for its improper and incomplete structure. At the same time, he should be receiving a strong program in English grammar in school to improve his natural conversational language.

Where oral communication is curtailed because of multiple handicaps or for other reasons, I believe reading and writing of Eng-

Language

Last Saturday Jane came to the my house early morning. Jane and I picked up the my room. After my mother called for horse ride back. The man said, "2:00 horse ride back." My mother said, "OK." My mother told me the you and Jane ~~will go~~ ~~gone~~ to the horse ride back at 2:00. After while My mother, Jane and I went to the horse ride back. We cannot gone to the too because the rain in the Canoge Park. We went to the

My Weekend

Last Friday, my grandmother and Cathy came to my school to pick me up to grandmothers house Friday night, my cousin, Cathy had gone to Salton Sea Beach for two day. My grandma had made popcorn. I watched the television About 10:00, I had gone to bed.

Saturday morning, my grandma and I went to the beauty shop to fix my grandma's hair. A lady, who fixes someone's hair is just look like Mrs. F___, who cooked in the caferitrica. When my grandmas' hair was all fixed I saw rain and hail. they hit very hard and the lighting zoomed quickly. I was scared.

figure 6. Compositions by two hearing-impaired children in sixth grade at an oral day school.

lish should be approached and taught in school the same as a second language would be, with strong emphasis on vocabulary, grammar, and syntax. Educators are experimenting with this approach with normally hearing children whose families speak an alien language at home or who come from ethnic and geographically isolated groups who have evolved colloquial versions of the English language which they speak among themselves.

Third, promote a continual flow of writing coming from your child, correcting his errors as he goes. Having been taught the proper structure of English in oral language and in reading, the ability to write clearly and correctly still depends on practice. I can't emphasize enough the value of writing often, from your child's earliest years into adulthood. Writing done in school is not enough; a hearing-impaired child must also be persuaded to write at home. What he writes should be corrected by you and then copied properly by him in a final draft. Establishing this routine early will set a pattern with which he feels comfortable and thus accepts throughout his school years. On your part, limit your corrections to grammar and spelling, and try valiantly to retain the thought, flavor, and style of his writing.

Perhaps the greatest single need in writing is to be able to write a letter well. So, begin when he's young making homemade valentines, and birthday, Easter, Father's Day, Mother's Day, and any-day cards. Remember them all, for his relatives and friends can all be written on one occasion or another, if only a sentence or two. Develop in your child a firm habit of writing short letters and thank-you notes. Correct his early letters, even though later your child will be inclined toward privacy. Suggest that he have a pen pal. At present, relatively few hearing-impaired individuals have access to or own a teletypewriter, but using it is an excellent incentive to write clearly in anticipation of a quick, well-formed reply.

Another method of promoting writing is for you and your child to keep a diary or journal. At first, this is a big notebook wherein you write short sentences, illustrating them with cutouts and drawings of important events. This can supplement your work with the calendar. Through the school years, the diary becomes more regular and more in your child's own writing, thereby progressively expanding and refining his language. Hopefully, he will continue to make occasional entries in his diary for years. It is interesting to note that creative writing classes often expect the students to keep a daily journal to develop ease and skill in writing. I read recently of a well-known author who has kept a personal journal for twenty years to keep his writing flowing freely.

I believe that whatever homework writing assignment is done by your child should be corrected by you and recopied neatly by him before being returned, for it's in the copying that he learns best by his mistakes. For your hearing-impaired child's first homework of this kind, it will be hard for him to form his thoughts and put them into words on paper—suggest words, but don't write them for him.

The report, the next most important type of descriptive writing to learn well, is first developed at school from fourth to sixth grades. It continues to be assigned and further refined throughout one's school years, and later will very likely be needed in business life. It will be a positive asset for your child to have the ability to write an organized and comprehensible report for his teachers and later his colleagues and supervisor.

Report writing gives your child the advantage of drawing from source material and from the vocabulary of that material, although it must be understood that the material should never be copied. The stumbling block is to learn to put the material into his own words. This is no small accomplishment for any child, and for a hearing-impaired child who has trouble learning to think out a problem for himself, it is almost insurmountable. We know that allowing a child to copy the material verbatim will not lead to a lasting learning experience nor earn him a good grade. This is the time when you can give your child confidence in understanding what is written by others, organizing it, and writing his own version of the material.

In this regard, I experienced an example of the value of repeated writing assignments. When Linda was in sixth grade, a very wise teacher assigned each child an individual report on Mexico or one of the Central or South American countries.

The first one was a nightmare. It was difficult enough to get Linda to find the material with as little of my help as possible, but even a greater task to get her to write one word on paper. Never had she learned to find material by herself, organize it, decide its relative importance, and then write it in her own words. We sat with an encyclopedia open to "Mexico" for literally hours. I would say, "There is an important paragraph. Read it—what does it say?"

No answer.

Finally, in desperation, I gave her a first sentence—by then it was long past her bedtime.

Eventually, before the week was over, somehow the report was finished. A travel bureau furnished free brochures with pictures she could use to make it more interesting. It was turned in and returned in a few days with a satisfactory grade—but next week, another report, this time Costa Rica! This procedure continued through six reports: look up the country in the encyclopedia; put something on paper in orderly fashion, borrowing vocabulary but not copying; and obtain pictures from the travel bureau (who by now knew us by sight). But wonder of wonders, by the fourth report Linda was writing about half the report alone, the fifth was three-fourths hers, and the sixth was all her own! All were corrected and then copied, as I have suggested, and each one showed improvement with fewer and fewer errors. The experience was exhausting, but from that time on whatever report was assigned, a format had been established and she completed it by herself with confidence. And we've been thankful to that teacher ever since.

A book report, critique, or similar assignment will fall into place if your child both learns a set pattern to follow and sticks to his chosen subject. A formula to remember is: state your theme, prove it, and finally restate it.

More specifically, these reports should include the following:

1. An introduction, which includes a statement of the theme with every word carefully thought out.

2. The body, which consists of facts, explanations, and at least three proofs of the theme with references to the book.

3. A conclusion, which restates the theme in different words, develops it a little further, and may include a personal comment.

Tell your child to keep aiming at the target as he writes these reports; including a lot of extraneous material unrelated to the theme because it happens to interest him is a common error. Have him devote very little space to describing the total contents of the book. The teacher is interested in what your child learned from and thought of the book, not what the story is about—the teacher knows the story.

An an example, suppose your child is reporting on Daniel Defoe's *Swiss Family Robinson,* and has decided that he wants to write about how the Robinson family used their own ingenuity to make themselves more comfortable on the island. After having stated his theme carefully in the introduction, he then proceeds in the body to give three examples of how the family invented various contraptions for their comfort. To conclude, he should restate the theme, and he might add that this book would be a good one for people to read today who are interested in survival techniques for backpacking into wilderness areas.

When a child learns to write a good letter and report by himself, he will have mastered the most important types of writing that he will use an an adult. Creative stories and compositions are more difficult for a hearing-impaired child, particularly those in which he writes about himself. In this regard, Linda was called upon to write an article about herself as she entered college. Even though by this time she could compose a letter without flaw and write an excellent report, she stumbled on this assignment about her personal history and wrote an astoundingly incoherent paper. I was amazed at this result, but often, their minds being factual, this happens when the hearing impaired try to write clearly about themselves. Evidently their stored memory for vocabulary and syntax gets blocked out by their personal feelings.

If you are determined that your child learn to write proper English with ease, give him a reason to write, and to write often.

ARITHMETIC AND MATHEMATICS

A matter of importance for continued education is your child's steady progress in arithmetic and mathematics. Going on to high school and maybe college, he must have a sound basis in these subjects. These are concrete, precise subjects that don't depend heavily on language and a hearing-impaired child can excel in them if he has some aptitude for figures and problems.

Even though this whole subject area tends to be combined nowadays under the term *math,* I prefer to be old-fashioned and differentiate between arithmetic and mathematics. To me, arithmetic is the art of using real numbers in addition, subtraction, multiplication, and division; mathematics is the exact science of applying these numbers in relative quantities, like fractions, percentages, and decimals, so important to practical use in the home and business. This may be an oversimplification, but I wish to emphasize the importance of groundwork in arithmetic, both in accuracy and in speed, before the study of mathematics.

Arithmetic is a subject that should be learned logically, step by step, without interruption or omission. Unless special classes are highly structured, I question whether the total time spent on arithmetic is enough or that continuity in teaching each step is maintained from teacher to teacher. For these reasons, arithmetic should be taught to the hearing impaired as often as possible in the regular classroom to take advantage of the curriculum material used by the school district. To leave out a step in the sequence, such as long division, will have the hearing-impaired child struggling to catch up all along the way. Keep your child interested in doing arithmetic problems during the summer months, as it will improve his proficiency for the coming school year.

Language is guaranteed to slip into arithmetic and mathematics sooner than you expect with word problems. Hearing-impaired children who are slow at reasoning have great difficulty with them, particularly when the language of a familiar problem is given in different words or in a new structure. That is, they do not readily see similarities if problems are presented in an unusual manner. Most children initially need extra help with word problems, and our hearing-impaired children need even more. At home, this can partly be accomplished by giving your child practice in arithmetic and mathematics through real-life situations.

For example, your desire to save grocery money can give your child some interesting problems: How much money will he save in each case if he buys a one-gallon jug of milk instead of two half-gallon cartons or four one-quart cartons of milk?

In a similar but differently worded problem: His dad bought four tires for $80.00 on sale. If he had bought them individually, they would have cost $25.00 a piece. How much money did he save?

Problems of different types and wording will help improve his language comprehension.

GEOGRAPHY AND HISTORY

Now, more than ever before, a firm knowledge of geography and history is essential to our children's appreciation of their heritage and understanding of other peoples of our world. Communication between areas near and far is now possible directly within moments by the use of the telephone and other sophisticated telecommunication devices. Jets can take you any place in the world in a matter of hours. This generation is traveling as never before; the world has become just a backpack trip away from almost anywhere. Our young people need to know geography and world history to be intelligent about world affairs, and they must have a good background in American history and government to become responsible citizens.

School teaches geography and history by beginning with our own environment and gradually extending its limits to encompass the world. It may be difficult at first for your hearing-impaired child to envision areas he does not see and the past he cannot experience. Following the progress of his school's curriculum, give some thought to how you can add to his understanding of the world and its history as it unfolds for him.

School begins to teach geography in first grade by describing where you are now; first, the school itself, by the teacher and students drawing a map of the school grounds and buildings so they can see on paper the very play yards, walks, and buildings that they know well. The class then walks around the mapped area, visualizing the reality of the big buildings when they are scaled down to the small drawing or map. The concept and reading of maps will increase in importance as the child grows older.

From here, the teacher will move to study the streets, the signs and signals, and the "community helpers" (firemen, policemen, and so forth). Where do you live? What is the street number on your house, the name of the street on the street sign at the corner, and then your full address? Where is the grocery store and school from your house? What route does the school bus take?

From this beginning, your child's environment is again scaled down to fit on a piece of paper, showing where he lives in the context of the community. Later, this map is extended to the nearby cities, eventually the state, and finally the whole country. By fifth or sixth grade the class has moved to the adjacent neighbors of the United States, and in turn to Central and South America. Ever expanding outward, the class looks at the globe, learns about hemispheres and continents, and forms the base for world geography in junior high school.

At home you can draw a map of your house and the area around it. You can introduce maps obtained from the Chamber of Commerce of your city, showing your child that what he sees on the map in inches is comparable to the miles you drive on your errands. On a family trip, follow your route with a road map. If possible, obtain an atlas and a small globe for reference.

Many of the early books your child will bring home from the library will be about a little Swiss girl, or a Dutch boy, or some other foreign child. Don't neglect to find the place, on the map, where the child in the book lives in relation to where you live. Your youngster can learn to understand the vastness of the blue of the ocean and expansiveness and colors of the land. Note the different clothes the children wear in other countries.

History is a concept that evolves later. The fact that anything happened before your child's young life, your life, or even Grandmother's life, takes time to comprehend. The teacher will introduce it slowly about fourth grade with the Pilgrims at Thanksgiving, explorers in early American history, and the trek west across the plains to the Pacific Ocean. At home, a short course in family history will help your child become aware of the passage of time, using the calendar and old pictures to explain. Initially, he will be more interested in his family's genealogy, because it is close to him, than his teacher's introduction to early American life. Also, compare what interests your child at present with similar items from the past, such as old cars, sailing ships, biplanes, antique dolls, and the clothes Grandmother wore.

There is one area that neither you nor the teacher can altogether bridge—the ever-increasing use of films, tapes, slides, and television in the classroom. The media are a valuable supplemental tool for the teacher to use to further enhance the subject being studied, but a child with a severe hearing loss will seldom understand the sound track of these teaching media. What your child will receive, unless the film is captioned, is an incomplete message. A teacher should be told your child's limitation in this area. However, the class discussion afterward will help considerably; through these discussions and the reading of the textbook, the pictures will then mean enough to make the film's content intelligible. And, if the teacher knows your child, he or she may allow him some leeway in an assignment based on a visual medium.

SCIENCE

Science is all around you—the bean seed sprouting in a milk carton, the calendar, the pouring rain, and the pollywog losing its tail in the fish bowl. Science is watching the birds fly and feed, and discovering the miraculous industry of ants. You need only to go out into the backyard or to the local park to see and hear and feel natural science, the very subject the elementary school teacher is bringing to your child. How much more vibrant is the study of the parts of a flower if one watches a rose open or a daisy grow day by day! Rocks are everywhere for the taking to break apart and observe the wonders within.

Expose your child to natural science, explaining its phenomena at every opportunity. Studying science within the four walls of the classroom will take on more meaning when you add firsthand experiences with nature to your child's knowledge.

I once taught six year olds in a school located near the ocean. In springtime I reserved a week or two to talk of the water and the beach and the words connected with them. I collected items for display: some seaweed, sand, shells, rocks, and saltwater. To this I added pictures of fish, crabs, and ocean scenes. Notes were sent home telling the parents what we were studying. One little boy arrived at school the next day with a shoe box clutched tightly under his arm and his eyes like stars. No one could touch that box, but he let us see his treasure. His mother had taken him walking for a half hour on the beach the evening before, and in his box was a shell, a rock, a piece of seaweed, and a leg and half the shell of a small crab. Sand was on everything and the smell of the ocean permeated the cardboard container. For that little boy, what I said about the beach and its vocabulary came alive that day.

chapter *15*

activities outside elementary school

When observing a child's pattern of social play at the kindergarten level, he can be placed in one of three categories, as one who: 1) plays alone or alongside the others, watching the other children play, 2) plays with one other child, or 3) plays in a group.

A child matures progressively, moving through all three categories at different times and rates. This development from single to group play is the way all children learn to socialize, and a child entering kindergarten can be in any one of the three stages. Neither intelligence nor age nor background seems to have as much to do with how quickly a child begins to play in a group as both temperament and personality. Children at this age are generally accepted by the other children as they are, and left to develop their social-play habits in their own way and at their own speed.

Kindergartners play happily alongside each other or together without any great need for conversation. They will usually accept a child with a hearing loss after a very simple explanation of his hearing aid and lack of speech. Your hearing-impaired child will enter the play like any other child at whatever level of social play he is in at the time, his hearing loss being less a factor than his personality.

However, as time passes, the give-and-take of conversation becomes more important in play, and it will probably always be easier for your severely or profoundly hearing-impaired child to play one-to-one, whatever his age. Because it's easier, he may linger in this second stage without progressing, slipping behind in social maturity. The only difference between him and the other children is his inability to hear the conversations that swirl in the background of his life, and it is likely that the lack of stored information gained from these conversations is a cause for a difference in maturity. With the help of everyone at home and your good neighbors, he should be encouraged to join group play in the neighborhood and organized youth groups to keep him socially in tune with children at his academic level. Sometimes it is recommended that a hearing-impaired child enter the regular classroom a year or two later in age than the other children solely because of his social maturity. This should be decided purely on an individual basis, and take into account that a child does better school work when he is comfortable in the classroom.

If busing your child away to a special school is necessary, then the problem of neighborhood play is confounded by the lack of the good school-related friendships that ordinarily develop between children. Your child will find it harder, but not impossible, to play in his home neighborhood with the other children, depending on his outgoing nature, ability to play fairly and to hold his temper, and the other characteristics that make up a young child's personality.

Often, parents of hearing-impaired children complain bitterly that their child is left out of neighborhood play. These parents can't afford to be complacent. From a realistic viewpoint, they should be prepared to give more of their time and energy, in their own home and yard, to the neighborhood children than the other parents do. Forget about whether or not another parent does his or her share of entertaining—don't expect an ideal fifty-fifty arrangement with neighbors and friends when your child has a hearing loss. Open your yard to the neighbors' children, lure the kids in for a special game, have cookies and juice on hand and popsicles occasionally. Even though the neighborhood children may not unequivocally take your child into their group, he will learn as a passive participant.

By all means, let your child learn by himself. Keep out of the play except for very special occasions, and try not to champion him or be picky about his faults more than is absolutely necessary. If he doesn't manage with other children now, it will be harder for him to adjust as he grows older.

A close friendship between your child and a normally hearing child is much desired. He will learn many things and especially new language that you can't teach him as easily. There exists a rapport and a common language between children. In addition, your child will exert a special effort to be accepted by his friend.

It is regrettable, but true, that children often accept a special child before their parents do, and surely before parents of neighborhood children. Like being diplomatic with the school administrators and teachers, exercise this same art within your neighborhood. Be a goodwill ambassador while explaining your child's hearing loss. This will also benefit others who have a hearing-impaired child, because for every person who understands this handicap there is one less uninformed adult in the world to call these children "deaf and dumb," or expect them (as I was once told) to be kept off the streets "for their own safety," or feel for some inexplicable or prejudiced reason that their child shouldn't play with your child. Lack of understanding is usually the cause of negative reactions to your child in the neighborhood. Therefore, the more they know about hearing impairment the better. If you explain about your child in a patient, friendly manner, you will get the positive results you want.

JOINING GROUPS

About second grade, your child is eligible to join a program such as Boy Scouts or Campfire Girls. This is a wonderful experience, and your boy or girl should have this opportunity if possible. It gives your child the chance to participate in a group situation with children his own age, as well as the prestige of wearing the club uniform and "belonging." However, these groups expect a parent's cooperation and participation, and for you it means, again, being prepared to offer more of your time and energy than the other parents.

There are many important considerations in choosing a group for your child. When a child goes to a distant school for special classes, there is often a decision to make between signing him up in a group from his school or in a group from his neighborhood. If he joins a group from school, he will know the children and relate to them better, but if he joins a neighborhood group he increases his list of friends, and these children, living in the vicinity of his home, will be the ones he plays with the most. Transportation and timing are factors. In the case of the group near his school, his regular transportation probably would not be available after the meeting and you might have to pick him up. But the choice may depend on your schedule, as you still might have to pick him up early at school to be on time for the neighborhood meeting. If it can possibly be arranged, the decision should be the neighborhood group, particularly if you feel your child has the potential, later on, to go to his own neighborhood school.

To illustrate my point, placing Linda in the right group turned out to be a happy, once-in-a-lifetime experience. While she was in a special day-school program some distance away, I thought she should have a group experience and chose Campfire Girls because this program, generally speaking, seemed less structured and competitive than the larger Girl Scout program. Linda was already integrated part of a day in regular classes, and our goal was for her to enter her own neighborhood school whenever appropriate. For this reason, I decided on our neighborhood group, even though there was a group she could have joined at school.

The next decision was whether she should join a group of girls her own age or one where the girls were a year younger but at her probable school-grade level. I floundered, made the wrong decision, putting her in the group of girls her own age. She was readily accepted by the leader, but as I watched her progress in school that year, I realized she was drawing closer to the day when she might integrate fully into her own neighborhood school, and that her school friends would be one year younger than she.

Upon contacting the younger group's leader to arrange for a possible move, I was very firmly told, "Yes, we'll accept your daughter, providing you are willing to help as assistant leader." So, I became assistant leader to the group, in spite of the fact that I knew nothing about Campfire Girls and had a new baby in a basket. The baby and basket went along, and Linda joined the new group.

For two years I assisted, and Linda seemed to enjoy it, even though she quietly followed on the fringes of the activities the majority of the time. For an anxious mother, this didn't seem as much as I had hoped for, but soon I knew that it was enough, because at fifth grade it was decided that she was ready to enter our neighborhood school. What mother doesn't suffer the fears of cruel retaliation or rejection of her hearing-impaired child when he first enters the regular classroom? I was no exception, but it just never happened, thanks to twelve dear Campfire Girls who reacted with absolute sisterly joy when told she would be in their class. They took her around and showed her everything the first day, treated her as one of their own group, and eased that first week in the new school as neither I nor the teacher could ever have done. My extra effort was more than repaid. The power of children with children!

For boys, there are Boy Scouts, Indian Guides, Little League, soccer, football, and so on; girls have their comparable clubs and sports. Sports are a real ego-builder for well-coordinated boys and girls, but Dad should help with the rules of the game and what to expect on the field. Remember when playing outdoors, language and sounds for the hearing impaired are affected by distance, air currents, and other sounds, and they dissipate quickly into the atmosphere.

Other interesting activities include baton twirling, gymnastics, drill team, folk dancing, square dancing, and other forms of dancing. Children with very severe hearing losses can follow a beat, which they may partly hear and partly feel through vibrations. I watched hearing-impaired children dancing at one school for the deaf where the stereo speakers had been placed under a wooden dance platform to increase the vibrations of the music in the floor. Hearing-impaired children can learn to follow the others in a regular dance group. They may be a split second behind as they get a cue from the person next to them, but with practice this becomes almost imperceptible.

Also, the best time for your child to learn ballroom dancing is when the other children he knows take lessons, around sixth grade. Ready or not, he will learn the steps and proper etiquette with his friends, acquiring the confidence he needs later to dance socially. Hearing-impaired children enjoy social dancing and become quite proficient. In schools for the deaf, dances are held regularly and are very popular in the upper grades. Therefore, your child should have no reason to hesitate to attend dances with normally hearing friends.

What is more, hearing-impaired children can and do learn to play musical instruments; and the child who doesn't shine in music may be great in athletics or in science, winning acclaim on the track or for a fine entry in the science fair. In a farming community, being active in a 4H Club is an excellent endeavor for a hearing-impaired child.

THE TELEPHONE

Parents may not be aware when their hearing-impaired child is small how much it will mean to him to be able to use the telephone when he's a teenager. A teenager's inability to communicate by way of the telephone further sets him apart from the other young people and becomes an awkward liability in his social life. When he is an adult, his inability to use the telephone can limit his achievement and the type of employment available to him as well as his opportunity for advancement in business. In many cases this need not be.

The value of training in the use of the telephone has been recognized by the National Technical Institute for the Deaf (NTID) in Rochester, New York, where hearing-impaired students beyond the high school level are trained for semiprofessional and professional employment. Diane L. Castle, Ph.D. (clinical research audiologist, Department of Audiology, NTID), described in a recent journal article, two courses available at NTID on the use of the standard telephone and teletypewriter (TTY) equipment (Castle, 1977). And in a subsequent 1978 issue Dr. Castle gave some revealing statistics on the number of young NTID students who could be included in these two courses:

> The following data are based on entry statistics for 1,070 NTID students enrolled as of July 1974 through September 1977. From this population, 844 students (79 percent) can learn to use some type of code or the oral/auditory strategies described in this article. The remaining 21 percent have limitations in speaking ability and/or phrasing the English language that prevents their independent use of the telephone. However, these students may improve their skills while at NTID and then become eligible for telephone training.
>
> Specifically, the data suggest that 329 students (31 percent) have the potential to learn to use oral/auditory strategies over the amplified telephone handset with strangers. These students meet the following criteria: a) they have used personal amplification in the earmold over the telephone for fourteen years, on the average; b) they have the ability to understand many words and sentences with hearing only; c) they have speech that is understood by most people; and d) they have good language skills.
>
> Further, 515 students (48 percent) have the potential to learn to use the "No," "Yes-Yes," or "Please Repeat" oral/auditory codes over the amplified telephone handset with family, friends, and others who know them. The data show that 302 of the 515 students meet the following criteria: a) they use a hearing aid in the ear used over the telephone; b) they are able to discriminate among a one-, two-, and three-syllable rhythm pattern; c) they have speech that can be understood by people who know them; and d) they are able to phrase questions which would result in the coded response.
>
> The remaining 213 students also would be able to detect rhythm patterns on the telephone except for the fact that they do not use amplification. The amplified telephone handset by itself does not provide enough loudness. If these students were using hearing aids, they would be capable of discriminating among the rhythm patterns. Instead, they learn to use a code method which requires the hearing person to call back so the deaf person can feel a prearranged number of rings when the hand is placed on the telephone. These students meet the required speech and language criteria for this method.
>
> It is important for deaf people to have options. These training programs acquaint NTID students with a variety of ways to use the telephone, including the use of the TTY. As informed adults, they can select from among the various possibilities depending on the situation. (pp. 119–120)

(Parents interested in reading about strategies for successful telephoning and a coded system for the telephone can refer to Dr. Castle's article and to an article by Raymond J. McLeon, Jr., and Martha Guenther in the December, 1977 issue of *The Volta Review*.)

In view of the added handicap that an inability to use the telephone places on a hearing-impaired adult and Dr. Castle's data on young adults that suggest far more could use the telephone with proper training than do so, the use of the telephone by your hearing-impaired child should give you reason for serious thought.

Let's consider first the peculiar qualities of the telephone. It is an instrument of communication entirely dependent upon speech and hearing. It is not a high fidelity instrument, like a good stereo or even a fine hearing aid. It covers a limited frequency range, from approximately 300 Hz to 3300 Hz, and has no range of volume except when coupled with a special amplified volume control (which, in itself, is limited for a person with a severe or profound loss) (Western Electric, 1980). What is missing in the frequency range is automatically supplied from a normally hearing person's memory, so that he's not aware that he's not actually hearing all the higher overtones of the sound *s*, for instance. Still, since the telephone is held at the ear, and, therefore, allows the ear to receive the optimum in volume and quality, it is a remarkably reliable instrument for transmitting voice.

A large percentage of people with a hearing loss can, surprisingly, learn to communicate on a telephone with varying degrees of adjustment. Each person works out the best way for himself. The combination of hearing aid together with an amplified telephone handset, available from the telephone company, can bring telephone voices within the hearing range of many of the hearing impaired. In 1971, I visited Mr. Roy K. Holcomb, Area Supervisor of classes for the deaf in the James Madison School, Santa Ana, California. I watched Mr. Holcomb, who is hearing impaired, talk on the telephone with such ease while using this combination that I was amazed, and inquired as to his degree of hearing loss. He showed me his audiogram which recorded a 90 dB loss for speech, adding that the telephone is not a handicap in his work in spite of his profound loss.

Our daughter, Leslie, with an 82 dB loss, improves steadily on the telephone with practice, but her understanding is uncertain when voices or subjects are unfamiliar or change in midstream. Daughter Linda, with a 97 dB loss, uses the telephone less, but does so with pride. She is unable to comprehend the full conversation. "Even when someone is helping me," she says, "I like to get the mood of the conversation by listening myself; I can enjoy moments of laughter only by using my aided hearing to listen. It is also a pleasure to recognize a familiar voice."

Further, using the telephone is dependent upon a hearing-impaired person having reasonably intelligible speech. However, for reasons beyond my technical knowledge, speech that may seem to be a poor candidate for good telephone communication comes over the wire with more intelligibility than expected. I would suggest you listen to a hearing-impaired person's voice over the telephone first before judging it unintelligible.

Profoundly deaf professional men, such as Dr. H. Latham Breunig and Dr. James C. Marsters, have learned to use the standard telephone service in their businesses with the help of a secretary and two telephones on the same line. The secretary listens through one receiver within sight of the person telephoning and repeats, in a low voice or without voice, exactly what the speaker says on the other end of the line. The telephoner speechreads the secretary and carries on his side of the conversation through his telephone. With one telephone, the same result can be attained through a third party using a watchcase receiver attached to the instrument. The hearing impaired can become so proficient in this method that it is difficult to tell that one of the parties cannot hear, except for an occasional slight delay in responding. Linda learned this method from Dr. Marsters, and now calls us with the aid of a friend who has mastered repeating the total conversation for her.

I find it difficult to be an adequate telephone interpreter. To be competent, one must repeat exactly what one hears, no more and no less. Somehow I keep forgetting this and add a word or two of my own in a motherly fashion, confusing both parties and spoiling the smooth continuity of the conversation. I am told that I'm not alone, that other people find it difficult to repeat conversation word for word. They end up paraphrasing what they hear or even jump the gun on the telephoner with an answer to what was said at the other end.

When our hearing-impaired girls were using body aids, it was some trick to position the hand phone upside down, one end near the hearing aid on the chest and the other at the mouth. They usually would take their hearing aid off and place it directly on the receiver end of the telephone. Linda has since purchased an old-fashioned telephone with the receiver and attached cord hung on the side of the upright instrument. This design allows more leeway in placing the receiver securely on or near the aid in the best possible position for reception, whether on a body or behind-the-ear aid. The use of a body aid with the telephone held upside down has the further disadvantage of appearing very strange to others; it can be embarrassing for a sensitive teenager to use the telephone in this way in public. Leslie recalls when returning at night to the school parking lot from an athletic event or bus excursion, she would wait until everyone had gone home before telephoning us to pick her up.

Dr. Castle's advice that one should have options is indeed well founded. A profoundly hearing-impaired person cannot always be sure that two telephones or the necessary help will be available. Only recently have we been receiving telephone calls that are more exciting to us than any before. One of us will pick up the telephone and hear, "Hello, this is Linda. I'm alone, but I want to tell you so and so. . . ." With this, she is able to understand short, identifiable replies like "Okay, "Fine," or "That's wonderful!" Goodbyes are said, and the communication has been most satisfactory. Linda has carried most of the conversation. This, we have found, is the secret to successful telephone conversations with both girls. The difficulty of rephrasing something they will understand better or of introducing a new subject, is best avoided, if possible, in favor of receiving the hearing-impaired person's message. Of course, if you have something really important to say, you may have to persist by trying several times to phrase the message in more familiar terms.

Numbers can be reached by counting ("I will pick you up at three o'clock—1, 2, 3") or by spelling, a method telephone operators often use. If desperate, use the alphabet. Linda described to me a method she used successfully with a friend for a prearranged conversation. She was to meet a friend at a bus station, but she did not know what day or the time of arrival. It was arranged that her friend call on a certain day at a certain time with this information. The conversation went something like this:

Friend: "I'll be coming on Tuesday at two o'clock in the afternoon."

Linda: "Sunday?"

Friend: "No."

Linda: "Monday?"

Friend: "No."

Linda: "Tuesday?"

Friend: "Okay!"

Linda: "In the morning?"

Friend: "No."

Linda: "In the afternoon?"

Friend: "Okay!"

Linda: "At one o'clock?"

Friend: "No."

Linda: "Two o'clock?"

Friend: "Okay!"

Linda: "Okay, I'll be there on Tuesday at two o'clock in the afternoon. Goodbye."

Linda has also had some satisfactory telephone calls with a friend helping her when there was no second telephone available. By holding the receiver away from her hearing aid slightly, a second person can hear the conversation with enough success to repeat it for speech-reading. An amplified handset would increase the volume, allowing the second person to pick up the conversation better.

Pay telephones tend to have less volume than a home telephone, and of course are not equipped with any optional volume control. Our telephone company admits that their recently installed pay telephones don't have the volume of their older instruments. To remedy this, they have developed an "adapter" appliance that, when attached by the caller, increases the volume of the new telephones. Check your local telephone company regarding availability of this item.

Use of a pay telephone for a long-distance call is a gamble at best, even for a person with a less-than-severe hearing loss. Going through the operator presents problems as, all too often, even after explaining one's hearing loss, the operator sounds rushed, clips his or her speech, and is sometimes rude. It is safer for a hearing-impaired person to have someone standing by to help if necessary with this type of call.

The use of tapes by some businesses to instruct a caller is a confusing experience for a hearing-impaired person who is unprepared for this strange answering voice. Typically, tapes have static and poor quality of voice, making it difficult, if not impossible, to understand them. After purchasing her first car, Leslie joined an automobile club, feeling it would give her added protection against emergencies. She did have a minor emergency and called them on a pay telephone, only to have a tape recorder answer in a jumble of unintelligible words. She hung up in confusion, and was fortunate enough to have a Good Samaritan come to her immediate aid. Later she learned that the tape had told her to wait, that all the lines were busy.

Anticipate that any preparation for your hearing-impaired child's use of the telephone will probably be up to you. What, then, can you do as a parent to prepare your child during the growing years? Certainly, all you do in the way of auditory training will improve your child's telephone communication. Work on his learning to understand from hearing alone such words as *okay, no, maybe, hello, goodbye,* and the numbers, as a bare minimum. As against *yes* and *no,* the two syllables of *okay* are easier to understand than *yes,* which is hard to distinguish from *no*. Or use an alternate positive and negative like *yes* and *no-no*.

Encourage your child to carry on conversations, as has been emphasized earlier, and in your own speech use the "fill-ins" that keep conversation moving along, so that he can pick them up and use them in the right places. On the telephone, lack of speech for even a few seconds leads to a worried "Hello, hello, are you there?" The fill-ins will preclude these blank spots and keep the conversation lively.

When your child is small, you can begin to play telephone with two toy telephones, or by just placing one hand to your ear and the other to your mouth. I found six year olds shy and utterly tongue-tied when I initiated this type of play in the classroom. So, we developed a little planned routine:

"Hello?"
"Hello, this is John. Who is this?"
"This is Candy."
"Can you come over to my house to play?"
"Okay. Goodbye."
"Goodbye."

This set pattern got them off block A, and their imaginations then led them to longer conversations. Although in a normal school day I couldn't pursue this thoroughly, it is an idea with which parents can experiment and expand upon.

During the early elementary school years, introduce your child to a real telephone. Have him listen to the dial tone and busy signal; dial the number for the correct time and listen; and dial a number you know answers by a short tape repeated over and over. Determine the best place for the telephone receiver near his hearing aid, and see how much he understands at its different volume settings. Experiment with the telephone control if there is one on his hearing aid. Sometimes this control is of value, and sometimes a person prefers to use the telephone on normal control. Those favoring normal control say that the telephone control cuts out all outside sound and, consequently, they can't hear their own voice. Look into installing an amplified telephone handset; one is usually set up in your local telephone company office where you can test its value for your child.

Go to a neighbor's house and call your child on the telephone. Of all voices, yours will probably be the easiest for him to understand. Close family members can talk to him a few minutes. If he has a good friend, perhaps you can get them started calling each other. The more confident and comfortable he is with the telephone, the less frightening it will be. Such preparation will ease the time when he will want to use the telephone to discuss personal matters. It is only natural that young people calling your teenager will not do so as readily if they know that their message will have to be relayed through someone else in the family.

Give him opportunities to have various telephone experiences: help him with pay telephones; formulate a planned procedure for calling a friend; let him participate in a call through the operator for a long-distance number; and discuss the standard tapes he might hear. When he has more courage, stand by while he answers the telephone himself the first few times. Then, let him experience for himself whatever comes.

At the Alexander Graham Bell Convention in San Francisco in 1968, I met Sister Nathanael Joseph of St. Joseph's Institute for the Deaf, St. Louis, Missouri. Sister Nathanael herself is hearing impaired. "Why," she said to me with feeling, "can't we have our telephone hooked into our home television set on a special channel?" The thought took my fancy, as it seemed a likely solution to telephone communication for the hearing impaired.

Since then, we have been able to plug into our television a regular area cable; a special cable showing movies, sports, and special events; electronic games; a videotape recorder; a TV captioning adapter; and a computer. Only the other day an article in the *Los Angeles Times* told of a plug-in now available allowing a person to watch home movies and slides on his own television screen. And not too long ago *National Geographic* reported, "In Lancaster, Pennsylvania, RCA engineers showed me tiny light-sensing electronic chips, known as CCD's, that they say may someday take the film out of photography and give us home movies we can view immediately." (Gore, 1978, p. 364).

To all the technical geniuses out there, Sister and I ask, "Why not the telephone through our home television set?"

RELIGION

The abstract quality of religious study is indeed difficult for a hearing-impaired child to comprehend. Parents should proceed slowly by teaching love, consideration for others, and moral values from their own example, as well as acquainting their child with a place of worship.

Some parents of hearing-impaired children will be deeply troubled by the possibility that their child will grow up unschooled in the tenets of their religious beliefs. This is a place for patience and tolerance. No doubt your child will take longer absorbing the basis of your religion, its history, doctrines, and the significance of services and ceremonies; but in time, with study, expanded language, and maturity, he will understand.

As your child's language grows, enroll him in Sunday School. He will benefit from new friends and the basic religious stories, especially if he has some preparation for the class in advance. Many denominations distribute specific lesson plans for Sunday School teachers to follow. Ask for a copy of each lesson in advance, and use it as a guide to teach your child in your own way before the Sunday class. Preparing your child yourself will enable him to learn the material thoroughly at a slower pace. Consequently, Sunday School will mean more to him.

You can expect that the singing, which is so important a part of most religious meetings, will be somewhat frustrating for your hearing-impaired child. When he is able to read, have him sing along with the others, following the hymn book as best he can. If he can't keep a tune or always follow the words, don't despair. In a large gathering his voice will blend in well enough with the other children and adults, despite drawing an occasional surprised glance from his neighbor.

Don't be overly worried about your child's adoption of religion. Embracing a religious belief is an experience that comes to each individual in his own time, and often in his own way. Indeed, I watched one of our hearing-impaired children, whom I considered ill-prepared to accept the concepts of religion, embrace a faith from personal desire when she was at college.

If you give your child a moral background, family support, and teach basic religious concepts as you know and live them, then surely with maturity, knowledge, and faith this door will open for him when he is ready.

PREPARING IN ADVANCE

Another time when advance preparation is well worth the effort is when your hearing-impaired child plans to see a movie, stage play, musical, or other performance involving a plot. The best speechreader has difficulty following the story on a movie screen, live stage, or TV. After purchasing tickets for a performance or when you know in advance of a select television screening, try to obtain a copy of the story for your child to read before he sees the show. Knowing the full text makes the experience doubly rewarding. Leslie, who loves drama, seeks out the script or the book on which the drama is based and reads it thoroughly before she goes to the theater—even a critique or review will give some idea of the story. This may spoil a surprise ending, but it is still better than not understanding how the ending came about.

Whatever the media, encourage your child to read the story (if available) after he sees any dramatized production; this will enable him to tie together the loose ends of the plot and other more subtle features underlying narrative and action.

"WHY AM I DIFFERENT?"

This question from your child throws many a parent off guard; it can be asked at any time, and is admittedly difficult to answer. Prepare yourself for answering this question, because you must give him an answer. Parents, their children, and the circumstances can be so diverse that it's not possible to propose a specific answer here, but explain to him the best you can, considering all the personal knowledge you have about his handicap and its cause (if known).

I can offer one suggestion that I found helpful in Linda's acceptance of her handicap: give your child the opportunity to be with children having other handicaps. Quite by accident, one summer, Linda had an experience that brought this strikingly to my attention. She attended a Crippled Children's Society day camp in the park with some of her hearing-impaired friends and encountered there, for the first time, children in wheelchairs and blind children. She discovered for herself that only the hearing-impaired children could run, jump, and play with abandon in spite of their handicap. She found herself pushing wheelchairs, leading the blind, and generally helping others. Any question of "Why am I different?" dissolved when she met children that she thought had more serious handicaps than her own.

The hearing impaired's handicap of communication, we know, is not one of the easiest to overcome, but it can be done, as Linda discovered at college when there were two blind girls living in her dormitory. They quickly became good friends, and Linda made up her mind about her own handicap for sure at that time. She found, in spite of her long, hard road to gain communication skills and education, that, in the long run, she was more self-sufficient than these girls. She could do more for herself and for others than they could. She could understand through speechreading most of what other people said; she could speak well enough for people to understand her; she could read books without the cumbersome size and translation problems of Braille; and she could drive a car.

My favorite story is the one Linda tells of how she and one of the blind girls liked to watch television together. Excitedly, the blind girl would ask, "What happened? What did they do?" And Linda, almost simultaneously, would find herself asking her friend, "What happened? What did they say?" Between them they found they understood the program and enjoyed it more than each one ever could alone.

CONTINUING INDEPENDENCE

During your hearing-impaired child's elementary school years, his mastery of new facts, communication, and other skills will be growing, as will his desire for independence. As he begins to test his wings, let him expand his horizons beyond the home. However strong your desire may be to protect him, his need to learn to cope with the outside world begins now. Overprotection makes the break from the family, that must come in time, all the more painful. Because of his hearing handicap, he may take a little longer to learn how to manage by himself, but the moment to break away should not be prolonged. Let him do for himself what he is capable of doing. Your confidence will inspire his own self-confidence.

There are many ways that lead to "cutting the cord," so to speak, and you, as parents, should foster their implementation. For instance, after your child has learned all the traffic rules for bicycling, he should be allowed to join his friends in riding around the neighborhood or to school in some cases. Of course, be as careful as you can in doing the groundwork before granting this authority—it may still come later than for his hearing friends, but it must come.

Soon he can be sent to the store when you believe he can negotiate the busier streets safely. Running errands for the family builds his confidence. He will feel genuine pleasure in accomplishment when he finally asks for an item behind the counter and the clerk understands and acknowledges his request. I will never forget, and surely the girls will never forget, the joy of that first moment.

As mentioned earlier, as parents of a hearing-impaired child you will undoubtedly be asked and want to participate in your child's first experiences with youth groups. However, after a year or two, arrange to step down in favor of another person. Your child should have an opportunity to relate to a group situation by himself, as it will give him further experience learning to get along with people.

These are small happenings to the majority of children, but to your hearing-impaired child they are great milestones. The day he first rides his bike in the street with his friends, his first trip to the store alone, and the day he is chosen the third baseman on the baseball team will be treasured memories.

part IV

the junior and senior high school years

"Dependence is the greatest handicap of all."

**Editorial, Indianapolis News,
June 27, 1974**

chapter 16

junior and senior high school

Modern education is placing more and more emphasis on the integration of hearing-impaired children into a normal school environment, no matter whether they are educated by the oral, aural/oral, or total communication method. Children may be assigned to a self-contained class, but now more often they are placed in regular classes and a concerted effort is made to orient the school to their needs. With the modern advances in hearing aids and teaching techniques, a hearing-impaired child should be able, barring other complications, to take his place in a regular classroom by the junior or senior high school level, if he has learned the basics of reading, writing, and arithmetic, and is able to keep his attention on a speaker for a reasonable period of time. Ideally, a child benefits most when he integrates fully by the fifth or sixth grade in his neighborhood school, so that he can start junior high with a nucleus of classmates that he knows.

For any child, the move from elementary to junior high school is the most traumatic experience of his school years. Consider that out of a single classroom situation the child is suddenly thrust into a whole new scheduled world, consisting of six or more teachers in six different classrooms, with strict time schedules regulating the classes and the short breaks between classes, staggered lunch periods, and the fast-change artistry of dressing for gym. If your school system has a separate junior high school, I would consider the time your child enters to be the crossroads in his school life, even more than high school, which is really a continuation in a similar, but larger, environment. Therefore, at the age of eleven or twelve a child suddenly must learn to stand on his own two feet as he has never done before. For a hearing-impaired child, it is that much more of an adjustment. Having fully prepared the previous environment for your child, you must now do it all over again for the new school. Set the stage as best you can by seeing the counselor in May before summer vacation. Again, have your child visit the new school, if not earlier with his sixth-grade class, with you or an older child just before opening day.

At this level, even more than elementary, there are absolutely no guarantees that teachers will know your child has a hearing loss; by the time you should visit the new school, after a week or two of letting things settle down, they still may not know. It can't be assumed that each teacher assigned to your child knows and understands just because the nurse does, the speech therapist does, or the counselor does. The teachers will have a large load to handle, many pupils to keep track of, and the chance of their having read your child's records is slim. Propose that there be a meeting of all of your child's teachers at which time they can be oriented to your child's handicap and his needs. This can be arranged best by the counselor, with the school nurse and the speech therapist participating. Even if there is such a meeting, you should still schedule individual conferences with all your child's teachers.

It will be an outgoing hearing-impaired child indeed who can find the words and courage to tell the teachers about his hearing difficulties by himself. You should do it at this stage, but, by the end of high school he will have to assume this responsibility with future teachers, instructors, professors, and eventually, his employers. It took my girls until their junior year in high school before they found the courage to explain their hearing problems to most of their teachers.

If possible, have your child's schedule arranged so that the subjects that require extensive speechreading, like history and English, are in the morning hours when your speechreader is fresh and rested.

Sitting near the front of the class is still the rule, but occasionally there are exceptions. One day, Leslie mentioned casually that she was sitting in the back row of her high school history class. I was quite disturbed until I learned that the room was small and the teacher had a large mouth, expressive face, and booming voice. What a delicious feeling it must have been for her finally to sit at the back of the room in a class!

Frequently, teachers comment that they like the attention a speechreader gives them, as their eyes continually stay on the teacher's face. They are pleased to direct their speech to one whom they are sure is paying strict attention. Many teachers welcome this opportunity to improve their diction and general presentation—it awakens them to the poor habits they may have formed. But, there will always be those who keep on talking into a book, to the blackboard, or out the window.

Teachers often ask with some concern whether or not your hearing-impaired child should be expected to take his turn speaking in front of the class when an oral report has been assigned. By all means! The experience of speaking before a group is excellent for gaining confidence, practicing clear speech, and learning to speak loud enough for everyone to hear. During the first year of junior high school Linda gave an oral report. I took the opportunity to check the clarity of her speech by asking the teacher whether she and the other students could understand her. "Yes," she said, "I understood her fairly well, and there was the most interesting reaction from the class—it was so quiet during the time she was speaking you could hear a pin drop!" Thus, the effort your child exerts to speak clearly and the effort made by the other children to listen harder are two distinct benefits gained from this experience.

Some time ago I attended a conference of parents of hearing-impaired children and listened to a panel of teachers. In the question-answer period, one parent asked, "My child is about ready to enter a regular high school, where can I find special help for him?" A teacher who knew that I had a hearing-impaired daughter in regular high school at the time referred the question directly to me. Being unprepared and flustered, I gave a simplistic answer, essentially saying no more than that my daughter was only getting help from her family.

All the way home in the car that day I scolded myself for the utter incompleteness of my answer. I should have said his child could get lots of help from outside sources, and it needn't be from a professional teacher of the deaf. There comes a time when a hearing-impaired child should have outgrown the need for such a special teacher, and certainly that time is in junior or senior high school. By that time, his speechreading and listening ability should be refined enough for him to learn from regular teachers and advanced students. What he may need is tutoring, possibly some supportive work in speech, and, of course, continued strong support from his family. In some cases, an interpreter, notetaker, and supplemental reading material may be advisable.

Your primary value to your child should not be in your knowledge of modern math, science, and history, even though you give some valuable assistance, but in your guiding him to where he can find the help and basic material he needs for these subjects, how to supplement with extra reading, and how to organize what he learns for tests and written papers. Many teachers of the hearing impaired are not sufficiently trained in these high school subjects, and consequently your child may receive better tutoring from a regular teacher or an advanced student. There is usually ample help for the asking within the school itself in the academic subjects. For speech, the school's speech therapist, with a keen ear and trained in the finer points of speech, can improve the speech of the older hearing-impaired child who already has a background in how to produce the basic speech sounds.

If you are fortunate, your school district will assign a teacher of the deaf to your child, and he or she can take over some of the supportive services that you would otherwise provide. Besides teaching speech and language, this teacher's great value lies in orienting other, regular teachers to deafness and the special needs of a hearing-impaired child, keeping in close touch with them on the progress of your child, and ironing out problems that arise.

Providing your child needs an interpreter or notetaker, these services can be arranged with school authorities. It is now a law that these services be supplied upon request. There is increasing enthusiasm for the use of oral interpreters who can, through more direct eye contact and well-enunciated speech, aid the speechreader in understanding a speaker who is difficult to speechread. A word-for-word interpretation of the lecture, instead of paraphrasing, will give your child the full context of what is said, and also permit him to add the enriched language of the speaker to his vocabulary.

The Registry of Interpreters for the Deaf, Inc. (814 Thayer Avenue, Silver Spring, MD 20910) is now in the process of building a nationwide pool of certified oral interpreters, thus adding to their large existing pool of manual interpreters. Some manual interpreters are training to be oral interpreters as well. Interpreters are trained to give either a word-for-word or a paraphrased interpretation, whichever is requested.

Use discretion in asking for an interpreter—a child should be encouraged to work independently insofar as possible. Consider that there will be classes in which he has a special knack or interest and can be expected to do well; others, like art and labs, where the work is not difficult to follow; and still others where the teacher is on top of his subject and easy to speechread.

Following what a teacher or interpreter says may take such concentration that it is next to impossible for the hearing-impaired student to take complete notes. If this is the case, a notetaker may be needed (or some prefer to make a recorded tape of the lecture which is later transcribed by a typist). Frequently, at the junior or senior high school level, a notetaker can be recruited from the student body at large; or even a fellow student in the class may be willing to put a carbon under his notes and give your child the copy; or occasionally a teacher will share his notes with a pupil. Linda and Leslie found that, in spite of having to watch the teacher's face intently, there were moments when he turned to the blackboard, hesitated, or was distracted when they could jot down a few notes. They often found their notes were better for them than deciphering another's notes. And they preferred a notetaker who caught the key points and organized his notes well as opposed to one who wrote down everything the teacher said.

GOING HIS OWN WAY

Your youngster has now grown to the age where he is able to take over his own destiny. He intelligently enters into the decision for purchasing a new hearing aid. He has definite opinions on the groups he wants to join, and even the school he wants to attend.

Time and again, a hearing-impaired youngster with an overriding desire to be socially acceptable will begin to chafe at the struggle, the extra effort, the heartaches that accompany him in a regular high school program. Add to this the normal problems of an adolescent, and everything looms large. He may long for a society of young hearing-impaired people like himself with whom he can be more relaxed and comfortable. He may ask to go to a school for the deaf for his secondary schooling, feeling that there he can learn more at his own pace, as well as enjoy a more satisfying social life. Perhaps he is also feeling the pull of a healthy, independent teenager to break away from the family.

I question the wisdom of fighting against this desire too strongly, no matter what your desires and goals are for him. In his early years, you chose his educational setting and guided his way. Now, he must begin to take a hand in the decisions for his future. For the parents who have raised their child in an oral atmosphere and who now see him turning to the manual mode of communication, trust his judgment about himself, and be comforted in the knowledge that the basic training you have given him will not be lost. He will draw on this background all his life, and will find it of special value when he enters the job market. His ability to manage in a predominantly hearing society will be easier because of your persistence in helping him with speechreading and speech.

There is comfort and pleasure from association with people with comparable handicaps. Our two hearing-impaired daughters, who are able to make their own way in a hearing society, at times seek this association and enjoy their relationships with their hearing-impaired friends. I see in this a need that is satisfied, but difficult for us to understand fully; it is a respite from the necessity of always having to try a little harder than the other fellow.

PHYSICAL ACTIVITIES

Physical education activities are an important part of junior and senior high school. With minor adjustments, a hearing-impaired teenager can participate in any sport and other physical activity with pleasure and even competitive skill. In fact, there is no reason why he can't enter and enjoy competition in his school activities, local recreational programs, Amateur Athletic Union (AAU) meets, and sponsored events, like church and "Y" activities.

In this context, competition teaches sportsmanship which builds character, concern for others, perseverance, self-satisfaction, and the desire to succeed, traits that serve one well all through life. The feeling of belonging to a group, with its possible successes being frosting on the cake, is one of the best panaceas for the shy, introverted, or insecure person. On the other hand, it can also calm and channel the misapplied energies of misguided and hyperactive youngsters.

For those who have little athletic ability and competitive spirit, playing just for fun can be a pleasant, wholesome experience. It opens the door to new friendships. A soft drink following a tennis match or the camaraderie of a team at the local ice cream parlor after a football game creates the right atmosphere for an easy exchange of conversation. A hearing-impaired youngster engaged in sports will notice that bias against his handicap is practically nil during and after game activities.

In addition to the opportunities for building character and meeting new friends, physical exertion plays an important role in relieving tension for the hearing impaired. A speechreader, who must put extra mental effort into communicating and who must strain his eyes and imperfect hearing to the utmost, experiences a degree of tension that we, who hear normally, cannot know.

Linda discovered the joy of athletics around sixth grade, competing in running and jumping events in school, AAU, and recreational programs. She later participated in organized college sports and in track and volleyball in two World Games for the Deaf at Belgrade, Yugoslavia (1969) and Malmo, Sweden (1973), each time bringing home a silver medal. Leslie mainly relied on dancing for her exercise throughout her educational years, and in high school she added competitive tennis. They both continue today with their physical activities, Linda in teaching her physical education classes and jogging, and Leslie seriously climbing into the higher brackets at her tennis club.

Linda and Leslie both attribute their present well-being and positive attitude to a large extent to their physical activities; they lose their frustrations, unwind their tensions after a busy day, and feel exhilarated in mind and body. Linda says that as she runs her muscles begin to relax and she feels free and light and very happy. Leslie "lets it all out" when she socks the tennis ball with all the power she has, yet controls its flight across the net. They believe that without this outlet their tensions, especially those created by communication problems, might lead to blowing a fuse.

It might be interesting here to parents of budding athletes to recount briefly some of Linda's experiences in track. She first began to run in elementary school in a few Recreation Department meets. In seventh grade she won a school sprint, and began to hear from friends about competing in AAU track meets. Now, instead of Campfire Girls or other service clubs, she joined a track club and learned to cope with loudspeakers, schedules, starting guns, pulled muscles, and team travel. The fine training she received from dedicated coaches, the friendships she made, and the wholehearted support she received from her Dad in all athletics were invaluable steps toward independence and adulthood.

Linda started a race with her head lifted enough to see the starter's hand rise for the "get ready" signal, and taught herself, through her hearing aid, to listen for the report of the starter's gun. There were problems, like the time she missed the race because she couldn't understand the loudspeaker directions and no one thought to cue her (usually, they went out of their way to be sure she was ready). Another time, the gun went off for the start and then was immediately followed by a false-start signal; the gun sounds were so close together that she didn't catch the second one and went right on running alone halfway around the track. The scene was straight from comic opera with a whole field of people (athletes, observers, and officials) frantically running toward Linda trying to stop her, while I stood in the bleachers helplessly waving my arms. Yet, none of these incidents were any more than momentary stumbling blocks in a wonderful experience! If she had never won a race in her life, just the joy of running in competition would have been worth it.

There has been such enthusiasm for sports among the hearing impaired that in 1924 the World Games for the Deaf were launched. These games, like the older Olympic Games, are funded by contributions and held every four years with many countries participating. In 1977 in Bucharest, Romania, 1,219 young people from 33 countries competed in a dozen team and individual sports, six of them for women. That year, 90 men and 45 women athletes with 34 coaches and team administrators made up the American delegation, and the United States team won 103 medals. The XV World Games for the Deaf were held in the summer of 1981 in Cologne, West Germany, where 184 American athletes participated in eight sports, with the aid of 29 coaches and officials. The Americans were the overall winner of the games with the most medals ever won by an individual team: 46 gold, 30 silver, and 35 bronze (Kruger, 1977, 1981). The 1985 World Games are scheduled to be held in Los Angeles, California. We should be very proud of our hearing-impaired athletes and give them all the support we can.

The officials make some adjustments for the competitors at the World Games for the Deaf. For instance, in track, many runners start by watching the fire and smoke of the gun instead of listening for the sound of the shot, the gun being held pointed downward so that it's closer to the eye level of the crouching runners. In volleyball and basketball, the officials use the usual whistle and hand signals, but implement them with signs. Naturally, the athletes also keep each other alerted to the officials' calls. When hearing-impaired young people from all over the world meet, those who know signs, find that, although not exactly the same, they are similar enough to bridge the language barrier. Linda made many new friends acting as an unofficial interpreter for the U.S. team on and off the field. Using her facility for speechreading and speech, she was a big help with communications in the hotels, restaurants, and shops on the European tour after the games.

Our other daughter, Leslie, participated in all forms of dance for physical exercise and pleasure during her school years and well beyond. However, she preferred the flow from movement to movement of freestyle modern dancing—it left her exhilarated and was the therapy she needed compared to a more disciplined dance like ballet. Then, and now in disco dancing, Leslie feels the music through the floor and hears some of it through her hearing aid. Her ability to follow the music varies according to its speed and strength of beat. A drum beat is the easiest to pick up, followed by music featuring one instrument. A discordant, fluttery orchestration, epitomized by Stravinsky's "Rite of Spring," is most difficult. Jazz is great fun, but following fast jazz music can be hectic. With any complicated beat, Leslie depends to some extent on closely following another dancer, and has become very deft at watching the dancer next to her from the corner of her eye. I believe that in dancing it is better for a hearing-impaired person to wear a hearing aid, but it is not imperative, as some dancers have done well without amplification.

One of the most amazing accomplishments in the field of dance was made by Helen Heckman, a severely hearing-impaired young woman, whose book was mentioned earlier. Long before the advent of the hearing aid, she studied dance under Ruth St. Denis and became a noted, professional concert dancer. The unique, methodical ways that were used in developing her impressionistic style are described in her book.

In general, it would benefit any hearing-impaired person engaged in a physical activity to have the use of an aid, of course, excluding water activities. A body aid is likely to fall out if it isn't securely fastened in the pocket of a tight-fitting harness. And a behind-the-ear aid poses greater problems; it can fall off the ear when not fitted carefully, and it can become damp with perspiration. Leslie partially solves these difficulties by wearing a sweat band on her head tucked between her hearing aid and skin to keep the aid dry, and a scarf over that to keep it all in place. She has learned to carry a towel with her to wipe her ear and earmold frequently, as perspiration gets into the opening of the earmold, travels into the tube connected to the aid, and cuts off the sound. (When this happens, the moisture can be cleared from the tube with a pipe cleaner.) For very active people, it is wise to check the instrument periodically for rust, as moisture may accumulate even though one has taken precautions.

Speaking of exercise, Leslie became a cheerleader in high school. This was not only a confidence-builder for her, it gave her the much-wanted feeling of "belonging"—playing an active part in the high school scene. From this experience, Leslie found that it is practically mandatory to have a good friend in the group who is willing to keep one up to date on everything. There are always sudden changes in rehearsal times and new cheers invented on the spot. And she needed someone to write out the cheers that others quickly learned by ear, and to work extra time with her on the tough routines.

The major sports along with golf, swimming, gymnastics, skiing, and ice skating are but a few of the activities enjoyed by hearing-impaired people—the list is endless. As a matter of fact, a hearing-impaired young man recently won an international ice skating competition in figure skating. There are unexpected bonuses from having a hearing-impaired youth on a school team, as this article on football in the *Los Angeles Times* "Morning Briefing" of November 8, 1978 (p. 2, part III), illustrates:

> Georgia Tech lined up to punt on 4th and 1, and Florida line-backer, Yancy Sutton tipped his teammates that it would be a fake. Sure enough, the Yellow Jackets tried to run and didn't make it.
>
> How did Sutton know?
>
> Sutton is deaf. In overcoming the handicap, he has become an expert lipreader and he read the lips of the Georgia Tech messenger who said, "Fake punt, run left."
>
> He's got some advantages I never dreamed of," says Florida defensive coach Doug Knotts.

chapter 17

refinement of communication skills

The personality changes that come with adolescence, characterized by self-consciousness and an unpredictable temperament, among other things, also include a new awareness of one's place in society and a desperate desire to be accepted. At last time is on your side. Now your teenager wants to be understood by his fellow classmates to such a degree that he will try as never before to speak more clearly and naturally. Time and again, parents are elated over the improvement in their youngster's speech during junior high and on through high school. The power of pure necessity has at last caught up with him, and what you may not have been able to accomplish through persuasion, he now wants to do for himself.

A GENERAL OUTLOOK

A poignant, true story comes from a teacher of the deaf: she recalls a hearing-impaired boy who at the second- and third-grade levels fought all learning with such vehemence that he once kicked her shins until they bled. But when he was a teenager, he made the effort to look her up and come by her home on his motorcycle to say, "I wish I had listened to you then. I wish I had learned the things you tried to teach me about speech. Can you do anything now to improve my speech?"

In an excellent film made at Lexington School for the Deaf in New York City, of all the scenes depicting a hearing-impaired child's education, the one that struck me the most was the one in which some high school girls were sitting around their counselor talking about their problems. One girl said, "I have been working to improve my speech by myself. Does it seem any better to you? I will graduate this year and must go out into the world and find a job and I am most anxious that people understand me."

Such a plaintive tone of genuine anxiety, need, and determination! With such a built-in incentive, a young person can improve even without much outside help. There have been many years of "lessons" from which a teenager can draw: basics of speech his parents have taught him, his teachers have taught him, and his classmates have taught him. Imitation of his classmates' speech will help him, and a parent can continue correcting his pronunciation, monitoring his voice, and serving as a good model at home.

Both our daughters as they became teenagers began to listen more intently, trying harder to discriminate between sounds for better understanding and speech. Linda, with her greater loss, learned to really listen for the first time in junior high school. She told me some years later how she used to test how much she could understand through hearing alone by following the text as the teacher read from a book. She still practices hearing discrimination with television commercials, which often first announce their sales pitch, then repeat it in print on the screen. Also, they both practice discrimination when watching captioned TV.

New ideas for improving one's listening ability should be tried, and practiced when proven successful. For instance, an audiologist told me about a young hearing-impaired adult who came to her for a hearing evaluation. He had an amazing ability to discriminate between speech sounds, considering the extent of his loss. He explained that he had trained himself by going to plays that were in rehearsal and asking for a copy of the script. By sitting in the almost empty auditorium and listening intently to the speech with the script for reference, he had vastly improved his ability to use his hearing for understanding speech.

An interesting procedure for speech improvement through hearing is described by Lady Ethel Ewing (Ewing & Ewing, 1964).

She and a young teenager would sit side by side with an open book. Then, using an auditory trainer, she held the trainer's microphone within six inches of her mouth and read a sentence from the book, while the student followed the written words as he listened without speechreading. Immediately afterward, the student would read the same sentence, trying to imitate exactly what he had heard. Lady Ewing would then correct his speech and repeat the sentence again, so that the student could attempt to improve his speech even further. This procedure can be duplicated at home using your youngster's hearing aid, and is an excellent method for refining speech.

Hearing-impaired adults who really enjoy conversation with all sorts of different people never stop trying to better their speech. In fact, they speak together frequently of a need for periodic speech training from professionals to sharpen their skills. Speech therapists can be used to monitor and correct individual speech sounds, and voice teachers have the necessary training to improve voice quality. It is remarkable how much clearer speech can be when it pours from the diaphragm instead of being blocked in the throat and nose. Refresher courses in speech training could be regularly supplied through colleges, night schools, and community service centers if enough people and organizations of and for the hearing impaired would request such services. When those who care follow the old axiom, "if you see a need, fill it," I'm sure ways to answer this expressed need will be started.

THE VOCABULARY OF CRAFTS

Courses in various crafts are offered during junior and senior high school, some of which are credited subjects required for graduation. Cooking, sewing, and woodshop are common requirements, and vocational training courses for typing, auto mechanics, drafting, graphic art, and printing are often offered as electives. These elective courses are very popular with students, including the hearing impaired, many of whom start their careers from these classes.

Each of these subjects entails a whole new jargon of its own. For a hearing-impaired teenager, his ability to profit from these classes depends in part on his mastering the vocabulary connected with the subject. This problem was of major concern to the special teacher in charge of the hearing-impaired students in the high school where I did my student teaching. She didn't have the time to work on the vocabulary of each craft with her young charges, and yet these courses were crucial areas for the hearing impaired, classroom situations where they were most able to integrate successfully and gain practical experience. Finally, she had to appeal to the parents for help with this particular type of vocabulary training.

I learned something of this vocabulary problem first hand when I was a resource teacher for hearing-impaired children at a junior high school. The girls who took sewing classes could sew well enough, but when it came to understanding directions or taking tests they failed miserably. This is an area where a parent can be of inestimable assistance. Mothers will know many of the words connected with sewing and cooking classes, and fathers the woodworking vocabulary. If you are unfamiliar with the vocabulary of the craft your youngster is taking in school, visit the class to find out the important new words that will confront him, like the names of machines, instruments, and tools, and the associated action verbs. Obtain a copy of any instruction sheets, procedure manuals, or lists of equipment related to the course. Then, go over this material at home with your youngster as the course progresses.

chapter 18

job market-bound

By the time your child is a junior in high school he should have an idea whether he plans to go to college or directly into the job market. If he chooses college, he should discuss with his counselor all the subjects he will need to prepare himself for higher education; and if he leans toward the job market, he will want to concentrate on vocational training classes. At this stage, if he chooses the latter, see that he doesn't leave out his full quota of academic subjects in favor of craft subjects. And, above all, do your best to influence him to graduate from high school.

Some youngsters, longing for the income and independence of a full-time job, will become impatient with school and want to drop out before high school graduation. This is most unwise, because a high school diploma is important in an employer's consideration of a job applicant. Repeatedly, advice to hearing-impaired young people from educators and employers is to stay in high school as long as it takes to graduate. If extra time is needed, it will serve to refine one's proficiency in communication and academic subjects. Many businesses today ask potential employees to take psychological and basic knowledge tests, and your youngster should have the confidence and knowledge to do well in these tests. In my opinion, it is imperative in this fast-moving age to have a good educational foundation in order to get into the job market, stay in, and merit advancement.

In recent years, there has been considerable concern in many states of the Union because high school students are slipping lower and lower on standardized test scores in reading, writing, and arithmetic. It is generally conceded that: first, the schools have lowered basic academic requirements in favor of more electives; and second, students are being passed along from grade to grade without having learned the material and made truly passing grades. Some eventually "graduate," nearly illiterate.

To counteract this trend, many schools are improving their programs by requiring more study in basic subjects and by systematically testing students at various grade levels for their ability in the three Rs. Students are no longer allowed to enter the next grade until they are able to pass simple, standardized tests.

Along with these tests, California school districts, for example, are required to develop a written list of minimum standards for graduation from high school. The standards developed by the small town in which I lived for a good many years are so practical and well stated that they bear repeating. They form a realistic, minimum basis by which parents can determine the progress of their hearing-impaired child. This list (Murphy, 1978), by and large, covers the skills he should master to allow him a fair chance in the job market and to live a productive life in his community.

MINIMUM STANDARDS FOR GRADUATION FROM HIGH SCHOOL

Reading

1. Understand a personal letter.
2. Understand a business letter.
3. Understand an instructional manual, labels, charts, schedules, abbreviations, and a traffic citation.
4. Identify parts of a newspaper, interpret advertisements correctly, and digest information contained in a news article.
5. Use a dictionary, phone book, and cookbook.

Writing

1. Write legibly in complete sentences, using proper punctuation, capitalization, and spelling.

2. Construct organized paragraphs.

3. Record, in writing, simple messages and directions.

4. Fill out common and standard forms, including a bank check.

5. Write common forms of business letters, including addressing the envelope.

Arithmetic

1. Add, subtract, multiply, and divide in whole numbers and decimals.

2. Figure pay rates, calculate interest and total purchase price for time purchases, make change, figure sales tax, and balance a checkbook.

3. Measure time intervals, objects, and figure the area for a two-dimensional surface.

4. Be acquainted with the common liquid, dry, and linear measurements.

You can provide practical applications for many of these skills at home. You may find that your child has missed learning some portions of the skills he needs; for instance, in measuring, he may know liquid measures but be hazy on linear measures. It would be presumptuous to think that all these basic skills are being taught to your child in school, so I find the above list an excellent one for you to check out as a parent.

Specifically, thinking back to when my children were in high school, I do not recall that they were taught how to write a check or balance a checkbook. They also needed initial help in making out forms, fumbling over what to write in the blank spaces after "citizenship," "race," and especially their "mother's maiden name." Pick up blank forms from such places as banks, schools, and state agencies (like the state employment bureau and motor vehicle department) and use them for practice at home.

I believe all girls should learn typing, for their own security. If one hasn't been in the job market, and suddenly needs to find a job, and has no other work skills, more opportunities will open up by having typing and basic office work capabilities.

By all means, have your child visit a "Career Center" if one is set up at his school or in the community. Such a center is equipped to determine the specific talents of a young person preparing to seek work and to give advice about the types of jobs that would best suit him. However, use your own good judgment in deciding how to apply this information to the ability and ambitions of your teenager.

THE NEWSPAPER

Mr. Jay Dozier, teaching sixth-grade hearing-impaired children at the Mary E. Bennett School in Los Angeles when I met him in 1963, was already well known for his use of the newspaper as a teaching tool. With it, he whetted more appetites for reading and knowledge in the pupils than I have seen before or since. During the school year, he built up an interest in the news of the moment by following important events in the newspaper. Soon his students were voluntarily bringing in clippings, and eventually his walls were crowded with articles, maps showing *where,* pictures showing *what,* and diagrams showing *how.* At the time I visited his class, Queen Elizabeth II of England was being crowned. The event dominated his bulletin board. Articles before and after the event gave fascinating details of the coronation and attendant ceremonies. It afforded Mr. Dozier an opportunity for history—"Who is she?"; for geography—"Where is England?"; and for an appeal to the children's imagination through the colorful costumes, pomp, and ceremony.

I can almost guarantee that every child leaving Mr. Dozier's class has become an intelligent newspaper reader. I tried his approach for a short time with students in junior high school with remarkable success.

And now, here it is among the "Minimum Standards for Graduation from High School"—to know the parts of a newspaper and understand the contents of a newspaper article! Again, I am reminded how sometimes we are lax in urging our hearing-impaired youngsters to become acquainted with the newspaper and to develop the habit of reading it for information. A newspaper will probably always be his best and most reliable source of news.

To start your child reading the newspaper, don't be too particular about what you first bring to his attention. Most likely, what will catch his eye and hold his interest will be the sensational. So say to him, "Did you know there was an accident on Main Street last night? Here is a picture. Look at that car! What does the article say about it?"

Newspaper articles follow a specific pattern in which the basic news is in the first paragraph, and the details follow. With practice, he will become familiar with the newspaper's vocabulary, language, and reporting format, finding pleasure in following the articles that are of particular interest to him. Have him take a timely article to school for class discussion. The next time there is a momentous event, like the astronauts' trip to the moon or the eruption of Mt. St. Helens, try following its progress through the newspaper. It can lead to historical, geographical, and scientific questions that will keep him current and add many new facts to his general knowledge.

chapter **19**

college-bound

Circumstances permitting, you should urge your hearing-impaired youngster to go to college. Today, business opportunities and success are more dependent on having a higher level of education than a generation ago. A young hearing-impaired person who has competed successfully with normally hearing children in a regular high school in English, history, mathematics, and science should be able to continue to do so in college, and he should be given the chance if at all possible. There is no justification in the notion that because your child has a hearing loss he can't go to college. The many hearing-impaired adults who have attended college and are established in various professions and well-paying jobs attest to the fact that graduation from college can be a realistic goal for the hearing impaired as well as the normally hearing.

Your son or daughter's chosen course of study and the family's economics, rather than the hearing loss, are first considerations in making a decision as to which college to attend. Any college of your child's choice is feasible, depending on its curriculum and his individual abilities and talents. Some hearing-impaired young adults may choose a college with a nationally acclaimed academic standing or one close by their home. Others may prefer one where there is a large enrollment of hearing-impaired young people and a faculty to accommodate them, such as California State University at Northridge, or Gallaudet College in Washington, DC, to name just two.

In going over requirements for college entrance with his counselor—these consultations should begin no later than his sophomore year in high school—your college-bound hearing-impaired youngster should seriously consider carrying a full schedule of English and a public speaking class. In my experience, hearing-impaired students should take English in all four years of high school, whether required or not. There's no substitute for this opportunity to soak up as much language, vocabulary, reading, and writing skills as possible, even to the extent of adding outside tutoring. Similarly, training in public speaking has increased value for the hearing impaired. Besides the excellent benefits this subject affords the student in gaining confidence and poise when speaking in front of people and preparing a speech, your child will gain practice in voice production. Learning how to project his voice to reach the last row of seats in a room will increase his vocal strength and resonance. At the same time, he will come to appreciate that he must speak slowly and clearly so that everyone can understand.

Admittedly, meeting college entrance requirements is exacting, but I found the greatest stumbling block for hearing-impaired college-bound candidates is the foreign language requirement; not because they can't learn a foreign language, but because of modern teaching methods. When Linda enrolled in French in high school, within a week, her teacher asked to see me. She did not feel she could possibly teach Linda the French language by the existing teaching methods, given Linda's hearing loss. She explained that the first year was to be devoted entirely to teaching conversational French through the use of tapes and recordings in a language lab setup, with no textbook. Today, this is still the standard practice in many high schools and most colleges.

Consequently, Linda transferred to Latin, and it was then that I discovered this "dead" language is tailored for the hearing impaired. Latin is taught by means of a textbook, with emphasis on grammar and translation, areas to which hearing-impaired students at this point in their schooling can relate. Since many English words are derived from Latin, students with a Latin background can better figure out the meaning of an unfamiliar word, thereby continually improving their vocabularies. Unfortunately, many small high schools usually don't have enough students requesting Latin to include it in their curriculums. But, at the same time, these small schools are probably not equipped with expensive language labs, and a student can still learn Spanish and French the traditional way with textbooks.

COLLEGE ENTRANCE EXAMINATIONS

A formidable barrier for the average college-bound student is the entrance examinations required for college admission. Nationwide, the most popular is the Scholastic Aptitude Test, commonly called the SAT. A shorter, preliminary test, the PSAT, is usually given in October of a student's junior year in high school, and the final SAT in his senior year.

The PSAT is principally given as a practice test for the SAT, but for a few high scorers it may lead to merit scholarships. The SAT test is divided into two sections, verbal and mathematics. The verbal section tests the extent of a student's vocabulary, and his ability to reason logically and draw conclusions correctly; the math section tests the student's ability to work with numbers and mathematical concepts. Some colleges also request a student take a selection of achievement tests in individual subjects. These may include tests in English, social sciences, any of three languages, any of three sciences, and higher mathematics. These achievement tests are generally used by the college for placement rather than being a factor in the entrance decisions.

Fortunately, in analyzing a young person's application for entrance into college, the student's SAT scores are of only secondary concern to many entrance committees. High school grades are the primary concern, but many other factors are considered, such as good citizenship, participation in extracurricular and community activities, and so forth, all of which make for a well-rounded individual. Occasionally, under serious consideration for admission will be the preferred major of a prospective student. As an example, if a young person wishes to major in art, and the college art department has ample space and faculty to accommodate new students, he may be accepted over a better qualified student who is applying for entry in a crowded department.

Hearing-impaired youngsters will probably make the lowest scores on the vocabulary section of the SAT. In spite of all the efforts of concerned parents, the vocabularies of hearing-impaired children seldom catch up with those of their normally hearing classmates. This shortcoming is not so noticeable in the classroom, but will stand out in test results. Since the final SAT score is based on the composite scores of both the verbal and mathematics sections of the test, it is possible for a low score in vocabulary to be balanced by a high score in math. Generally, these tests for a hearing-impaired teenager will not truly show his full aptitude or abilities, and a "just passing" grade should be considered satisfactory even for an above-average hearing-impaired student.

I have never found any really satisfactory way to prepare for the SAT vocabulary test except to be sure your youngster is getting continuing work in vocabulary in his high school English classes. Some forward-looking high school districts specifically plan for the SAT vocabulary tests with pretest work. Whether your youngster is fortunate enough to have college pretest work or not, vocabulary should be emphasized all through high school; it will benefit not only the students who will be taking the tests, but also those for whom these high school years may be their last classroom opportunity to expand their vocabulary.

CHOOSING A COLLEGE

The summer before the senior year of high school is a good time for looking into various college programs and visiting their campuses. By September, your teenager should have decided on which colleges he would like to attend and have sent for the necessary entrance forms. He should fill in and send the applications himself, with guidance from you and his counselor where necessary. Some colleges ask for the applications to be returned as early as September of the year before high school graduation, and some also show preference to early applicants. Most public libraries have material on colleges, both directories containing summary information on colleges and catalogs of some individual colleges. These books will list requirements, majors available, housing information, and costs. If in doubt, write directly to the registrar of each college for information. It is safer to apply to three or four colleges rather than one, so that a reject will not leave your youngster crestfallen and frantically applying late to a second choice.

There are an amazingly large variety of scholarships available for college students. For local scholarships granted by clubs and individuals, inquire of the counselor at your teenager's high school. For those awarded by specific colleges, inquire of the registrar of that college. For scholarships available for the hearing-impaired in general, inquire of the Alexander Graham Bell Association for the Deaf, or the National Association of the Deaf (see Chapter 2 for addresses). Also, your state Board of Education may have information on scholarships available for the handicapped through its rehabilitation department. And check the American Legion's pamphlet *Need a Lift.*

It is hoped your teenager will have, by now, an idea of what study area he wants to pursue. If he seems confused and uncertain, or does not have the grades, a two-year college may be the way to go. After two years, his chance of being admitted to a four-year college as a junior is better than if submitted earlier with the crush of freshmen applications, and he will have determined his particular study interest by then.

Securing the services of interpreters and notetakers can be arranged through the college authorities. In a large college, there are usually specialty counseling services to help handicapped students solve their problems. However, in general, your college-bound teenager should expect to have to fill in where needed with extra reading, and to encounter occasionally an apparently unsolvable problem, such as the professor who does not use a textbook, expecting the student to pass the tests solely from lecture notes. Linda had such an experience in a required course. She and the professor, after discussing the problem amiably, concluded it was almost unsolvable. He recommended she relax, do the best she could with notetaking and read on the outside. She took his advice, stuck in there, and completed the course with a "C." And Leslie was forced to drop an art history class in college because the entire course consisted of the presentation of slides in a darkened room, the professor refusing to honor her request that he speak either in the light of the podium or the projector. Today, an oral interpreter might have solved both these dilemmas.

chapter 20

stepping stones to adulthood

In commenting on the quotation from an editorial in the *Indianapolis News*, June 27, 1974, that "dependence is the greatest handicap of all," Dr. H. Latham Breunig added, "Whereas a hearing loss is a disability, and not necessarily a handicap, excessive dependency on others can, indeed, be a very handicapping condition" (Breunig, 1978, p. 203).

The steps you and your child have been taking toward his freedom from dependence—that most debilitating of all handicaps—will accelerate at high school age. He will be ready, if he has had an opportunity to make decisions and act on his own in his elementary school years. In high school, young people begin to run their own show with less supervision in school and at home, and to earn and save their own money, keep their own books, and make their own plans. Your hearing-impaired youngster will have more and more desire to be independent, and he will find it attractive to join his friends' activities away from home.

With parental judgment, allow him to expand his horizons with an after-school job, a trip to summer camp, a convention, or a sporting event. Give him freedom to move further and further from home. Each new experience will pave the way toward building a strong, independent adult, able to care for himself and make his own decisions.

DRIVER'S LICENSE

Your youngster takes one of the giant steps forward when he applies for a driver's license. Hearing-impaired persons, meeting the age requirement, are eligible to drive and make very good drivers. In fact, their record as a group is excellent according to casualty insurance companies. There should be no problem in obtaining auto insurance, but if there is, contact other companies or ask for help from a hearing-impaired adult group. (Parents and hearing-impaired adults have done much in breaking down prejudices in the insurance field.)

Certainly, it is better to be overprepared than underprepared for driving. If your teenager wears a hearing aid, it is presumed he will not drive without having it on, as he will be better able to hear an insistent horn or a siren and act in an emergency. One reason that hearing-impaired persons have good driving records is the caution that many take to be sure they are following the flow of traffic. Like the hearing-impaired dancer who watches the dancer to the side of him, a wise hearing-impaired person does not pull out at a stop signal until the car next to him does. In this way, if there is a danger signal he does not hear, he will not drive directly into the intersection and possible trouble.

So, let your teenager drive for you as much as possible during the "learning permit" period—there is no substitute for experience. In California now, for example, young people must pass both a driver's education class in school and a driver's training class at the wheel of a car before they can apply for a permanent license.

If your teenager is in a regular high school, you may meet driver's training instructors who have had no experience with hearing-impaired youngsters, and even oppose their learning to drive through the established program. It would be advisable for a parent to acquaint a driver's training instructor with their hearing-impaired child's communication problems. The instructor must understand, for the safety of the training car and its occupants, that the hearing-impaired youngster will not be able to understand oral instructions from the instructor on his right side without fleetingly taking his eyes off the road. This can be hazardous, but it can be kept to a minimum by the instructor giving explicit directions in advance of the driving lesson as to where to go and how, and devising simple hand signals between the student and himself. Further, he should also realize that the instructions he gives in the front seat will not be absorbed by the hearing-impaired student when he is observing from the back seat. Therefore, he should count on a short time at the end of the lesson to review important points for the hearing-impaired student.

As a case in point, Linda was refused driver's training on the grounds that it was dangerous for the other students in the car. Since driver's training was not mandatory at that time, we didn't argue, but taught her to drive ourselves. By the time Leslie was ready to drive, it was a state law that she must take driver's training in high school. The elderly man who was her instructor couldn't quite fathom how she was going to understand what he said and drive at the same time. I would get frantic phone calls after lessons: "I don't know what to do, she turned left before I intended her to, right into a parking lot!" I must have put on my best diplomatic hat, because the driver's training sessions were extended to allow her extra instruction after the other young people had left. This eased the pressure for her. Leslie soon came up to his driving standards, and he signed the necessary papers.

At the time of the actual test, in front of the examiner for the Department of Motor Vehicles, all you can do is explain to him your youngster's handicap and anxiously await the results. For me, it was a pleasant surprise to find that the DMV examiners had had experience testing hearing-impaired drivers and were very understanding.

SEX EDUCATION

Telling your child about the "birds and the bees" is a personal matter, but parents of a hearing-impaired child cannot afford to short-change him on the subject of sex education. Omitting any portion of the information relating to sex may backfire. Hearing-impaired children tend to think in factual, absolute terms. They have difficulty visualizing from a few vague facts and grasping the whole scenario. These children don't always learn from other children the background knowledge that normally hearing children may learn. And a "good friend" may give him misinformation, which is worse than none at all.

High school teachers of hearing-impaired youngsters are frequently appalled at their student's lack of knowledge of sexual matters. I have often wondered if this may be blamed on the peculiarity of a hearing disability rather than the neglect of the parents in explaining these matters to their youngster. The parents may have conscientiously tried, and thought their adolescent understood when he actually didn't.

On this subject, hearing-impaired children need new vocabulary, extra graphic descriptions, extra time to comprehend, and extra help in visualizing something that lies in the future. I suggest that every means available be employed, from films and sex education pamphlets offered in school to supplementary books that you supply. The U.S. Government, for one, through the Department of Health and Human Resources in Washington, DC, prints excellent pamphlets for children on this subject, according to age level. The Department will send them to you upon request.

Nothing, however, will take the place of a heart-to-heart discussion between the two of you. Even if it causes embarrassment, answer questions fully, draw pictures, and leave little to the imagination. Most important, a book won't tell him about the beauty of a sexual relationship nor give him a warm touch of reassurance.

APPLYING FOR A JOB

Young people everywhere can do with some advice from adults when applying for their first job. In most cases, they have had very little contact with the business world, and are still too young to approach it wisely. They need to discuss with experienced businessmen and women how they will appear to a prospective employer and be reminded of the generally conservative attitude of the business community. You, as parents of the young job applicant, can be of great assistance in directing him toward a positive approach along these lines. Whether your advice will be welcomed and heeded depends upon the rapport you have developed with your young adult. It is hoped he will listen to you and others before his first job interviews.

Assuming your young job seeker goes to a large company, he will probably be interviewed by the personnel manager or one of his assistants. Providing he has an appointment, he should be on time (in fact, five or ten minutes early). His experience may be minimal, so he may not have a résumé, but if he does, he should present it at this time. Otherwise, he should have well in mind his personal history and work experience. To the interviewer, a young job seeker appears to better advantage if he: is neatly dressed, not tacky; is cheerful, not gloomy; walks smartly, without shuffling; sits up straight, not slumped over; is attentive, not dreamy; is confident, but not overconfident; and, above all, shows a willingness to learn. In any interview, whether it is with a personnel department employee or an executive, one should try, without noticeably clock watching, not to take up too much of a busy person's time. Be appreciative to the interviewer and his secretary when leaving. The job applicant's impression on any company people he meets will be important.

Following this scenario, a job candidate is usually then asked to fill out a company application form. He should have all the necessary information with him, including his social security number, physical data, and education and work records. Remind him to read instructions on the application very carefully and advise him of the following: where it says, "Print," print. Where it says, "Print last name first," follow the directions, and watch for instructions in the sections on education and work experience that often request the applicant to begin with the most recent experience by date and go backward (he will need to have with him beginning and ending dates, and the names and addresses of schools and companies). In addition, an applicant should be prepared to furnish the names and addresses of his family doctor and three or four character references (family friends, school teachers, or past employers) willing to provide a good recommendation.

If your young job seeker prepares a résumé, have him type it neatly, with personal data first, followed by his schooling and job experience. He should include everything he can think of that he has done, including odd jobs, summer jobs, and volunteer work. The résumé should be as brief as possible and arranged for quick, easy reading, preferably on one page. Businessmen and women like to glance quickly over a résumé without having to hunt for important points. At his discretion, hearing loss need not be mentioned in the résumé.

A young person, particularly a hearing-impaired person, should seek a personal interview with any prospective employer, even if it means traveling some distance. No amount of correspondence will take the place of a face-to-face meeting, where character and feelings come into play. This is an opportunity for a hearing-impaired candidate to brush away the film of ignorance overlying the attitude that an employer may have about a person with a hearing loss. Given that everyone has weaknesses, one should stress one's strengths: detail his abilities and show self-confidence, self-respect, and optimism.

The fact that this young person has a hearing loss will, in some cases, make it more difficult. There will always be the employer who is afraid to hire someone with a disability for fear that, among other things, he himself cannot cope with the situation. However, there are many more employers who are open minded and interested in the ability of a person rather than a disability (which may not even be related to the work to be done). Occasionally, an employer considers a hearing impairment an asset because the young person is not distracted by the sounds around him. Also, the handicapped are usually punctual, steady workers. There are antidiscrimination laws now governing employers and a strong trend prevails toward hiring the handicapped. Have your job seeker watch for job ads that say, "An equal opportunity employer."

The greatest difficulty in finding a job, even if a person is able to communicate with reasonable ease, is the telephone. Yet there are many positions where a telephone is not needed, or where it is seldom used and a fellow worker can handle any calls. In fact, Linda taught at a university, and she found the administration most cooperative regarding her telephone problem. She was given the services of a student aide for two hours each afternoon to help her with her telephoning, and a department secretary took care of messages the rest of the day. If the question of the telephone comes up in a job interview, a suggested answer might be: "I have a hearing loss and wear a hearing aid, but I have partial hearing and can speechread well. I may need some help with the telephone, but I'm sure I can handle the job."

On an application, if the young person's speech is good, he should state that fact. Linda found that when a prospective employer contacted one of her personal references, the employer's greatest concern was whether he would be able to understand her speech.

On a panel discussion of oral hearing-impaired adults on the subject of applying for a job, there were two opposing opinions on filling in the part of a formal application form that asks about disabilities. One young man said that he leaves that space blank, finding that his chances are better if he gets the job first, then proves himself in the job before explaining his hearing loss to his employer. A woman totally disagreed. She felt that it is better to face the question openly, filling in the section on disability rather than having the employer think later that she had not been totally honest.

Another debatable but noteworthy point was brought up during this panel. A certified public accountant was upset because, when competing with another CPA having the same qualifications for the job, his chances of not getting the job were increased due to his hearing loss. He was adamant in demanding the same chance from employers when applicants are equally qualified, exclusive of hearing loss.

By all rights, he should have an equal opportunity. However, I maintain he has to face these realities: first, in the hard world of business, a hearing impairment often is a strike against the job seeker; and second, rarely are two applicants for the same position truly "equal" in their qualifications. Realistically, a hearing-impaired job seeker should anticipate that he must not only be fully qualified, but more-than-fully qualified to successfully compete for a specific job over other applicants. To upgrade his qualifications, he should seek more knowledge and experience in his field through additional schooling, summer jobs, and apprenticeships. In fact, all sorts of previous work experiences can set an applicant above the average young job seeker.

Company response to your young job seeker's application will likely come in a telephone call, whether written notice has been requested or not. Therefore, if he has difficulty with the telephone, suggest that when he's filling out the application he either leave the telephone number space blank or give the telephone number of a friend or relative who will take the message. Also, there are services, principally in large cities, to accommodate the hearing impaired with telephone needs. For example, Leslie was looking for a job in San Francisco and asked "Deaf Self-Help, Inc." to telephone for her to arrange interviews with employers whom she had previously written.

Vocational educators of the hearing impaired have long been concerned with not only the problems connected with hearing-impaired young adults trying to find jobs, but also their ability to keep their jobs. Educators say that surveys of employers show that many are not favorably impressed with the attitudes of the hearing-impaired worker. I doubt that this impression is categorically true, but I know that attitudes toward one's work, fellow employees, bosses, and company are important factors in holding a job and showing progress.

Raymond G. Doane once spelled out the requirements of industry in a paper entitled "Industrial Requirements for Young Deaf People":

> Strange as it may seem to some people, research findings reveal that the development of personal-social traits is the most important industrial requirement.
>
> One of the personal-social traits commonly discussed by others is attitude. Industry would like to have all workers develop a sense of responsibility, a sense of independence, a respect for fellow laborers, a respect for management, personnel, an ability to work with others, a habit to keep their surroundings clean, orderly and safe, a sense of obligation for punctuality and good attendance, and an indebtedness to do a day's work for a day's pay. (Doane, 1957)

The development of such healthy attitudes begins in the home.

LIVING ALONE

In preparation for the great adventure of living away from home, the first important step your hearing-impaired youngster should take is to determine some way to get up in the morning in time to meet his responsibilities. Few people are endowed with a built-in alarm clock infallible enough to be trusted at all times.

As the day approached for Linda to go to college and live in a dormitory, we discussed and tried several wake-up ideas with her. We bought a small, hand-wound Big Ben alarm clock that shook all over when it went off. First, we placed it under her pillow, but by morning it had become dislodged and was on the floor. Then, I sewed a pocket on her pajamas to hold it; this was lumpy and, besides, the clock fell out. A vibrator under the mattress seemed to be the best solution, but she preferred not to use one, and eventually depended on a roommate or someone in the dormitory to wake her up. While some individuals have tried a vibrating wristwatch, they've been similarly dissatisfied. What's more, as a sound sleeper, Linda feels that the effectiveness of a mechanical device may decrease as one becomes used to it.

Much later when she was looking forward to her own apartment, Linda's solution was to obtain a smart, little dog whom she named "Ruido," the Spanish word for *sound.* With the help of her roommate, Linda trained Ruido to waken her by having him jump up on the bed when her alarm clock sounded. He also runs to her when the doorbell or telephone rings and generally compensates for her hearing loss when she's alone. Recently, concerned groups in various parts of the country have begun to train dogs to perform similar functions for the hearing impaired, and to provide protection as well.

On the other hand, Leslie, when first living in a dormitory, turned to the use of a vibrator the first time her roommate forgot to wake her up for class. A vibrator, primarily sold as a massager, can be attached to a clock and placed between the box springs and the mattress, where it vibrates the bed as the alarm goes off. It can be purchased from specialty shops that sell devices for the hearing impaired. The clock has to be equipped with a jack into which the vibrator is plugged. Another activator for the vibrator can be an electric timer of the type commonly used to turn house lights on and off at preset times when the occupants are away from home. Some people depend on a lamp by the bed connected to a timer; it shines in their face to rouse them, even uses a bulb that flickers on and off. Both girls found this annoying.

Mr. Joseph Wiedenmayer, a seasoned U.S. career diplomat who is hearing impaired, tells a most memorable story about getting up in the morning. One day when he was in a hotel in a foreign country and had to waken very early for an airplane flight, he attached a string to his ankle, ran it through the keyhole of the door, and arranged for the hotel keeper to pull the end of the string at the desired time in the morning until he responded (Wiedenmayer, 1965). It worked fine! Today, one has only to walk the corridors of a hotel at night where there is a convention of hearing-impaired adults to know that Mr. Wiedenmayer's idea is still widely used. There are the strings, not from an open keyhole any more, but showing from under many a door.

Indeed, an assortment of devices is available to alert the hearing impaired when they are alone. One hearing-impaired young woman's apartment was described to me as being "positively rigged." This would aptly describe Leslie's present small apartment, where she has: a light for the doorbell, a light for the telephone, a volume control on the telephone, a teletypewriter, a gadget that directly transposes volume on the TV set to her hearing aid, and a vibrator under the mattress. Her budget for the future includes a television adapter for captioned programs.

A person living alone should take the sensible precaution of ensuring that whoever has a key to the apartment, like the manager, will alert him in case of fire or other emergencies. Getting to know your neighbors and doing odd favors for them will serve him in turn with added protection and assistance, such as telephoning. An unlisted telephone number for a hearing-impaired person is another protection, as it screens out nuisance calls, although there is an added cost.

Again, the telephone itself initially poses obstacles. Linda has purchased a standard-type answering system on which she has recorded her own voice requesting that callers leave their messages on the tape. This particular system has an added remote control device that she can detach and take with her when she knows there is a message on her machine. Someone can then attach this device to another telephone, dial Linda's telephone number, and hear the recorded message. This added feature enables her to go for help wherever a person is available to listen to the message for her, rather than requesting their presence at her apartment.

The teletypewriter (TTY) is increasingly popular with the hearing impaired as a reliable substitute for the telephone. One can be purchased or rented from the telephone company. However, it is expensive both to buy outright and to operate. A message by teletypewriter takes much longer to transmit by typing than by voice over a standard telephone; thus, the telephone bill quickly adds up. Many hearing impaired are working within their group organizations with the telephone company to effect a special rate for those using a teletypewriter, especially for long distance calls.

Obviously, the teletypewriter is only useful when calling a person who also has one. To increase the value of this type of communication and for their own convenience, the hearing impaired are working toward having teletypewriters placed in key offices of public service and utility companies. In recent months, government departments and large companies are complying one by one. Our phone book has a listing on the first page as follows:

"Special Assistance for the Handicapped
Teletypewriter (no charge to calling party)
Dial 1 + 800 242–4570."

There are also social-service offices opening up that take TTY messages in their area and send them on to the proper party by telephone, or take a telephone call and relay it to one with a TTY.

No doubt, having a roommate is the easiest way for a hearing-impaired person to manage away from home, but for one who treasures the freedom of living alone, you can see that there are ways to adjust.

ADULTHOOD

At the end of your youngster's high-school education, his "raising" should be over. Whether your young adult goes on to college, trade school, or a job, you must let him go his own way, even though for a while your pocketbook may still be his financial security.

No child, any more than your hearing-impaired child, will grow into adulthood if coddled. The greatest, single fault of the families of handicapped children is overprotectiveness. The success stories we usually hear involve the mentally retarded, blind, hearing impaired, cerebral palsied, and so on, whose parents knew how to foster independence, letting go of their young adult at the proper time.

Problems may still arise, but now your child must squarely face them himself. He must determine his own future, learning by his mistakes and growing confident through his successes. There will be times when he will need your help—extend this help willingly, but make it clear you will not be his ever-present crutch.

Be reassured that improvement of a hearing-impaired person's communication skills does not stop when he becomes an adult. Having learned the basics of these skills, he will, from desire and need, continue to improve himself. Constant use of one's speech to participate actively and effectively in business, social, and community affairs is strong motivation for continued self-improvement. Linda, for instance, finds that her voice improves in strength and quality with her lecturing at the university. Most noticeable to her is the difference between the quality of her voice each fall when classes begin in comparison to her voice before summer vacation. And, each year she must renew her ability to speak clearly and project her voice to reach students in the back of the class.

Moreover, a continuing desire to communicate spurs a young

adult to try harder to improve his ability to understand through his hearing. During a recent family get-together, the girls compared notes and found that both were experiencing an exciting improvement in their ability to understand speech through hearing. Linda noticed that she is supplementing speechreading more and more with her aided residual hearing. Being less dependent on speechreading than in the past, her accuracy in understanding a conversation has improved. She also continues to understand a little more of the conversation each time she uses the telephone.

Leslie at first thought, incredulously, that her hearing was improving, but came to the conclusion it was not her hearing but her ability to discriminate between sounds. The plots of old movies on television that she had watched earlier now became clearer, and she found she could understand some of the conversation she had been unable to make out before, presumably through both better concentration and discrimination. To catch a punch-line now was fun!

Linda observed that she is just learning about TV off-stage sounds (such as a door slamming) that meant nothing to her before. With the help of a friend explaining and illustrating the off-stage sounds she hears, she can identify them the next time she hears them, making TV plays and the like more understandable.

A heartwarming overtone that often filters into the personality of an adult who has struggled to overcome a severe handicap can be described as a certain depth of values and human understanding and love for mankind. I saw it in the strong, confident handshake of our family doctor of many years who stuttered so severely that he wrote his diagnoses and instructions to his patients in letter form. I saw it in the warm, reassuring smile of another doctor whom I first met at the door of an emergency hospital room at three o'clock in the morning, and helped with the heavy swinging door because he had braces on both legs and a crutch under each arm. I see it in Linda's eyes when she tells us of the parents of hearing-impaired children she has met and encouraged. And I see it in the words that Leslie gave me to use in the section on applying for a job: "Everyone has weaknesses; stress your strengths."

YOU

And now, it is time to take a look at you. All these years you have been developing habits of your own in order to further your child's learning. Now you may have to undo a few.

You've been aware of the need for talking—and now you probably talk too much, repeat yourself, and may still have a tendency to lead the conversation toward the subject of hearing impairment. Such habits are not as acceptable in adult, social conversation as they were in your conversation with your hearing-impaired child and those individuals with similar interests.

There comes a time when your corrections are more annoying than beneficial, and your former, good habit of giving your child a cue to the conversation in a group becomes offensive to him as a young adult. In his desire to be independent, the attention this brings to him, as you repeat what has been said and everyone looks at him, is embarrassing. I have been told, "Don't do that, Mom, unless I ask you."

True, your hearing-impaired child has been dependent on you for a good many years and your time and energies have been devoted to him. But now, form the new habit of treating him like an adult. As my hearing-impaired children came into their adolescent years, I noticed that, when two of us were together, a third party tended to talk to me rather than to my youngster. Their eyes were directed to me almost exclusively as my daughter and I listened, even though the conversation was purely for my youngster. This happened at the doctor's, dentist's, audiologist's, and hearing aid dealer's offices, and confounded the problems of my young speechreader who often felt left out. My strategy at this point was to no longer accompany either of them into the inner sanctum of an office. The positive results from this turnabout were astounding. The young adult on his own rises to the occasion far better than expected. If he flounders, he learns at the same time. The significance of this independent action for his maturity and personal ego greatly outweighs the deflation of your own ego when you finally realize that you are no longer really needed. It is time for you to follow those other interests in life that you've been dreaming of all these years.

epilogue

"Friday night's dream on a Saturday told,
Is sure to come true, be it never so old."

Old Saying

With the publication of this book my dream comes true, and I hope it will play a part in seeing your dreams come true as well. May it bring food for thought, hope, and encouragement to all those parents of hearing-impaired children who have read its pages.

My special thanks go to Linda and Leslie who collaborated on various sections where the experience of each as a person with a hearing loss was invaluable, and to my husband, Pete, whose editing smoothed many a sentence. Further, I am deeply grateful to the many others, family and friends, who contributed and kept saying "put it on paper."

Writing this book has been a pleasure, and I trust that within its contents you will find several messages just for you and your child. Hold on to Friday's dreams—they are precious. One of these days they will come true.

references

Associated Press. Parents as primers. *Reader's Digest,* June 1975, p. 10.

Bitter, G.B. (Ed.) *Parents in action: A handbook of experiences with their hearing-impaired children.* Washington, DC: A.G. Bell Assn. for the Deaf, 1978.

Breunig, H.L. The right to independence. *The Volta Review,* 1978, 80(4), 203–205.

Castle, D.L. Telephone training for the deaf. *The Volta Review,* 1977, 79(6), 373–378.

Castle, D.L. Letter to the editor. *The Volta Review,* 1978, 80(2), 119–120.

Dashiell, J.F. Perception. *The Encyclopedia Americana* (Vol. 21). New York: Grolier, Inc. Americana Corp., 1979, p. 569–570.

Doane, R.G. Industrial requirements of young deaf people. Paper presented at the meeting of American Instructors of the Deaf, 1957.

Ewing, A., & Ewing, E.C. *Teaching deaf children to talk.* Manchester, England: University of Manchester Press, 1964.

Ewing, I.R., and Ewing, A.W.G. *Speech and the deaf child* Washington, D.C.: The Volta Bureau, 1954.

Falberg, R.M. *Attitudes and their importance in the vocational placement of the deaf.* Speech given at the 41st meeting of the Convention of American Instructors of the Deaf, 1963.

Gates, A.I. *The improvement of reading, a program of diagnostic & remedial methods* (3rd ed.). New York: Macmillan Co., 1947.

Gore, Rick. The wondrous eyes of science. *National Geographic* 153(3), March 1978, 360–389.

Griffiths, C. Amplification for infants and toddlers. Proceedings of a conference on *Developing home training programs for hearing-impaired children.* Albuquerque, NM: The Indian Health Service and the University of New Mexico, 1976, p. 13.

Haycock, G.S. *The teaching of speech.* Washington, DC: The Volta Bureau, 1961.

Heckman, H. My life transformed. New York: Macmillan Co., 1928.

Indianapolis News, editorial, June 27, 1974.

Josephson, M. *Edison.* New York: McGraw-Hill Book Co., 1959, pp. 322–323.

Kirsh, R. Reading and pleasure principle. *Los Angeles Times,* November 30, 1978, part IV, p. 4.

Kruger, A. Olympic Gold! *The Deaf American,* 1981, 34(2), 26–34.

Kruger, A. Hello, Bucharest. *The Deaf American,* 1977, September, 15–17.

Liepmann, L. *Your child's sensory world.* New York: Dial Press, 1973.

Linehan, E.J. The trouble with dolphins. *National Geographic,* 1979, 155(4), 506–540.

Ling, D. *Speech and the hearing-impaired child: Theory and practice.* Washington, DC: A.G. Bell Assn. for the Deaf, 1976.

Ling, D. Hearing and other senses in speech perception and speech production. Address given at the regional conference on the auditory approach to speech development, sponsored by the A.G. Bell Assn. for the Deaf and Oralingua School for Deaf Children, Los Angeles, CA, November 3, 1978.

Lowell, E., & Stoner, M. *Play it by ear!* John Tracy Clinic, Los Angeles: Wolfer Publishing Co., 1960.

Martin, V. Decisions, decisions! . . . and other facts of life with a hearing-impaired child. In G. Bitter (Ed.), *Parents in action.* Washington, DC: A.G. Bell Assn. for the Deaf, 1978.

McArthur, L. Learning to be self-sufficient. *The Volta Review,* 1967, 69(*4*), 259–261.

McCarry, C. Kyoto and Nara: Keepers of Japan's past. *National Geographic,* 1976, 149(*6*), 836–850.

McGinnis, M.A. *Aphasic children: Identification and education by the association method.* Washington, DC: A.G. Bell Assn. for the Deaf, 1963.

McLeod, R.J., & Guenther, M. Use of an ordinary telephone by an oral deaf person: A case history. *The Volta Review,* 1977, 79(*7*), 435–442.

Morkovin, B.V. *Through the barriers of deafness and isolation.* New York: Macmillan Co., 1960.

Morning briefing, *Los Angeles Times,* November 8, 1978, part III, p. 2.

Murphy, T. New writing standards would stress simplicity. *Ojai Valley News* (Ojai, CA), April 5, 1978, p. A.1.

Murphy, T. Minimum standards being set to graduate from high school. *Ojai Valley News,* April 19, 1978.

Newby, H.A. *Audiology.* New York: Appleton-Century-Crofts, 1958.

Nix, G.W. (Ed.). *The rights of hearing-impaired children.* Washington, DC: A.G. Bell Assn. for the Deaf, 1977.

Numbers, M. *My words fell on deaf ears.* Washington, DC: A.G. Bell Assn. for the Deaf, 1974. p. 190.

Pollack, D. *Educational audiology for the limited hearing infant.* Springfield, IL: Charles C. Thomas, 1970. pp. 68, 75.

Ross, M., & Calvert, D.R. The semantics of deafness. *The Volta Review,* 1967, 69(*10*), 644–649.

Sanders, J.W., & Coscarelli, J.E. The relationship of visual synthesis skill to lip-reading. *American Annals of the Deaf,* 1970, 115(*1*), 23–26.

Schimmel, D., & Fischer, L. *The rights of parents.* Columbia, MD: National Committee for Citizens in Education, 1977.

Sheils, M. Why Johnny can't write. *Newsweek,* December 8, 1975, 86(*23*), 58–65.

Thorndike, E.L., & Barnhart, C.L. Pronunciation. In *Thorndike-Barnhart dictionary.* New York: Doubleday & Co., 1965.

van Uden, A. *A world of language for deaf children. Part I, a material reflection method.* St. Michielsgestel, The Netherlands: St. Michielsgestel Institute for the Deaf, 1968.

Watson, T.J. The use of residual hearing in the education of the deaf, IV. *The Volta Review,* 1961, 63(*10*), 487–492.

Western Electric. Letter dated August 22, 1980, signed by Mark G. Dill, Public Relations Associate.

Wiedenmayer, J. Let's wake up. *The Volta Review,* 1965, 67(*3*), 233–234.